EDUCATION FOR ALL

By

Veeramachaneni Venkateswara Rao

M.A.

Veeramachaneni Vijaya Lakshmi

M.A., M.Ed.

Veeramachaneni Vamsi Krishna

M.B.A.

Ravindra Bharathi Educational Academy
Ravindra Bharathi Public School
Ravindra Bharathi Play School
Vijayawada–520 011
Andhra Pradesh

Editor

Dr. Digumarti Bhaskara Rao

M.Sc., M.A., M.A., M.Ed., Ph.D.
Reader
R.V.R. College of Education
Srinivasa Nagar Colony
Guntur–522 006
Andhra Pradesh
India

SONALI PUBLICATIONS
NEW DELHI-110002

Edition : 2024

ISBN 81-88836-30-3

Published by

SONALI PUBLICATIONS

4228/1, Ansari Road,
New Delhi-110 002 (India)
Phone : 23266109
Fax : 91-11-23283267

Printed by :

Navya Digital, Delhi-110092

Preface

'Education for All' is relatively a new concept. This is our academics' dream for universalising education in this country, which is enthusiastically supported by the Government also. As per scholars' view, education is the foundation, on the basis of which the future of a country is largely determined. The direction of a country is directed according to the education, people receive there. Elementary education is the basic foundation of education on which the future of a student largely depends. In providing elementary education. Special emphasis should be placed on the methods of teaching and other measures, particularly required for first generation learners and for reducing the number of dropouts.

Needless to say that education has a crucial contribution to make towards promoting national integration, understanding and a sense of togetherness and harmony. There is, therefore, great need for an integrated and value-oriented education with a national perspective. Eradication of adult illiteracy and the development of a programme of continuing education is a major thrust area in the annual plans.

The task of covering all the illiterates in the age group of 15-35 years, is a formidable programme, also to be linked effectively with various development programmes. The expansion and effectiveness of adult education provides a further impetus to this growth.

No doubt, there are books on various aspects of Education in the market, but there is a dearth for comprehensive books on Education for All, as a movement. Hence, this work, for the benefit of scholars, students and volunteers in the field of Education. Hopefully, this humble effort would suffice the need for a good book on the subject.

Author

Contents

1

Introduction

The World Conference on Education for All was held in Jomtien in 1990. This marked a new start in the global quest to universalise basic education and eradicate illiteracy. Through the Jomtien Declaration and the Framework for Action, commitments were made and directions set for a decade of large-scale and sustained efforts. Agreements were entered into by countries, intergovernmental organisations, and NGOs to work together throughout the decade. The Jomtien message, setting it in a global context of social and economic development and environmental change.

Several cooperative ventures were launched in order to monitor student learning achievements, to share knowledge and experience and to drive the Jomtien agenda forward. Countries in their pursuit of the Jomtien goals were invited to set their own specific targets according to their situations and capabilities. Thus, there are many country-specific differences in the kinds of material that have been prepared, the topics that have been treated and the issues that have been identified. The Jomtien Declaration was grounded in fundamental values and principles, several of which proved extremely difficult for a number of countries to sustain.

This period witnessed the important contextual changes both positive and negative for the achievement of the EFA goals: the collapse of political regimes, civil war, scientific and technological advances, major economic fluctuations, and others: These changes had quite different impacts on different countries and regions. Analysis of the success or otherwise countries have had in achieving the Jomtien goals forms the main body of this Global Synthesis.

Arising from experience in trying to achieve their targets, a number of crosscutting issues have emerged:

- how to overcome barriers to improve access and greater equity; strengthening the quality, relevance and effectiveness of education;
- new patterns of shared responsibility and decision-taking;
- ways to mobilise resources and use them more effectively;
- the creation of a new educational knowledge base.

This in fact is quite in line with the original agreements and expectations. The targets were defined as directions to which countries would relate their own goals and strategies. There have been setbacks and failures, including a lack of commitment and leadership, poor planning and management, neglect of critical problems. It cannot be concluded that, from a global perspective, the targets have yet been reached or reached in quite the way they were thought about a decade ago. Nevertheless, in the following ways there has been real progress towards achieving the Jomtien goals:

- Significant improvements in achieving enrolment, and participation targets for basic education at all levels of education including early childhood care and education;
- Big reductions in some countries in inequities, notably in the area of gender, disability and ethnic minorities;
- Big reductions in a small number of countries in volumes and/or rates of adult illiteracy;
- New policies, frameworks, legislation and resources in several countries to pursue one or more of the EFA target directions;

- Greater involvement of non-government organisations, community groups and parents in decision making, action programmes and the operation of child care and education facilities;
- Big improvements in educational information and in analytic and evaluative capacity;
- The targets, although not achieved or fully achieved, are more attainable than a decade ago. Whatever the failures and setbacks, there is more than enough here to demonstrate the massive achievements and value of the EFA movement and to inspire confidence in the future.

The representatives of the global education community met in the World Conference on Education for All and embraced a new vision. More than a unique event, this Conference signalled a powerful movement which, while picking up on many threads from the past, sought to weave a strong new fabric.

The World Declaration adopted at Jomtien went far beyond a renewed commitment to earlier targets set for basic education and adult literacy. It spoke for universal access to education as a fundamental right of all people, for fair and equitable treatment of all learners — infants, children, youth and adults. It underlined the need for better learning environments, for new partnerships, for improved quality in educational procedures and results — and for both more resources and improvements in resource utilisation.

Together with the accompanying Framework for Action to Meet Basic Learning Needs, also adopted at Jomtien, the World Declaration on EFA set goals and priorities. Strategies were adopted which would tie commitment to action, mobilising all possible resources.

It was a remarkable achievement for the world education community to reach this policy consensus and agree on the set of aspirational goals. The Jomtien agreements and decisions outlined broad programmatic directions designed to substantially improve opportunities and raise the level of educational performance in all countries.

For the first time, there was a framework which, however ambitious, set clear directions for purposive worldwide action. Preparation for the Jomtien World Conference involved agreements among UNICEF, UNDP, UNESCO and the World Bank, subsequently joined by UNFPA, and included nine regional consultations. In 1991, following the World Conference, an International Consultative Forum on Education for All was established. Its mandate was to serve national follow-up action and support it effectively and seek to maintain the spirit of coöperation amongst countries, multilateral and bilateral agencies, as well as NGOs.

The EFA Forum was conceived as a series of global meetings for the EFA partners to discuss progress, and matters of mutual concern. Also established for operational purposes were a Forum Secretariat and a Forum Steering Committee, and subsequently, a Management Committee. Of signal importance is the widely representative a nature of the EFA Forum, a unique global mechanism of consultation and co-operation among countries, multilateral and bilateral development agencies, non-governmental organisations, the private sector and media.

A preliminary meeting in Paris in 1991 was followed by one in Delhi in 1993, when nine of the world's most populous countries and some others, together with donor countries and agencies, established a working alliance of developing countries with large population the E9 initiative. These countries have met regularly at ministerial level, for collaborative action and information sharing. At Amman, Jordan, the world education community met again in 1996, to review progress and to pinpoint the major obstacles still in the way. Regional meetings and data gathering preceded the Amman Meeting.

Four issues that have persisted since were raised: the need to balance quality learning with the attention being given to years of schooling; concerns over the quality of data; insufficient recognition of the activities of non-governmental organisations; and the need to maintain the EFA momentum at country and regional levels.

Countries have been grouped into trans-national regions by the EFA Forum and syntheses prepared to point up trends and issues, region by region. A most impressive, indeed unprecedented, body of information on world education is the result. In a wealth of national reports, regional and sub-regional syntheses, thematic studies and a statistical document, masses of both quantitative and qualitative data have been assembled and reviewed. Trends have been defined and developments arid setbacks reported. Gaps and deficiencies have been frankly addressed. Significant issues have been raised for further consideration. The time has now come to pull these strands together. It is impossible to do justice to the richness of all this material in a global synthesis.

Not to be overlooked in reviewing the decade is the substantial growth and refinement of knowledge about education trends and the conditions which either enable or inhibit attainment of the goals that have been set. At the outset this major achievement in capacity building, analytic power and understanding must be acknowledged and warmly welcomed. The Education For All movement has likewise demonstrated the value of global collaboration through the EFA Forum.

Much has been learned from the experience of addressing the Jomtien agenda on the ground and from the processes of analysis and evaluation of results. There is a clearer understanding now both of what the Jomtien commitments actually meant in practice and of the nature of the challenges that they posed. A firm platform has been established for future action. The basic messages of Jomtien remain, but adjustments, elaborations and further undertakings based on the experience of the past decade are now called for. The Dakar World Education Forum together with its Framework for Action, in providing the opportunity for a strongly renewed commitment to practical action, also enables new targets to be met.

Many different routes can be tracked from Jomtien to Dakar, as countries reached towards the goals and values of Education for All. Differences of culture, tradition, environment, social, political and economic conditions and educational systems have profoundly influenced the ways countries went about achieving the Jomtien goals, and their rates of progress. A key issue is the level of commitment, and leadership, resourcefulness and determination in face of the challenges.

There have been failures and setbacks, stagnation as well as progress, and these must be put in the balance. Overall, the studies and appraisals that have been made of the decade of effort since Jomtien both underline the need and give renewed hope for the continuing development of education worldwide. We can again unite in determining future directions and continuing responsible action to achieve the goals.

The extent to which the Jomtien decade has been a success in achieving the targets set in 1990 is the subject of the overall EFA 2000 Assessment of which this Global Synthesis forms part. 'Success' has been variously defined, since countries were expected to work within a framework, setting their own targets.

In many countries these targets were reached or sometimes exceeded; in others there are very big shortfalls. 'Success' in these circumstances, requires interpretation from many different standpoints as well as complex judgements about a large and varied body of data.

There have been major achievements. In three quite clear ways, as a process, the Jomtien decade can be deemed a success:

(1) Mobilising global action to improve education;

(2) Developing the knowledge base and analytic capacity;

(3) Identifying and clarifying the areas requiring further concerted action.

But

(a) commitment and involvement have been uneven,

(b) not all targets have been pursued with the necessary vigour,

(c) despite the overall improvements, in some countries education reform stood still during the 1990s or there have been declines.

The commitments and undertakings made at Jomtien were premised on quite fundamental values and beliefs:

- People everywhere have basic human aspirations and needs: these include nurture, health, training and education in order to fulfil themselves and live well in their families, their communities and as citizens;
- Injustice, poverty, disease, war and violence are inimical to the satisfaction of basic human needs;
- All societies have fundamental requirements and they have obligations towards all their members, whose rights as affirmed in the Universal Declaration of Human Rights include education;
- There is a bond between people and society of mutual rights, responsibilities, duties and commitments; education serves to strengthen and enrich this bond. The movement of Education for All (from Jomtien to Dakar and beyond) affirms:
- The right of all people everywhere to basic education;
- People's needs and responsibilities as learners;
- Society's expectations and requirements of its members as learners;
- The need for commitment, leadership and change in the education environment and wider context to foster and facilitate learning.

The overriding purpose of the global movement of education for all is no less than the achievement of a better life for all people, grounded in civilised values and human rights and responsibilities.

The goals set and the strategies adopted have, as their rationale, global agreements and commitments to make a living reality of a vision. That reality, however, must embody and express the principles underlying the Jomtien Declaration and Framework for Action.

These principles are ethical, humane and civic; they are culturally and socially sensitive. Mutual obligations and responsibilities bind people and communities together. They can be described as a set of social virtues; combining goodness with efficiency.

These virtues include:

- equity and justice;
- fairness;
- empathy and considerateness;
- peace;
- the valuing of difference; and
- active democratic citizenship.

They combine in the ideal of a full, good life for everyone, to achievement of which is the goal of education. But have learning opportunities for all people everywhere — infants, children, youth and adults-been provided. For the EFA 2000 Assessment, there are questions to raise about rates of progress and the directions pursued in achieving the goals. As these questions are addressed, it is also necessary to ask how far and in what ways have equity, justice, peace, and democracy been advanced.

Achieving universal basic education poses very different challenges for different countries and regions and for particular groups within countries. Even so, it was agreed that there could be a common set of target directions for all countries. Countries were invited at Jomtien to set their targets for the 1990s in terms of six dimensions. Countries have provided data for each of these targets which have been analysed in reports on each major regional grouping: Asia and the Pacific; the Americas; Arab States and North Africa; Europe; Sub-Saharan Africa; E9 (the nine most populous countries). These targets have been operationalised and analysed in the Statistical Document, through 18 core EFA indicators. These indicators are designed to describe and measure the main components of basic education as envisaged and agreed at Jomtien, and progress over the decade.

Despite the active encouragement and support to countries and the EFA regions to provide data through these 18 indicators as well as in many other ways, there are, inevitably, many gaps. In the statistical data and in the country and EFA regional reports there are considerable variations in coverage and topics discussed.

A set of highly authoritative special thematic studies, commissioned by intergovernmental organisations and NGOs, draws upon statistical data, surveys, the research literature, anecdotal evidence and other sources in providing rich insights and judgements about trends and issues that lie at the heart of the EFA movement.

A number of reports on specific topics and projects have been prepared, including information on student performance in several reports on the UNESCO-UNICEF project, Monitoring Learning Achievement (MLA). But despite freely acknowledged deficiencies, the knowledge base is vastly better in 2000 than 1990. The six dimensions of EFA targets are given below:

- Expansion of early childhood care and developmental activities, including family and community interventions, especially for poor, disadvantaged and disabled children;
- Universal access to, and completion of primary (or whatever higher level of education is considered as basic by the year 2000);
- Improvement of learning achievement such that an agreed percentage of an age cohort attains or surpasses a defined level of necessary learning achievement;
- Reduction of the adult illiteracy rate to say, one half its 1990 level by the year 2000, with sufficient emphasis on female literacy to significantly reduce the current disparity between male and female illiteracy rates;

- Expansion of provision of basic education and training in other essential skills required by youth and adults, with programme effectiveness assessed in terms of behavioural change and impact on health, employment and productivity;
- Increased acquisition by individuals and families of the knowledge, skills and values required for better living and sound and sustainable development, made available through all education channels including the mass media, other forms of modern and traditional communication, and social action, with effectiveness assessed in terms of behavioural change.

The declaration suggested, target directions and hence the statistical indicators are part of a larger framework of concepts, ideals and ideas, and strategies of action which were incorporated into the Jomtien Declaration and Framework for Action. The key concepts of learning and of learning in different settings and in a variety of modes, were treated in the Jomtien documentation in considerably broader contexts than schooling and the provision of formal education through school-like instrumentalities. Countries have not, however, often reported as comprehensively on learning as was expected.

Other considerations that were raised at Jomtien include: cost effectiveness and improved efficiency; local empowerment and community action; the disabled; partnerships; the terms and conditions of service of teachers; child care and development; education in the context of cross-sectoral policies; and private and voluntary funding sources. Overall, albeit often implicit, there has been a clear set of expectations for the 1990s: improved human development policy; appropriate legislative and regulatory frameworks; well-managed systems and procedures; competent personnel of integrity; transparent and accountable use of resources; enhanced public awareness; and better learning opportunities and outcomes. That in many countries one or more of these expectations could not be met or was not reported, would in no sense be a reason to forego or dilute them in future planning.

At Jomtien, attention was frequently drawn to the political, social, economic and cultural environments which both condition educational policies and practices and are interactively informed and modified through education. Satisfaction was expressed over progress towards peaceful entente, greater co-operation among nations, the increasing recognition of women's rights and capacities, growth of information services and scientific and cultural developments.

The beginning of the 1990s were conditions and forces which could jeopardise future progress: mounting debt burdens; threats of economic stagnation and decline; rapid and unsustainable population growth; widening economic and other disparities within and between countries; war, occupation and civil strife; enforced migration; violent crime; widespread environmental degradation; and the preventable death of millions of children. Especially-but not only -in the least developed countries these negative forces had resulted in major setbacks to education throughout the 1980s.

Today, a decade later, that context has undergone transformations. In the changing environments of the 1990s, topics scarcely considered at Jomtien or developments not anticipated have come to the fore. Their seriousness and impact will require some reshaping of the new agenda and hence of target directions for the next phase of EFA. To mention only some of the most dramatic changes of the era: the political, social and economic shifts in Eastern and Central Europe; the rapid development of the Internet as a pervasive lever of change for the organisation of life, commerce, entertainment and education; the emerging new economy based on intangible capital and calling for much increased adaptability to rapid change and a new repertoire of entrepreneurial capabilities and attitudes; dramatic developments in the life sciences with far reaching implications; the voluntary and enforced movements and mixing of people and cultures; the growth of poverty and increasing debt around citadels of increasing affluence; and the swift advance of economic and cultural globalisation.

Whole countries and regions within countries have experienced either economic decline and collapse or unprecedented growth cycles; war zones and areas of civil unrest have spread with whole population held to ransom; and in some regions, notably Sub-Saharan Africa, there has been the disastrous spread of the HIV/AIDS pandemic. It seems, also, that there has been an intensification of natural disasters attributable to climate change, underlining the need for much improved emergency services. Most of the issues raised at Jomtien remain highly relevant but they need to be treated as it were in a new key due to the changed environment.

There is basic continuity from Jomtien to Dakar and beyond, but these and other contextual issues call for a revised agenda. A new Framework of Action is required to reinforce the mission, to continue with unfinished business and to take up the new challenges. Strategic reinforcement of the EFA mission and of the expressed need for further sustained effort has come from several different sources: first, the continued growth of systematic knowledge including increased understanding of changes in the wider environment impacting on education; second, a succession of world conferences throughout the 1990s which have both documented and given prominence and publicity to major world issues, many of these having quite direct educational implications; and third, changes in communication, trade and international finance which heighten public awareness of global interdependence and imbalances.

The advance of educational knowledge and understanding is of particular relevance to the fulfilment of the Jomtien mission. While not an explicit target at Jomtien, knowledge building has in fact proved to be one of its most positive outcomes with highly significant implications for future strategic capability and the ability to target action and mobilise resources. By the end of the decade, there are much more advanced systems for data collection and analysis in many countries than existed at the beginning. There has been a real effort by the UNESCO Institute for Statistics, working closely with national and other statistical agencies around the world, to come to terms with previously existing deficiencies. Country reports, regional syntheses and the special studies provide numerous examples of improved data sources and advances in knowledge. The problems have not all been solved but they are, at least, much better documented and understood. This should be seen as a crucial step towards overcoming them.

Of course, not all improvements in educational knowledge are attributable to Jomtien, but there have been several important gains consistent with the Jomtien Framework for Action and supportive of its goals. For example, the initiative for the development of an international set of education indicators by the Organisation for Economic Co-operation and Development (OECD) predates Jomtien and has proceeded largely independent of it, as has that Organisation's procedures for reviewing educational trends and developments in member countries and others. Likewise, the education statistics work of the European Union (Eurostat), its reviews and those of the Council of Europe and other international bodies are freestanding. They can, however, all be counted as major regional achievements supportive in various ways of the EFA mission. They have a potential extending far beyond the regions in question.

The Jomtien Declaration must be interpreted in the broadest possible sense of learning-formal, non-formal and informal — and at any stage of life. Learning takes place in and out of school in the home, the local community, the work place, and in recreational and other settings. Not confined to childhood and the formative years, it extends from infancy throughout the whole of life. What is 'basic' is no longer confined to the primary school or formal education.

An important achievement of the EFA movement is the closer attention being given especially by NGOs and voluntary bodies to the foundations of learning in the period. Care, nurture and encouragement of all round child development at this stage are increasingly being recognised as essential for subsequent growth and hence of satisfactory basic education. Increasingly, also, there is a challenge to find appropriate structures for supporting and recognising different kinds of learning previously disregarded or given scant recognition in formal education systems.

Most countries are still at a relatively early stage in developing new procedures for assessing competence and awarding new kinds of qualifications that give credit for experiential learning that takes place outside formal education institutions. For education of all kinds, there is scope for much greater use of a variety of media and settings and hitherto untapped resources, as pointed out in several of the special studies.

During the nineties many countries have improved their capacity to gather and analyse educational data and evaluate performance: preparation of the EFA indicators and the national and regional reports and of the UNESCO World Yearbooks of Education have been a stimulus. National systems are introducing new structures or strengthening existing ones.

Examples include the National Qualification Framework in South Africa, the Office for Standards in Education in England and Wales, the system of observatory and evaluation reports in the National Ministry of Education and Culture, France and the expanded evaluation role of the National Institute for Educational Studies and Research, Brazil. By participating in the UNESCO/ UNICEF Monitoring Learning Achievements project, more than fifty countries have gained a better understanding of pupils' learning achievements. The issue of the diversity of learning and the danger of equating 'learning' with 'schooling' having been noted, it remains true that organised schooling provides, for most people, essential foundations for learning over the life-cycle. As many of the country reports point out, schooling builds on a platform of early childhood care and education (ECCE).

It is succeeded by vocational preparation, tertiary education and organised adult, continuing education which have reached a highly advanced stage in a growing number of countries. Schools and school teachers are also a resource for adult literacy and continuing education programmes, not only in developing countries where they have a vital role. While there are indispensable, major contributions to education and learning by all kinds of voluntary bodies, community and self-help organisations, however, the provision by public authorities of schools of good quality, access to schools, and opportunities and active encouragement for all to succeed and progress in and through schooling remain the essential and central ingredients of EFA.

The commitment of EFA is to basic education. But this is not a fixed or clear-cut concept and countries were advised at Jomtien to determine their own definition. Most but by no means all have chosen to restrict 'basic' to primary, schooling, meaning the first stage of formal schooling -which so many have yet to attain. 'Basic', in an increasing number of countries, however, now connotes not only early childhood care and education and primary schooling.

In Nigeria, 'basic' education refers to early childhood care and pre-primary education, primary schooling and the first three years of secondary. Throughout Europe, North America and Australia, Japan and parts of South East Asia, 'basic' includes both primary and secondary levels.

In a small but growing number of countries, some kind of post secondary or tertiary education is almost becoming 'basic' in that it is seen as a foundation for working life or further studies for all youth. There are moves to incorporate all levels and forms of education within a framework of 'lifelong learning for all'. These require a reconsideration of just what is best taught and learned in childhood and youth, as a foundation for continuing learning.

Difficult — indeed unnecessary — as it is to maintain clear cut distinctions, for ease of communication as well as target setting, basic education does need to be redefined, with reference to technical, specialist, higher, tertiary and lifelong. Here, basic is refers to the competencies, knowledge, attitudes, values and motivations that are deemed necessary in order for people to become fully literate and to have developed the educational foundations for a lifelong learning journey. Basic education commences at birth and may be achieved through either formal or non-formal means and agencies.

Competencies, skills and substantive learnings defined as basic, when provided for in schools and similar institutions, are usually cast in the form of a core curriculum which while it includes and builds on literacy includes numeracy, social and scientific knowledge, physical and health education and the arts and crafts.

Dimensions like visual and aural literacy and racy in a world where multi-media are pervasive are no less basic than verbal and numerical skills. In short, the four 'Delors pillars' learning to know; learning to do; learning to live together; learning to be-are all basic. The length and nature of schooling that have been defined as 'basic' by countries vary: from a bare minimum of 3-4 years of primary school to a nine year school, or completion of full secondary schooling.

Programmes and campaigns of adult literacy are an example of non-formal basic education, as are community health campaigns, parental education in child care and educational campaigns conducted through the mass media. 'Basic' with reference to these minimum levels, should be treated as the very early stages of a process that needs to continue and grow. The Assessment reports indicate, education and especially schooling is firmly grounded in the historical, cultural, social, economic and political conditions of countries and regions within them. These constitute environments, which profoundly affect not only policies, legislation, regulations and resources, but also the quality of the curriculum, the capacity of teachers and the conditions of teaching and learning. Countries are not affected equally, nor are regions, groups, families and individuals within countries.

A question arises therefore as to just how far goals and targets can be described as 'common' when such varied meanings are attached to the term 'basic' and where circumstance for attainment vary so widely, not only between but also within countries. The six target directions were outlined at the beginning of the decade with such generality as to be applicable universally, although with a bias in a couple of them towards countries with low rates of participation and literacy.

The translation of these broad general targets into country and regional-specific policies and programmes was properly left to the countries themselves as was the anticipated rate of progress in attaining them. Thus one of the most problematic aspects of EFA — the pursuit of common goals and the implementation of strategies in circumstances of enormous diversity-must be kept to the fore in assessing the achievements of the Jomtien decade. Inevitably, rates of progress from quite unequal starting points and in a great variety of environments differ dramatically. While global, regional and national indicators tell important stories, they cannot completely capture either the full range of conditioning factors or the diversity of provision, resource and response within countries. It is by attention to environmental conditions as reported in the variety of documents assessing progress and problems that the diversity can best be understood.

Many countries, in responding to the Jomtien challenge and in pursuing their reform strategies, adapted targets to the diverse circumstances. For example, extreme regional inequalities in Brazil have seen the national government in a federal system playing a differentiated provisioning and redistributive role. In China, there are different targets for length of primary schooling in different parts of the country.

These presumably would eventually be amalgamated within the overall target of the nine year compulsory school, but that is not at all imminent.

Inevitably much of the concern that has been expressed in the reports of progress since Jomtien relates to the difficulties many countries or parts of countries are experiencing. Making adequate provision for access and participation by learners and for teachers to be adequately prepared, equipped and resources to carry out their work is still a monumental challenge in many countries and areas. These difficulties reflect conditions and circumstances which in part are beyond the education system itself.

Although frequently not open to direct action through educational policies and programmes, they must however be addressed, both as conditions for the realisation of EFA goals and as susceptible over time to influence, if not complete redirection, by a well educated populace. The need for a renewed commitment is evident in those countries where little if any progress has been made.

Educational policies which squarely address the key issues are needed and can work, as has been shown in those countries that are making progress. Educational reform can itself be a potent means for achieving much more effective use of resources and for improving economic and social conditions, which are often seen as a barrier to educational development.

What is at issue in the EFA movement is nothing less than a continuing transformation of educational values, structures and procedures in many parts of the world. The focus is education and learning; but changes in social and cultural context, in economic and financial conditions and in the ways communities go about their daily lives are also at issue. For even the most educationally advanced countries, there are profound challenges to meet if the improvements that are sought are to occur in the quality and relevance of what is provided. The goals of universal access and effective, continued learning for all are a constant reminder of unfinished business not only in the poorly resources and less well managed systems.

The experience of the Jomtien decade has given rise to a multitude of questions and issues as countries and agencies have pursued the targets they set themselves. The way has often not been smooth. There are uncertainties, for example, about how to make the most educationally effective use of the new technologies in conditions of scarcity. Partnerships have not always been as comfortable and cooperative as desired in relations at times between governments and NGOs, or among donor agencies, or between governments and communities.

Differences in belief systems and ideologies and community traditions are to be respected and valued for their diversity and cultural richness. They do not, however, always align well with or provide support for the Jomtien targets. Sometimes they are completely at variance, for example traditions and customary practices regarding the roles of women and girls and their educational needs. The preference expressed for family rather than institution based child care raises important issues about community choice and the interaction of universalist values and the particularist preferences of individual cultures and subcultures. They are also a constant reminder of scarcity : choices are often forced on families and on children due to unrelenting financial pressure as well as traditional customs.

Attainment of the Jomtien targets calls into play a great number of contextual considerations whose variety and impact go a long way towards explaining the continuing, worldwide differences in the attainment of targets. The numerous educational trends, concerns and issues discussed at Jomtien were, for the purpose of target setting, combined into six target dimensions.

The Framework for Action document was prepared as a reference and guide for national governments, international organizations, bilateral aid agencies, non-governmental organizations (NGOs), and all those committed to the goal of Education for All in formulating their own plans of action for implementing the World Declaration.

This statement was followed by suggestions for intermediate goal setting, specific time-bound targets and measuring progress. However, these were to be based on a realistic appraisal of possibilities. Countries with low literacy and enrolment rates and very limited national resources, will need to make hard choices in establishing national targets within a realistic time frame.

Countries were invited to set their own targets for the 1990s in terms of the six target dimensions. Thus there were two closely related but nevertheless different challenges:

(1) to set realistic national and local targets within but not necessarily incorporating all of the Jomtien target dimensions; and

(2) to aspire in that target setting to implementation to meet the full range of Jomtien targets and at the level of attainment specified or indicated.

Reporting on progress over the decade has not usually drawn explicitly upon that distinction. But it is extremely important in assessing success or otherwise to recognise that while all those who adopted the Jomtien Declaration were committed, they were committed to target directions, and not to precisely the same targets in substantive terms.

Some of the harsher judgements that have been made do not respect that distinction. On the other hand, the distinction cannot be used as a justification for indifference, misdirection of resources and poor organisation and management.

These six target dimensions need to be examined from the several perspectives adopted in these reports. Data on trends are not always consistent, nor do they permit reliable comparisons over time or within countries and parts of countries.

In many instances, the data that have been assembled are still provisional and subject to correction. With due allowance for these considerations, the data do permit snapshots, for example the achievement of literacy targets in a single district, urban/rural disparities in access to primary schools, or learning achievements across a range of countries.

The new information and communication technologies and the supply and utilisation of educational materials are obvious examples. Mapping exercises undertaken in the Asia Pacific region graphically illustrate educational opportunities at specific points of time. For example, geographic and gender inequalities are shown in maps of primary school net enrolment ratios in Nepal, in 1996. These clarify the issues of the markedly lower net enrolment of girls as against boys in many societies, and the lower enrolment of both in rural as against more urbanised areas. Overall trend analysis based on statistical returns forms part of the accompanying

Statistical Document and these trends are identified in general statements in the following discussion. However, there are as well numerous specific developments of considerable importance in building up a comprehensive picture of what countries and organisations have achieved in the quest of education for all. A number of these have been selected for illustrative purposes.

There is a definite need for new ideas and strategies to bring education from the periphery to the centre of people's lives and of political and social action programmes. Many of the plans and programmes for educational development and reform that countries have adopted during the 1990s draw together several of the Jomtien target areas and interrelate a number of the over-arching themes.

Extensive bodies of both quantitative and qualitative data have been gathered and analysed for all six target areas. There are three of them-early childhood care and education, participation in primary education and adult literacy-where the information provided in the EFA Assessment is fairly inclusive, if still quite variable. However, there is much less information available on the quality of children's performance in school, youth skills development, and education for a better life. Appraisals of the latter three would require both output data, which are generally either limited or completely lacking, and a considerable amount of values-based judgement.

In Mexico, a National Agreement for the Modernization of Basic Education, in 1992, constitutional reforms and a new education law, in 1993, set the framework. The most important reform was the decentralization of basic education and teacher education. The broad goals, definition of contents evaluation and compensatory policies were retained by central government, while administration of the operation of education institutions was for the states. Social mobilization occurred through participatory councils.

Compensatory policies for poorer communities were introduced and special attention given to bilingual education. In

Brazil, a ten year Education for All plan was established for the period 1993-2003. It was strengthened by a constitutional amendment which reorganised basic education funding to improve equity and earmarked more resources for education; a new National Education Law including new evaluative procedures; a new National Plan referred to the Congress for approval in 1998.

In China a new Five-year Plan for Educational Development and Long Range Development Towards the year 2000 was established, shifting the focus from universal primary education to universal 9 year compulsory schooling. This was supported by central regulations and guidelines. Numerous measures were introduced to speed up universal primary schooling either in full or 3-4 year programmes in remote areas and to improve provision for girls, the disabled and the children of migrants.

In Pakistan, targets were set in a National Education Policy 1998-2010 for universal enrolment and compulsory attendance and a completion rate in primary schools of 80%, public- private partnerships, increased levels of investment, assessment of basic competencies and decentralised management.

2

Right to be Educated

Schools and institutions of religion combined proselytizing with literacy, compulsory education later became a duty rather than a right of the child. And yet, getting all children to school is still mistaken for their right to education, although they can be brainwashed, indoctrinated, abused, harmed for life. All rights of the child apply to education and in education. If they do not, human rights will not be achieved through education.

A great deal of attractive rhetoric about integrating human rights education into all education has been generated during the past decade. Teachers are expected to be its conveyers in school, while parents are expected to send their girls to school because it is — in theory — an excellent idea. Bridging the abyss between theory and practice necessitates looking far beyond education to identify all factors which hamper girls' education.

Women's Condition

The girls' right to education is inextricably linked with the rights they can gain through education, but these lie beyond education strategies. A glimpse into detrimental effects of formal schooling on the girls' marital prospects in Uganda and Nepal, demonstrates the need for main streaming all human rights in education strategies. The intrinsic value of education, which is so optimistically assumed in all international strategies, clashes again social norms which confine girls to early marriage, negotiated between their parents and those of the prospective bridegroom.

The price which the girls' parents have to pay to the bridegroom's family, as lamented by a Nepali mother, increases with the girl's formal schooling. It is easy to ignore these real obstacles to the schooling of girls because they are assumed to have been eliminated, that all the rights have already been recognized for all women and girls. Human rights instruments are, as the term 'instrument' indicates, tools which ought to be used to secure equal rights for girls. Trying to promote the girls' right to education without heeding the obstacles to their right to marriage or property diminishes the value of the girls' education for their parents, thus closing off an obvious road towards change.

The advantage which human rights have over the fragmented visions of advances which can be made in isolated areas, such as education, is considerable. The human rights approach forces designers of development strategies for whatever isolated sector to look at all human rights and fundamental freedom. A large number of articles of faith accompanies schooling for girls. Primary education for girls aged from six to eleven is expected to delay marriage, lower fertility, improve the health of the next generation. It is a counter intuitive argument that eleven year old girls, after merely five years of schooling, would not marry and bear children since there usually there is no alternative for them.

Education of girls requires much more than getting girls into schools — it necessitates altering gender roles. The prospects which girls have after schooling influence the attractiveness of schooling for the girls and for their parents. These prospects are determined by the ability of girls and women to exercise all their human rights — from equal political participation and representation, to equal access ,to bank loans. It is by focusing on the gender dimensions of education that we learn how much change is needed to transform education into rights-based education. Frank Dall has pointed out how detrimental "the classroom-centered model designed to service a pre-industrial European society" has been. One visible feature of this model are square schools, even if all huts around them are round.

There must be schools whose size and shape fits the environment, but the iron rule of school-building is to make them square. Building schools is usually the first step towards providing education for children, although there is no evidence that the building itself, expensive as it may be, has any effect on children's learning. School uniforms constitute a considerable expense for parents and, again, no association with children's learning has even been established. Taking children away from their family for full-time schooling -especially girls — has often proved impossible but it was only in the 1990s that adjusting the time-table to children's lifestyle started prevailing over the conventional idea of full-time schooling, away from home, with a schedule designed for industrialized countries, and with expectations to match.

Vocational education is twice or even four times more expensive that general education and, when given instead of general education, which parents see as the ladder leading their children to white-collar jobs, tends to become seen as a problem rather than a solution. Many adults recall their school days as exercises in futility, when they were forced to memorize the names of national heroes, the dates of important battles, the exact length of rivers. Ronald Dore caricatured education in 1976 as "ritualistic, tedious, suffused with anxiety and boredom, destructive of curiosity and imagination; in short, anti-educational."

It must be incomprehensible to children why we are forcing them to learn exactly the same things which we neither enjoyed nor found useful ourselves, except for passing exams. Much as the aims and purposes of education are beautifully defined in theory, the practice for most children is drudgery and they alternate from voting with their feet and truanting or going through the ritual of memorising masses of useless data and hating it. Their right to question and challenge is not theirs, except in theory. Their voice is seldom heard. A boy aged 8 has feared becoming "the smallest unclever" in his family and pursued memorizing things which he found "very boring."

A Bosnian boy aged 13 has agonised over the muddle in his head created by having to memorise all the varied information which the syllabus has inflicted upon him, and has pursued as well. Their own experience is likely to result in their inflicting the same kind of drudgery upon their children. Giving children a voice while they are still at school would make all the difference, as the Convention on the Rights of the Child anticipates. School should be child-friendly, based on the right of the child "to be curious, to ask questions and receive answers, to argue and disagree, to test and make mistakes, to know and not know, to create and be spontaneous, to be recognized and respected."

The enormity of the task embodied in this vision clashes against the reality of schools that may be grappling with the lack of running water and sanitation, with the incompatibility of the school timetable with family and community life, with violence against and among children, with curricula and syllabi that force children to spend their schooling years constantly fearing that they will mix up the masses of information which they are forced to memorize. From the human rights viewpoint, education is an end in itself rather than merely a means for achieving other ends. Some economists, such as Alain Mingat, define education "as efficient production of human capital and its purpose is then structuring the supply of qualified people over a long period of time to make it more in line with economic demands."

The contrast between the human-rights and human-capital approaches is best illustrated taking children with physical and learning disabilities as example. They may be excluded from school because providing wheelchair access might be deemed too expensive or their learning deemed not to yield a sufficient marginal return on investment. This type of reasoning obviously challenges the very assumption of human rights, namely the equal worth of all human beings.

Is the recognition of the role of "human capital" adequate for understanding the importance of what has been called "human development," to wit the development of the capability of people to do the things they have reason to value and choose? There is a crucial difference here between means and ends. Seeing human qualities in terms of their importance in promoting and sustaining economic growth, significant as it is, tells us nothing about why economic growth is sought in the first place, nor much about the role of enhanced human qualities in making it directly possible for us to lead freer and more fulfilling lives.

Human beings are not only the most important means of social achievement, they are also its profoundest end. Being a fine piece of capital is not the most exalted state that can happen to a human being. Human capital is commonly defined as the sum of economically relevant attributes (knowledge, skills, competences) held by the working-age population. A human rights response ought to be forged lest the postulate of the International Labour Organization that labour is not a commodity risks falling into oblivion. Furthermore, accepting underlying market value of human capital risks turning upside- down the idea that economy should serve people rather than the other way around.

Theodore Schultz examined in 1962 risks embodied in an imbalance between non-human capital, such as land and physical capital, and human capital, which meant a healthy and educated population at the time. Schultz advocated investing in people so as to raise their capabilities. The literature on human capital has evolved in the past decades from the relationship between education and income, focusing on the economic value of schooling and/or the rate of return on schooling, especially private, to then affirm the productive utility of human knowledge.

This is only one out of many purposes of education. Such reductionism precludes defining education in terms of the full development of human personality, frustrating the very foundations for human rights education which require sharing knowledge rather than trading it and co-operating rather than competing. The human-capital approach moulds education solely towards economically relevant knowledge, skills and competences to the detriment of human rights values.

Education should prepare learners for parenthood and political participation, it should enhance social cohesion and tolerance and more than anything, it should teach the young that all human beings – themselves included – have rights. A productivist view of education depletes it of much of this purpose and substance. The human-capital approach has, however, revealed the importance of public investment in education as well as disparate prospects for attaining knowledge-based economies.

The current international priority for basic education has led to a halt in financial support for post-basic education. This fares ill against findings that the foundation necessary to enable individuals 'to build up their human capital' is upper-secondary education. Moreover, without secondary and university education, what education will teachers have so as to be able to teach children?

We have not enabled all children and young people to go to school and discussing the right to education thus requires exposing and opposing the abyss between the normative and empirical worlds. Children, more than adults, should but often do not have the right to education. Recognizing and guaranteeing their right to education thus remains priority. Once in school, children can be subjected to indoctrination as well as beaten into submission hence merely getting them into schools secures only one part of their right to education.

International human rights law has therefore from the very outset guaranteed fundamental freedom in education. Mere respect of such freedom, without guaranteed access to education for all children and young people, leaves the poor condemned to illiteracy or schooling of such poor quality that it cannot meet even the most generous definition of education.

The right to education straddles the division of human rights into civil and political, on one hand, and economic, social and cultural, on the other hand, thereby affirming the conceptual universality of human rights. Both the right to education and rights in education thus ought to be recognized and protected. Moreover, many human rights can only be accessed through education, particularly rights associated with employment and social security. Without education, people are impeded from access to employment. Lower educational accomplishment routinely prejudices their career advancement. Lower salaries negatively affect their old-age security.

Denial of the right to education triggers exclusion from the labour market and marginalization into the informal sector, which is accompanied by the exclusion from social security schemes because of the prior exclusion from the labour market. Redressing the existing imbalance in life chances without the full recognition of the right to education is then impossible. Moreover, illiterate people are routinely precluded from political representation. In many countries, literacy in general or in a particular language is prerequisite for becoming a candidate in elections. As recently as 1985, illiterate people were precluded from having a right to vote in Brazil. There is thus a large number of human rights problems which cannot be solved unless the right to education is addressed as the key to unlock other human rights.

Education operates as multiplier, enhancing the enjoyment of all individual rights and freedom where the right to education is effectively guaranteed, while depriving people of the enjoyment of many rights and freedom where the right to education is denied or violated.

The right to education is easiest to analyse by focusing on the corresponding governmental obligations on two levels:

- on the level of individual states as is customary in human rights, and
- on the level of global and regional intergovernmental structures within which governments act collectively.

While individual states are held primarily responsible for ensuring that human rights are effectively safeguarded, global economic and fiscal policies can constrain both the ability and the willingness of individual governments to guarantee the right to education. The identification and elimination of obstacles -especially financial — to the realization of the right to education is the key to progress. There is, nevertheless, no commitment to the right to education by international financial institutions such as the World Bank and the International Monetary Fund, nor the international donor community as a whole. The main reason are corollary duties and responsibilities.

The collective voice of governments has been supportive of education but less so of the human right to education, indicating that there is a difference between the two. This difference is epitomized in the post-war history. An international commitment to universal primary education for all children in the world was made once per decade. None materialized. Each betrayed pledge was followed by a similar pledge, which was also betrayed. The difference which human rights bring can be expressed in one single word — violation.

The mobilizing power of calling a betrayed pledge a human rights violation is immense. Moreover, legal enforcement of human rights obligations makes violations expensive. Resort to legal enforcement requires pre-existing individual and collective commitment to the right to education. The turn of the millennium has been marked by attempts to forge consensus within the international community on diagnosing problems faced by the whole world and devising solutions for them. High hopes have been focused on these global summits, hopes that a global vision of our common future will emerge and that commitments will be made to translate it into reality.

The established practice has been convening a follow-up global conference for each issue — women, environment, social development, or children — where one was held in the 1990s. The one on education was held ten years after the Jomtien Conference in 1990 had instilled a great deal of optimism by forging a set of global commitments.

The Fourth Global Meeting of the International Consultative Forum on Education for All took place in Dakar on 26-28 April 2000. This meeting has been referred to as Jomtien+10 in popular parlance as it was based, as the title of the final document indicates, on the acknowledgment that commitments made at Jomtien in 1990 had not been met.

The 1990 commitment had been to achieve universal primary education by the year 2000 but the target year was postponed to 2015. Whether we will do better in the first decade of the new millennium than in the last decade of the previous one is an open question. Answers tend towards pessimism unless corrective action is urgently undertaken. The 1990 Jomtien Conference was convened against the diminishing coverage of primary education in the 1980s, especially in Africa, where the proportion of primary-school age population in school declined by 10%. Further retrogression was feared and could only be halted through parallel measures at the global level and in individual countries.

The Jomtien Conference was a historic event intended to enhance priority for basic education through a global mobilization around time-bound targets. The language of the final document adopted by the Jomtien Conference merged human needs and market forces, moved education from governmental to social responsibility, made no reference to the international legal requirement that primary education be free of-charge, introduced the term 'basic education' which confused conceptual and statistical categories.

The language elaborated at Jomtien was different from the language of international human rights law. Those who saw Jomtien as a donor-driven process were proved right because donors' support for education did increase in the immediate follow-up to the Jomtien Conference.

Programmes and Policies

As a corollary, many developing countries started elaborating education-for-all strategies through assessments of basic learning needs (in the Jomtien jargon) and estimates of the associated resource requirements. The gap between the needs and the funds did not diminish much although the Jomtien meeting noted that "the downward trend of falling enrolments that we witnessed during the 1980s has been reversed." Reversing the retrogression of the 1980s necessitates profound domestic and international changes: Too few have taken place as yet and retrogression, was only halted, perhaps temporarily. While individual governments were traditionally deemed capable of complying with their human rights obligations if they exhibited the necessary political will, the tumultuous 1980s showed that the political will of many individual governments of poor countries was no longer sufficient to halt and reverse previous retrogression.

A great deal of global mobilization, within and outside the United Nations, was necessary to 'adjust adjustment,' to challenge and change the fiscal austerity which had badly affected primary education, making the right to education an un-affordable luxury in open contradiction to the international human rights law.

Human rights obligations demand that the maximum of available resources be allocated to human rights, thus explicitly targeting fiscal austerity. This line of reasoning would have been immensely helpful in drafting education strategies at Jomtien and, ten years later at Dakar, but was absent from both.

From the human rights perspective, no significant improvement was achieved in the year 2000. The status of the right to education in these global education strategies was obviously controversial because the formulations that were ultimately agreed upon in Dakar replicated 'the language of Jomtien.'

Suggestions to adopt the language of international human rights law, with its definitions of rights and obligation, violations and remedies, were apparently not heeded. References to human rights and to some treaties in which these are defined were more numerous than they had been in 1990, but the corresponding obligations were not mentioned.

The process of negotiating the final text adopted at Dakar had started in 1999 from a 30-page draft to end with a 5-page text in April 2000. Difficulties in reaching an agreement on collective commitments which the Dakar Conference was to finalize thus must have been considerable. The consequences of defining education as a human right are corollary duties and responsibilities, entailing changes in policies and practices of the respective agencies. Rights entail corresponding obligations as well as remedies for violations.

There were few financial commitments to carry out whatever transpires to have been agreed in Dakar; the $300 million was apparently spent to review the situation and reach an agreement that ultimately could not be reached — what to do after the conference has ended to reverse the ill fate of education, especially in the allocation of public funding. A sideshow was a heated debate as to whether education was or was not a human right. On the positive side, the advocates of selling and purchasing education lost the battle as references to the right to education were included in the final document. On the negative side, the advocates of buying and selling education won the war because there has been no financial commitment needed by the millions of poor children to get education as a matter of right.

The Dakar Conference has not done much to eliminate barriers in the way of the right to education. These are easy to articulate and this is done here by presenting a series of misconceptions, starting from the key obstacle which is routinely singled out for hindering the right to education -poverty. Similarly to the reluctance exhibited by the key actors at Jomtien and Dakar, barriers that need to be overcome on the road to the right to education can be traced to the price which recognizing the right to education entails. In the case of international agencies such as the World Bank or the International Monetary Fund, their policies have to be adjusted to making free primary education available and accessible to all children. This is costly for them because it often interferes with debt servicing by the respective governments, while they are owed much of this debt.

In the case of individual governments, budgetary allocations have to be adjusted to the requirements of international human rights law, education law has to be altered to recognize children as the subject of the right to education, curricula and textbooks have to be altered to accommodate all human rights for all, methods of instruction hindering human rights have to be eliminated. In the case of parents, accepting that their children are not their property but people with rights necessitates challenging the world-wide heritage of denying that children have any rights.

The way to the right to education is long and uphill. It is necessarily a relay-race because obstacles are many and diverse. First and foremost, economists and statisticians are needed to facilitate creating rights-based economic and fiscal policies and the associated statistics.

A range of professions and academic disciplines are necessarily involved in moulding education so that it can contribute to poverty eradication. It is, however, the principal task of the human rights community to dismantle misconceptions about linkages between poverty and human rights and these are addressed first.

At the beginning of the new millennium, the new vocabulary of donors' policies in education includes human rights and poverty eradication. Neither of the two is new but the linkage between them is novel. Clearly and powerfully articulated human rights-both in education and in poverty eradication-are necessary in order to prevent the current focus on poverty from lowering the goals of international development co-operation.

The changes in donors' policies have come at a time of constantly decreasing aid hence this fear. The shift from development to poverty eradication may lower the goal of helping individuals, communities and countries to develop by merely halting impoverishment. The shift from education to basic education focused donors' funding to the lowest rung in the education pyramid, sometimes also diminishing the age-range of beneficiaries from the previous 6-15 to 6-11.

Investment in education for all children was historically assigned to the state because it yields economic returns with much delay and, moreover, only in combination with other assets. The history of compulsory education did not revolve around economic arguments alone but these carried considerable weight. The need for a large pool of literate people was a driving force behind compulsory education during early industrialization as was the need to keep children out of the labour market thus enabling adult workers to negotiate and uphold fair wages. The economic rationale behind compulsory education also included ensuring that people can support themselves after leaving school lest they become a financial burden on public authorities.

Nevertheless, today education rarely attains the priority in budgetary allocation which international human rights law requires, and where it does, allocations tend to favour higher at the expense of primary education. South Korea is a favourite example of the sound economic rationale for investing first in primary and then secondary education, with two-thirds of public funding having been allocated to primary education in 1960-1975, followed by allocating one-third of the total to secondary education in 1975-1990.

The importance attached to secondary education differs from the current global emphasis on primary education as the passageway out of poverty. The example of South Korea is important because disappointments with education which has been ill-suited to income generation have been many. Recently they have been evidenced in Eastern Europe, where the generally high levels of education have not proved to have been a sound economic investment. It is indicative that only one in seven young people in Central Europe has rated education as essential for getting ahead in life. With scarce natural resources, Korea has relied heavily on human resources to develop its economy. Education being a major source for trained manpower, educational policies have changed in accordance with the types of human resources demanded by a changed economy.

In the 1950s, when low-level skilled workers were needed in manual industries, efforts were geared to undertake a massive scale literacy campaign to produce a manual workforce. In the 1960s, skilled workers were in great demand for light industries, and the focus was shifted to expand vocational education at the secondary school level. As the importance of heavy industries grew in the 1970s, technicians who could deal with complex modern manufacturing processes were in demand. The government responded by expanding junior technical colleges. The number of junior colleges nearly doubled in this period.

Economic Factors

In the 1980s, economic competitiveness based on high level technology and information industries became fierce and this challenge urged the Korean government to strengthen research and education in basic science and technology. Though there have been some mismatches, it is generally agreed that secondary school enrolment and investment in education have a positive and crucial relationship with economic growth in Korea.

Expansion of secondary enrolment and public investment in secondary education were very important in offsetting diminishing returns to investment in physical capital, and thus made significant contribution to achieving sustained per capita income growth. It is often pointed out that the positive effect from public investment in secondary education was made possible because Korea had a universal elementary education and had, as well, comparable rates of investment in physical capital along with export-oriented growth strategies. In other words, Korea expanded and universalized elementary education followed by secondary education, and only after achieving this, shifted its emphasis to the expansion of higher education.

The economic rationale for education in South Korea what Korea did right in the 1970s was that it spent four-fifths of its education budget on basic education, while countries with similar level of economic development focused on higher education. One significant effect of this improvement in basic education was that due to increased number of women with a basic education, the number of school age children remained stable.

Thus a growing amount of resources could be devoted to a stable number of children, allowing for improvements in the quality of education. In contrast, other countries which neglected the importance of basic education observed a growing number of school age children, and had to direct their educational resources to build more schools, with less resources left to improve the quality of education. Amongst the other ingredients of the relatively successful story of Korea's educational development, a right choice of policies, and an undisrupted implementation of these policies are deemed to have been crucial.

Disillusionment with education which is producing armies of unemployed graduates is well known throughout the world and demonstrates the necessity of adapting education to the children's future, to their prospects for supporting themselves. When this is not done, the parental choice not to send their children to school easily falls into the pattern described for Burkina Faso:

People who do not send their kids to school cannot solely be discarded as 'ignorant' but might have made a rational choice. Firstly, education is conducted in French, the official language, which is not spoken by most people. When children come to school, they first have to learn French before they may be able to access other subjects. Secondly, unemployment is common among the youth with years in school.

The economic incentive to send children to school is thus less convincing today. A main problem is that many children who go to school do not return to farm work any longer. To send children to school might constitute a double loss: first they cannot participate in farming and herding and thus contribute to subsistence, and, second, they might be able to get a job after school but would be unwilling to accept farming again.

A contribution to poverty alleviation of thus-designed schooling is unlikely because of the abyss between educational systems (as these have historically developed) and poverty reduction strategies (which have started in earnest at the turn of the millennium as a condition for debt relief). Educational systems were routinely designed to enable children to progress to post-primary education and ultimately acquire jobs, for which — as in Burkina Faso — French was essential as was migration to cities where post-primary education, and later the jobs, were. The most likely employer was the government. Redesign of formal schooling so as to enable young people to create their livelihood in rural areas, and to make it attractive for them to do so, remains a challenge yet to be met.

Education alone cannot even start addressing key problems. Poverty-alleviation strategies anticipate meeting this challenge and, to do so effectively, they would need to analyse the process of impoverishment (and enrichment) so as to discern the chain of causality. This is seldom done and poverty remains a notion that is not deemed to be man-made, which it almost always is. The statement that poverty is a human rights violation sounds good because people can intuitively sense that poverty and human rights clash against each other. Everybody can feel that something is wrong when children cannot go to school because they are too poor, and nobody is today publicly advocating that primary-school children should be working as was done in earlier times.

Going to school in comparison to working is idleness, and the longer boys continue in this easy sort of life, the more unfit they will be when grown up for downright labour.

The change in the past two centuries has been profound; although children are often forced to work, nobody is openly demanding that they should do so. On the level of rhetoric, there is agreement that children should be at school until they reach the minimum age for employment, usually set at the age of 15. There is no underlying commitment to make this happen, however. Poverty is routinely cited as the major cause of child labour.

Conventional wisdom relates the lack of access to education to poverty and sees the solution in throwing money at, the problem. A recipe of pouring money into countries where too many children are precluded from going to school might -paradoxically — do no good. Suffice it to mention that only 60% of educational budgets in Benin, Burkina Faso and Mali were spent in the late 1990s 16 although the need for additional funding was — and is-constantly emphasized.

Increasing an educational budget of a central government does not automatically translate into funding to teachers, schools, textbooks, and everything else that children need. Most children are not in national capitals hence their schooling necessitates a functioning country-wide educational system.

Problems are inversely related to the proximity to the national capital — the more distant, the less likely they are to be addressed. The willingness and ability of governments to raise funds and use them to educate children varies a great deal; neither should be presumed to exist already.

Child labour constitutes a huge obstacle for. children's education because it is mostly poverty-driven as children have to contribute to the survival of their families. Our fragmented manner of addressing these issues leads to singling out poverty in some regions and territories while not in others.

Myopic images of peace-making, as they were put into practice in Kosovo, have revolved around ethnicity and religion, autonomy and statehood, but not about education for the young and the price which children and young people have to pay when the survival of their families is jeopardized.

Unsurprisingly, "adolescents out of school and work request intensive courses for computer and foreign language skills so that they become qualified to work for international organizations" and these adolescents have pinpointed the core problem:" if parents had jobs, adolescents would have to work less."

To attain meaning, statements positing that poverty is a human rights violation would have to be followed up by identifying the actor (more likely, actors) who are perpetuating, or even increasing poverty. This is not the case and poverty becomes like the weather – everybody is complaining about it but deeming it to be beyond anybody's control. All donors are today committed to the eradication of poverty but so they were in the 1970s and there is not much to be shown as successful eradication of poverty. Something did happen, however. Poor school children seeing donors and their employees driving in their shiny four-wheel jeeps have learned one important lesson.

The then Norwegian minister of development co-operation has found that children have a very good idea how not to be poor after schooling:

In a classroom in Tanzania, the pupils were asked what they wanted to be when they grew up. Everybody answered: aid worker.

The flip-side of the statement that poverty is a human rights violation implicitly equates the antipode of poverty (which must be wealth) with the realization of human rights. Children whose parents purchase for them the best education that money can buy are then assumed to have their right to education recognized and realized. If the parents are at same time paying tax for an education that should but does not exist, they will not think so. The children are paying the price of corruption twice: firstly, they have been deprived of education, and, secondly, they will have to pay back the loans which successive military governments had taken and spent.

The placement of corruption on the agenda of international financial agencies and the donor community promises a change, but making this change happen will require a great deal of courage and determination. The postulate of international human rights law whereby governments should use the available resources to their utmost to secure all human rights for all serves as ready-made guidance.

International co-operation is defined as the principal means for facilitating the realization of the right to education but its prospects are hampered by a vicious circle. The volume of aid is at its lowest in history. The constantly diminishing aid flows include assertions that much aid is misappropriated or misused. Alongside corruption, nuclear weapons are a frequent target of critique. Amartya Sen, Nobel laureate in 1998 for restoring an ethical dimension to vital economic problems, has been asked about India's resources and priorities. He has suggested that the government should prioritize education, health care and land reform. Asked where India would find the money, Sen replied:

"If one has any sense of priority, to say that India does not have the money is absolute, utter, unmitigated nonsense."

From the recipient's perspective, the glaring discrepancy between vast aid needs and minuscule aid flows does not give donors moral credibility to demand accountability. In its extreme, such attitude becomes give-us- the-money-and-go away. Children who cannot go to school because the dialogue between donors and recipients has worked itself into a blind alley have no voice.

Getting the children, their parents and teachers involved in securing that funds for education reach their destination is not a particularly difficult task. It would rupture the vicious circle of enrichment of intermediaries and impoverishment of beneficiaries which aid often sustains.

Rights-based development is a syntagm that has spread within international development co-operation at the turn of the millennium. The term indicates that development should be founded upon human rights. Previously, the rights of actors funding and carrying out development interventions were asserted and protected but not necessarily the rights of beneficiaries.

These beneficiaries were treated as objects of development interventions (developees) with developers retaining all the rights. It is against this heritage that the term rights-based development has been coined. In the words of Claire Short, Britain's Secretary of

State for International Development, there are three particular changes that ought to be made so as to make development aid rights-based:

- if we want to work for human rights we must be willing to take risks and reach out where we can, rather than sit smugly at home and feel good about hectoring governments that oppress their people;
- this new approach also has implications for the way we work. In our White Paper, the Government commits itself to a rights-based approach to development. This means making people the central purpose of development. Not by speaking or acting on their behalf, but by allowing them to speak for themselves – to articulate their own interests and needs;
- strategies for development should not be a secret deal between governments – done behind closed doors.

The heritage of changing vocabularies in international development co-operation entails a risk that human rights language may be appropriated without its contents. There are no self-activating safeguards against abuses of the term 'rights' or 'rights-based.' As these terms have been divorced from their grounding in international human rights law, there is a risk that 'rights' will become a weasel-word into which almost any contents can be fitted. The process whereby this is done is well known and entails exercise in power. It would thus benefit from the application of human rights simply because human rights are safeguards against abuse of power.

Partnership has become a keyword in international development co-operation, also at the turn of the millennium. Partnership between indebted governments and their creditors assumes a relationship of equals. Where one side desperately needs a cheque while another holds the cheque book, it takes a great deal of creativity to define such a relationship as one of equals. The language of partnership assumes relationships which would have made human rights work redundant from the outset. The term 'partnership' disguises inequalities and hampers identifying, exposing and opposing abuses of power. Those who wield power may abuse it hence human rights safeguards are necessary, always and everywhere.

Human rights NGOs have been established to expose and oppose human rights violations, and this role neither will nor can be taken over by governments, individually or collectively. Moreover, human rights work cannot always be carried out in partnership with governments. There is an adage shared amongst human rights NGOs whereby one cannot work in human rights and be popular with governments. Human rights work necessitates identification of those who wield power so as to be able to prevent or remedy its abuse. Despite this new language of rights-based education and partnership, the practice of selling and purchasing education is gaining ground, embodying a risk that education will be moved from international human rights law to international trade law. Contemporary changes can be illustrated by an increasing resort to the term 'rights' to denote shareholders' or creditors' rights 28 rather than in the sense attributed to this term in international human rights law.

In education, UNESCO has thus defined the danger of depleting the rights-language of its original meaning:

In so far as the 'right to lifelong learning' is understood to include a 'right' to continuing education, it would seem in practice to amount to little more than the 'right' of any citizen to participate, at his or her own expense, in the market for goods and services generally, with more or less encouragement from public funds depending on the situation in individual countries.

This process of transforming the rights-language so as to make it fit the prevalent ideological commitment to the free market is accompanied by broadening and deepening inequalities in access to education. Donors' concentration on basic education has made universities, particularly in Africa, starved of funding. The profits of exporting education services to people who have no access to them in their own countries dwarfs aid for basic education.

Moreover, information and communication technology is referred to as a global phenomenon, although only 5% of people in the world have access to it.

A new term — digital divide — has been coined to depict this new abyss. Public investment in education has led to the completion of upper-secondary education by more than half of the working-age population in the OECD countries. The OECD has moved to almost all-encompassing enrolment at the secondary level, while for most developing countries not even data on enrolment are available.

Children aged 5-15 constitute 13% of the population in OECD but 30% in developing countries. UNESCO has perceptively observed that adults in the OECD countries are running out of children to educate and attention has thus switched to prolonging their own education ('right to life long learning'), which fits the aging populations.

In developing countries, meagre funds have to be stretched to educate a large proportion of children. As a consequence, virtually all children will complete 11 years of compulsory education in the OECD, while in developing countries all-encompassing primary education has yet to be attained; providing 11 years of education to all remains a distant dream. The abyss between knowledge-based and education-deficit regions is not likely to be narrowed spontaneously but rather to increase. International trade in education services is emerging as a principal means for increasing this abyss.

The globalization of professional and academic qualifications has been based on "a relatively uniform culture, set of business practices and language" and has re-actualized the phenomenon of brain drain. The linkage between aid for education and trade in education services is evidenced in donors' allocations for students from developing countries, which makes such funding into both aid and export revenue. Diminished aid for higher education in developing countries leads to increased numbers of students going to study abroad.

A further link is diminished public funding for higher education in the donor countries themselves, which pressurizes educational institutions to seek ways to overcome financial shortfall, including through exporting their services. This circulus inextricabilis has attracted attention but too little is known about it as yet.

Data ought to be compiled and collated from a maze of public and private institutions, with a further difficulty inherent in the protection of commercial confidentiality of such data. More importantly, the underlying conceptual change treats education as a commodity to be sold and purchased and necessitates reaffirmation of education as a right. Another conceptual change has been brought about by sanctions, which are imposed against a particular state but, because the state is a legal rather than real-life concept, they harm the country.

Sanctions against Iraq have been particularly long and comprehensive, and their effects on education harsh. There have been pronouncements of human rights bodies on this issue, with the Committee on Economic, Social and Cultural Rights lamenting that humanitarian exemptions do not encompass access to primary education, and the Commission on Human Rights reaffirming that food and medicine should not be used as tools for political coercion, but not mentioning education. Deprivation of education can be encompassed by sanctions which would then, according to Marc Bossuyt's study for the Sub-Commission on the Promotion and Protection of Human Rights, constitute a violation of the right to education.

Children are a popular object for fund-raising because they elicit a sense of guilt when deprived of food, water, schooling, or clothing. Statistics on children deprived of access to school are used a great deal, even if they show two sides of the coin. On the one hand, such data reflect this sense of guilt towards children who we have failed as adults. On the other hand, these data show that we really do not know how many children we have failed, not even to the closest ten million. The full scope of investment necessary to make schools really rather than nominally available is hidden because the most frequent internationally used indicator — enrolment — does not capture either out-of-school children or the real-life schools.

A UNESCO/UNICEF pilot survey of primary schools in the least developed countries has revealed that electricity or piped water is an exception rather than a rule, while many children finish primary school without ever seeing a single textbook in their mother tongue. This reality is often hidden behind the existing education statistics — nominally available schools are counted in, children registered at the beginning of school year are counted as if they attended school the whole time, teachers are presumed to be teaching although their salaries may not have been paid for months or even years.

Quantifications have become a hallmark of every international strategy; education is no exception. A desperate search for the exact number of children precluded from schooling yields precise, if varying data -from 100 to 150 million. The purport of such exercises is to demonstrate precision, to delineate the scope of the problem and assess the effort needed to solve it. No matter how much they vary, the numbers of out-of-school children are numbing and tend to elicit apathy or frustration rather than decisive action. Moreover, poor starving children tend to be portrayed not as subjects of rights but objects of charity.

The effects of their marginalization spring to global attention when they strive to make their way to rich countries or get involved in wars which are seen as senseless from these rich countries. The tendency to romanticise poverty interferes with common sense.

Rather than seeing poverty as brutalising and dehumanising, with the instinct for survival pressurizing people towards selling their children or their own organs to survive, poor people tend to be portrayed as waiting for a solution to their problems while patiently starving to death. A widespread approach has then emerged prioritising the counting of poor people so that measures could be devised to somehow alleviate their poverty. Education has become part of the package which routinely follows from this approach.

A commonsensical approach holds true that education could be the first step on the ladder out of poverty, but unless additional steps are in place, education on its own cannot do much, if anything. Teaching landless peasants the alphabet does not lead to their land ownership or to productive use of that alphabet unless they can create some way of earning their livelihood. The full range of issues to be built into education strategies often turns out to be too complicated or costly, and sights are then lowered to getting children to school. A drawback is that nobody knows how many children are out of school, where they are, who they are, how old they may be, why they are not in school, which language they understand. A hunt for figures follows, with varying outcomes.

Counting the children makes obtaining the figures costly in time and resources because it requires field-work. Mathematical modelling comes to rescue by facilitating the creation of data which exhibit the desired precision at low cost. Would it really make a difference if we knew that precisely 107,982, 346 children lack access to any education whatsoever? It is unlikely that we could ever get the figures right because quite a few children would die while being counted because they regularly lack not only education but also food, shelter and safe water. Those children who are encompassed by enrolment statistics, and thus counted as having access to education, do not necessarily have their right to education recognized. The way from access to school to education that is compatible with human rights is long and progress is impeded by another set of conceptual obstacles.

The assumption that education is inherently good is as prevalent as it is unfounded on reality. Images of education not being good-and-desired are rare. One has been unearthed by Victoria Britain in Angola: "When a soba (chief) explains that people do not want to send their children to school because they see that those who go become politicians or businessmen and are thieves and liars, you know you have got a really fundamental need for a change."

Because negative images of education are rare, the assumption that it is inherently good is widespread and seldom, if ever, challenged. Discussions about Education Statistics is governed by the rule of correlation: it is the least available for those countries where education is also the least available and the need for data is thus greatest. The consequence is resort to technological short-cuts. Mathematical models are applied to invent the size of the population of Angola or Afghanistan. Nobody can fault it because nobody knows how many people there may be in these two and many other countries.

Statistics on school enrolment are created by estimating the numbers of children in each age bracket, pupil-teacher ratios are construed by associating the statistically created numbers education tend to focus on how to provide it and how to increase the provision. Any subject which is taught can be abused. Anti-human-rights messages can be found in mathematics as these examples show:

- In Hitler's Germany, a mathematics textbook nudged learners to calculate financial savings that would ensue from eliminating mentally ill people: "The construction of a lunatic asylum costs 6 million DM. How many houses at 15,000 DM each could have been built for that amount."
- One maths book, printed in the US during the Afghan war for use amongst Afghani refugees, offered the following mathematical problem: "If you have two dead Communists, and kill three more, how many dead Communists do you have?"
- A school textbook in Tanzania in the 1970s included the following mathematical problem: "A freedom fighter fires a bullet into an enemy group consisting of 12 soldiers and 3 civilians all equally exposed to the bullet. Assuming one person is hit by the bullet, find the probability that the person is (a) a soldier, (b) a civilian.

The widely shared belief that getting all children into school is always a solution, never a problem persists, however. Parents whose children have been beaten in school so badly that they ended up in emergency ward to be treated for injuries know better. Abuses of education became institutionalized through re-education camps, where political dissidents were (still are) brainwashed into regurgitating the dogma espoused by the powers that be. Throughout history, education has been particularly effective in the militarization of boys. Participation in warfare has been part of traditional initiation rituals, through which boys become men.

Glorification of war continues through history textbooks which are dotted with wars and war heroes, through the promotion of violent sports, and limitless commercialization of computerized war games. Education for war has, unfortunately, a much longer tradition and commercial attractiveness than education for peace. An image that education is good and one just needs to secure additional funds to provide more of it could never be endorsed by the indigenous peoples in Latin America, who have experienced education as oppression.

Those who dared to rupture the denial of education and ventured to school were severely punished. Women who remain openly indigenous while schooling children have three layers of prejudice to overcome. A judgment about the contribution which education made to the genocide in Rwanda by creating and reinforcing mutual Hutu-Tutsi prejudices is pending.

The UN Special Rapporteur on Rwanda at the time has noted how successive governments conditioned the population to the acceptance of ethnic discrimination and moulded education to fit this aim: The schools took it upon themselves to develop actual theories of ethnic differences, based on a number of allegedly scientific data which were essentially morphological and historiographical. In the first case; the two main groups can be differentiated by appearance, as the Tutsi are 'long' whereas the Hutu are 'short'; the Tutsi are handsome, genuine 'black-skinned Europeans' while the Hutu are 'ugly', genuine 'Negroes'.

The fact that the Hutu occupied the country before the Tutsi makes them indigenous, whereas the Tutsi, as descendants of

Europeans, are invaders. These purportedly scientific data inevitably created a psychosis of fear and mistrust which gradually became a veritable culture of mutual fear and led to another theory, that of pre-emptive self-defence based on the 'kill or be killed principle'. This theory was a major factor in the 1994 genocide.

Using human rights safeguards to constrain the power inherent in writing history books, from which the coming generations are going to learn their own history, is often needed but lacking. The issue is deemed to be 'technical' regardless of its often being a veritable political minefield. Regarding the discrimination that still affects the indigenous woman, in her traditional skirt, the Vice-President of the Republic, Victor Hugo Cardenas, made the following statement in a press interview: "Cardenas recognizes that progress is slow, though tangible, and does not deny that indigenous communities still suffer from Dubravko Lovrenovic, a professor of history at the University of Sarajevo, has recalled a voice which euphorically told him by phone on the eve of the war: "It is now our turn to write history."

Writing history to describe to both Tutsi and Hutu children what happened in Rwanda, how and why, will inevitably be as difficult as it is important. The emergence of truth commissions has played a pioneering role in quite a few countries by re-writing recent history, often negotiating a history that can be accepted by the victims and their victimizers, by the oppressed and their oppressors. More than fifty years after the end of the Second World War, the pre-war history is being re-written throughout Europe. Moreover, the role of education in conflict-generation is seldom portrayed in history textbooks. They tend to remain confined to consequences, especially violence, while keeping silent about the myriad of factors which generated and facilitated the underlying conflicts.

The initial enthusiasm for mass education at independence soon gave way to the institutionalization of inequality. Mass enrolment at the beginning of primary school did not lead to mass persistence throughout primary and secondary education to continue at the university and education was slanted towards the interests of the narrow elite whose children actually made it all the way up to the university. Frustrated expectations of early school leavers – especially boys – have been shown to lead to criminality, violence, and warfare. Their abandonment by the system of education to their own fate was accompanied by the paucity of lawful methods for securing livelihood and the attraction of pursuing unlawful ones with impunity.

The abundance of bad models to imitate and the absence of good ones made the choice of many adolescents a foregone conclusion. The neglect of adolescents, highlighted in Sierra Leone, has been an unintended consequence of the priority for primary education in global education strategies as of the 1990s and will hamper efforts at peace-making unless it is reversed. An important obstacle to universalizing the right to education is a view that education is not indispensable for human survival nor required for subsistence, that families can function with children labouring rather than learning.

The Exploited Ones

The absence of education for victims of armed conflicts and disasters dooms them to remain recipients of assistance while preventing them from becoming self-sustaining. Water, sanitation, medical services, shelter, clothing and food constitute the 'survival package' which is offered through humanitarian relief. Including education in this package is a development of the 1990s, but overcoming the previous 'ideology of survivalism' has yet to become institutionalized. Arguably, the most negative aspect of Sierra Leone's elitist system of education has to do with a complete failure to cater for those who do not make, it within the system.

School drop-outs are simply not provided for in any serious or meaningful way. Thus, those who do not survive and rise to the top of this narrow and competitive system simply become the 'forgotten aspirants' in a very elitist educational process. In situations where only a tiny minority can get a complete and reasonable quality education, the price of ignorance weighs more heavily on those who have some schooling than those who never had access to school.

The role of education in spawning warfare Sierra Leone aspirants', which is turn could serve as a time-bomb waiting to explode. It is not surprising therefore to find 'forgotten aspirants' playing a role as combatants on both sides of the rebel war in Sierra Leone. Because of the demonstrated impact of education in promoting social mobility in newly independent Sierra Leone, wrong signals have been sent to the subsequent generations. This has given rise to unrealistic expectations about what can be achieved by virtue of mere school attendance and certification. At independence in 1961, the drive for indigenisation meant that nationals with little more than secondary level qualifications were catapulted to top positions. Later, the new and expanding population of university graduates were guaranteed high-level jobs regardless of specialisation.

Most secondary school graduates could also be certain of reasonable jobs within the public sector. When economic growth and job creation began to lag behind output of universities and schools, reality dictated that educational qualifications *per se* could no longer be a guarantee of any job, much less top level jobs. Unfortunately, expectations continued to fly in the face of this new reality. The belief that schooling leads to good jobs could not be questioned. Hence a strong sense of delusion persisted amongst learners that society owes them something once they have gone through the education system.

Designing rights-based education necessitates eliminating barriers which keep human rights separated from education. It is not only parents and children but also teachers who have rights. The status of teachers can be forgotten in education strategies and it often is. It is much too easy to define teachers as a production factor in the manufacturing of human capital and forget that they are people with rights.

Probing into the teachers' fate can reveal that neither their labour rights nor their trade union freedom are recognized and that their salaries are much too low to enable them to teach as they have to combine three or four full-time jobs to be able to feed their families. Although it is possible to imagine schooling taking place without schools but not without teachers, the attention to schools and textbooks in international education strategies is immense while they are relatively silent about teachers.

The advantage of teaching being labour-intensive is that employment of large numbers of people is possible — necessary — to educate the millions of children and young people in the world. Since teachers are locally trained, hired and paid, the additional benefit is that there is no need for foreign exchange, different from schools or schoolbooks that may be provided through loans which ought to be repaid. It seems, however, that instead of being seen as an actor indispensable for schooling, teachers may be perceived as an enemy of their own vocation.

One reason for viewing teachers as a burden rather than asset is the proportion of education budgets allocated to teachers' salaries. In a country where school-age children represent one third of the population, a ratio of one teacher per every fifty children makes teachers 0.6% of the population. As there is little besides teachers in the schooling process in many poor countries, teachers salaries necessarily form the bulk of the education budget. The consecutive crises through which education has passed in the recent decades triggered a constant search for cutting down education budgets. Because teachers' salaries constitute the bulk of education budgets, they were the obvious first target for budgetary cuts and an ideological rationalization has followed. The protection of human rights of teachers sometimes slips into oblivion if teachers are defined as an education- production-factor rather than being treated as people.

The applicable international human rights standards are many because the problems teachers encounter are complex and multi-layered. They range from the application of the internationally prohibited grounds of discrimination to teachers' recruitment and deployment, to the protection of their professional and academic freedom, or to the role of teachers in human rights education. Problems in enforcement have ranged from the teachers' status as civil and/or public servants leading to the denial of their trade union freedom, or a definition of teaching as an essential service leading to the denial of their right to strike.

The expectations upon teachers to integrate human rights education throughout the curriculum, against the background of denials of their own rights, demonstrate why human rights are indivisible. Acknowledging that all human rights ought to be recognized and protected clashes, however, not only against human-capital approaches but also against the trust in democracy as a substitute for human rights.

Without human rights correctives, resource allocation in education looks pretty much the same worldwide. Most money goes to universities, whose learners are the most expensive to school, the fewest in number, and the most likely to pertain to the country's elite.

The lack of political voice of primary-school children, especially in rural areas, makes the allocation of funds for education a foregone conclusion. University students are present in national capitals, politically articulate, and regularly come from the wealthiest segment of the population.

The language of rights effectively favours university students and fits into the paradigm depicted by Massimo Cacciari through his homo democraticus, who has all the rights but no corresponding duties, is unwilling to accept any limitations upon his freedom, including freedom of spending to satisfy all his desires, easily setting aside the needs of the next generation because they do not have a political voice.

Low budgetary allocations are typical for categories that lacks a political voice hence human rights law strives to alter this pattern by remedying the lack of political voice through bestowing legal rights. Primary school children cannot form a political party, get elected to parliament and secure budgetary allocations for themselves.

International human rights law requires progressive realization of the right to education where primary education ought to be made free of charge, and this should gradually extend to post-primary and, ultimately, university education. This approach is known as progressive realization and is exactly the opposite to results of political processes taking place in the absence of human rights correctives.

Retrogressive realization of the right to education then provides those at the very top of the education pyramid with most funding while ultimately precluding those at the bottom – the youngest – from even getting started. The proportion of children in the northern part of the world is small and their parents can secure funding for education by combining their political voice with paying tax. In Africa, children constitute the majority of the population but obtain a vote after becoming adults and joining the minority who has the right to vote.

Few of their parents pay tax, many because they earn too little, and their vote seldom affects budgetary allocations, often because there is too little to distribute after foreign debt has been serviced. Children's right to education thus goes beyond national and regional borders, it is universal and addresses governments collectively. It also highlights what an abyss there is between democracy and human rights, which have erroneously become treated as they were one and the same.

The absence of an enforceable claim upon governments to allocate a specific amount to education highlights the need to focus on the procedure whereby allocations are decided upon. Human rights are seldom costed because human rights standards do not determine how much should be spent on specific items, but define substantive and procedural human rights standards; the latter encompass the process of decision making. Exercise of political rights thus becomes the necessary instrument for attaining economic and social rights, imposing upon those who exercise them a duty towards others.

University students are politically vocal, primary school age children are not, and the latter can easily be neglected in the allocation of resources. The proverbial preference for university students in budgetary allocations within education (in the extreme exceeding up to one thousand times the allocation for primary education) vividly illustrates the necessity for introducing the human rights rationale throughout the process of resource allocation, from global to local.

As adults we should (but never do) acknowledge that we routinely abuse our power over children. International human rights law affirms the parental choice for education of their children, but requires states to constrain it where this choice jeopardizes the best interests of the child. This postulate has yet to be translated into practice. A visiting Martian would have a great deal of difficulty understanding what the humanity, as species, is really trying to do.

In one country we are expelling girls from school because they are wearing a headscarf, in another we are precluding them from access to school because they are not wearing a headscarf. Nobody would be able to persuade such a visiting Martian that we really care about our children's education or about their rights.

Assuming that advancing human rights is easy clashes against conflicting rights, as is often the case with parents and children. In a rare case where a child, sixteen years old, has been accorded the right to challenge parental disagreements about the choice of school for her, justice Dalcq in Bruxelles has acknowledged that the best interest of the child should prevail. The case involved a girl whose divorced parents disagreed as to which school she should attend. The girl had ultimately refused to attend the school chosen by the mother (who exercised parental rights) and ended up attending no school, to then legally challenge the mother's attempt to force her to attend the school which her mother had chosen.

The child's choice of school was judicially vindicated so as to prevent further jeopardy of the child's right to education. An implicit agenda of schooling may be to keep children conformist and deferential, forcing them to kneel when addressing adults, training them to recite the, official dogma without allowing them to ask questions, getting them to accept physical punishment for faults which children often cannot even understand.

A textbook for Christian religious education used in East Africa highlights obedience as the explicit purpose of education: "At school we have to obey people who are not our parents and this is real preparation for life." An excerpt from a textbook on children's accounts of their childhood, used by fifteen year old Ugandans in the 1970s, describes the fearful, uncomprehending obedience which was instilled through schooling.

Children were trained from their earliest years to be respectful, obedient and mannerly, these being the standards by which adults became acceptable in society. All parents, and fathers in particular were very stern with their children who in any way departed from such standards. Furthermore the punishment for children who misbehaved, however harsh, had to be accepted without question or complaint. Thus the children, respectfully submissive, learned to fear their fathers as harsh and severe. Strong feelings of dislike though dutifully suppressed were very frequently mixed with this fear.

Inculcating obedience easily leads to children's following orders without questioning them, especially when punishment accompanies failure to do so. Corporal punishment socializes children into accepting violence, and the combination of obedience and violence easily makes them ideal child soldiers. The curriculum is often design to accommodate what the closely involved adults, principally parents and teachers, are comfortable with rather than what children need and nominally have a right to get.

There are few explicit assertions of children's right to learn about sexuality in school, a rare example was included in the

Children's Charter, which was adopted on 1 June 1992 by the Children's Summit of South Africa. It posited that all children had the right to adequate education on issues such as sexuality. This was a courageous and immensely ambitious statement, at odds with the adults' proverbial intransigence regarding children's access to sex education. The 10-year United Nations Girls' Education Initiative, launched at the Dakar Education for All Forum in April 2000, requires a great deal of human rights input in responding to the Secretary General's challenge to empower girls to protect themselves against HIV/AIDS.

Prevented from going to school, girls are denied information about how to protect themselves against the virus. Without the benefit of an education, they risk being forced into early sexual relations, and thereby becoming infected. Thus, they pay many times over the deadly price of not going to school.

There is no need to point out how controversial human sexuality, an inevitable part of HIV/AIDS-education, has been, and how much effort is needed to design and put into practice educational modules acceptable to all relevant actors. Progress is evident from the attention paid to children's right to obtain knowledge necessary for their self-protection, which has replaced the silence of the past decades.

Education law has traditionally treated children as objects of education, specifying the rights of parents, teachers and the state. The affirmation of the rights of the child has not yet been accomplished in most countries. There is a welcome move in this direction, which prioritizes the best interests of the child as a step towards child's rights. The Supreme Court of Canada has affirmed that restraint should be exercise by adults, particularly parents, in order to mould education towards the best interests of the child.

For a child who is young or unable to communicate his or her needs or wishes, equality rights are being exercised on his or her behalf, usually by the child's parents. Moreover, the requirements for respecting these rights in this setting are decided by adults who have authority over this child.

For this reason, the decision-making body must further ensure that its determination of the appropriate accommodation for an exceptional child be from a subjective child-centered perspective, one which attempts to make equality meaningful from the child's point of view as opposed to that of the adults in his or her life. As a means of achieving this aim, it must also determine that the form of accommodation chosen is in the child's best interest.

The Supreme Court of Colombia has taken this rationale one step further, holding that school children should have the possibility to express their personality. It was examining a case involving a boy, who had been wearing an earing in class, whereupon the teacher commented that this earing suggested that the boy was a homosexual. The Court faulted the teacher's inappropriate behaviour and insisted that relations between pupils and teachers should be altered.

The subjects of the educational process are not divided into passive recipients of knowledge and active depositories of wisdom. The constitutional principle which guarantees the free development of personality and the right to participate in the educational community have transformed the learners into active subjects who participate in education through their rights and duties ....

The relation of pupil-teacher is not based upon the authority which the teacher can exercise as the ultimate depository of wisdom or through his hierarchically superior position, but rather upon reciprocal respect of the subjects of the educational process with the same possibility for free expression, under the sole condition of not jeopardizing the rights of others or the just order.

The most far-reaching interpretations of the rights of the child have focused on children with disabilities. These overruled the previous exclusionary approach, whereby children had to fit into the existing schools and, if they could not remain out-or-school or be segregated into special schools. Children relying on wheelchairs for their mobility could not access schools which were built without access for wheelchairs. Children unable to conform to criteria of linguistic proficiency or successfulness in testing were segregated into special schools. A veritable conceptual revolution has been created by turning around such premises, whereby the school had an implicit right to turn away the child because the child did not fit. Affirming the best interests of each child, and gradually equal rights of each child, has reversed the premises for decision-making — it is the school which has to adapt to the child, not the other way around. The German Federal Constitutional Court has affirmed the need to design specific solutions through explicitly balancing all pertinent human rights dimensions.

The current state of pedagogical research does not indicate that a general exclusion of disabled children from integrated general schools can be constitutionally justified.

Education should be integrated, providing special support for disabled pupils if required, so far as the organizational, personal and practical circumstances allow this. This reservation is included as an expression of the need for the State to consider all the needs including the financial and organizational factors, of the community in carrying out its duties.

Globally, under all categories, the children most frequently excluded are girls. Gender continues to be the major causal factor in children being left out, and pushed out, of school. The denial of a girl's right to education remains a pernicious and persistent characteristic of many societies on a purposive basis, for reasons of culture and family choice.

Beliefs that the formal education of girls is inappropriate or unnecessary, and failures to make schools safe, secure and empowering places for girls, continue to create systemic gender bias in who goes to school and successfully completes a basic education. Girls are excluded by cultures insisting on early marriage and preparing for that role by young years focused on domestic chores, caring for siblings and protecting virtue. They are excluded when, due to pregnancy, they are forced to drop out of school and rarely given support by either home or school to return.

The figures are well known but none the less dramatic: approximately two-thirds of the 130 million primary-school-age children not in school are girls. In Africa, almost 26 million girls are out of school.

In Afghanistan, under the Taliban, net primary attendance is only 36% for boys, but a tragic 11% for girls; while 47% men are literate, only 15% of women are. In the Lao People's Democratic Republic, of the 64% of adults who are literate, only 35% are girls and women. In Yemen, girls' participation is only about 31%, some 42 points behind that of boys. They are the especially vulnerable. Children limited in realizing their full potential for learning by being denied access to a good quality education are also children who are physically, intellectually or emotionally vulnerable. This includes children who have been put at risk by the inadequate pre- and post-natal care available to their mothers, by their own nutritional deficit or by an early home environment that failed to nurture or stimulate them. The 120,000 children who survived iodine deficiency disorder in 1990 and are now afflicted with cretinism; the 250,00() who survived vitamin A deficiency and are now blind; and the thousands who are manned annually by landmines, are all children whose right to learn and be educated to their full potential has been put at risk.

Children are also systematically excluded in many cases on the basis of what the society and school define as disability. Like much else about exclusion, beliefs and actions around disability cause a great deal of suffering, but few clear answers.

Of an assumed 10% of children in a population with some form of disability, it is estimated that as few as 3% of those in developing countries have access to rehabilitation services. Globally, it is the tragedy of these children that along with the special efforts they themselves have to make in order to participate, they have to deal with education systems which define them out by failing to apply a framework which creates environments better suited to all learners.

Children are excluded where no provision is made to support them when physical, emotional or intellectual difficulties interfere with their learning. It is estimated that only 1 % of such children are in school. In more-industrialized countries, where they do often have access to school, the participation of these children may still be marginal.

The poor pedagogical training of teachers can limit both the effective management of the particular learning needs of these children and their integration into the social relationships of the class. Elsewhere, these problems are exacerbated by an overall lack of resources, child-accessible facilities and expertise.

Most insidiously, perhaps, these children are excluded by being rendered statistically invisible: not included among the potential total school-going population and, therefore, not missed when they do not turn up.

In near-crisis proportions for some countries and new since Jomtien, the answer to the question of who is being excluded is children affected by HIV/AIDS. Clearly traumatic for children in terms of their health, HIV/AIDS is also having tragic impacts on their right to be protected by and participate in their society, and on their ability to protect and manage themselves. One of the enduring traumas for affected children is that the discrimination associated with HIV/AIDS can put certain of their rights (of access to care and learning) at jeopardy of others (their right to confidentiality).

Children are also being negatively affected when their parents and other family members are infected and die. AIDS has created over 8.2 million orphans between the critical school ages of 6 and 12), a figure that is expected to reach 40 million by 2010 (UNFPA, 1998, p. 18).

HIV/AIDS is thus creating children who are suddenly responsible not only for their own protection and care, but also that of younger siblings and other infected relatives, and with few human or financial resources to bring to bear in doing so. With an HIV/AIDS affected family typically comes a downward spiral of exclusions: economic problems, leading to inability to pay school fees and dropping out; food insecurity and difficulties with other basic needs; sometimes loss of land and possessions to relatives, and a move into the street where vulnerabilities increase exponentially.

Children's ability to access services, and the quality of those services, are most certainly being affected. This includes limiting their ability to go to, and stay in, school and the ability of schools to ensure that the teachers will be there when the children do come. In Zambia, 680 teachers were reported to have died of AIDS-related illnesses in 1996, 624 the following year and 200 in the first few months of 1998, 'figures which translate into more than 2.1 % of trained teachers or almost two per day'.

Monitoring the progress and impact of the epidemic on different groups of children at risk and on their learning is fundamental to ensuring appropriate action on their behalf. As education systems fail, however, any mitigating influences for children in terms of the nurturing, knowledge, skills and protection that might come from education are being even further reduced.

They are minorities and indigenous. Children excluded from education are frequently the children of ethnic minorities and indigenous groups. These two types of community are often distinguished in terms of the intensity, persistence and scope of their exclusion from mainstream societies. Common to them in terms of their children's education, however, is the serious risk that many are facing from schools which fail both to treat children equitably as learners and to respect their cultures as valid systems of knowledge and values.

For both indigenous communities and long-standing ethnic minorities, the fact of exclusion is real, and it is serious. In 1994, 70% of Peru's Quechua-speaking people over 5 years of age had not been to school; in Guatemala, 80% of the rural indigenous population was illiterate. In China's Qinghai Province, an area of nomadic herders, attendance at the secondary level has dropped more than 66% over the last decade, largely as a result of rising school costs and fewer jobs, making these costs less tenable. These are not rare instances.

The questions for education concern the nature and impact of this isolation on quality of life, and how the situation should be addressed to ensure effective learning and equity. The questions go beyond issues of poverty and marginalization. They include how the rights of these children and communities will be preserved, and their best interests ensured, when their very history, culture and language serve both to exclude them and to put them at risk of never being able to achieve 'inclusion'.

In most cases there is no reasonable possibility of these communities remaining outside the mainstream. Without the dignity of any choice, however, education systems are excluding these families and their children by leaving them to handle the balancing of socio-cultural integration, assimilation and disintegration as best they can.

Many of these children will not go to school; most who do go, will not stay. The Karimojong of Uganda provide a cogent example. A semi-nomadic people in a 'highly fragile and precarious ecological environment', the formal primary school:

> . . . has failed to provide . . . children with the necessary knowledge, attitudes and skills relevant to their roles and livelihood . . . which neither equips them to become productive members of their society nor prepares them to take up meaningful life outside it undermines their values, traditional knowledge and skills, cultural traits and form of education which are crucial to survival. The curriculum is generally irrelevant does not stress preparation for self-reliance, (a) positive image of pastoralism for the emergence of traditional and modern pastoral cultures which would enhance the economic contribution of pastoralism to the national economy . . . . The formal primary-school education continues to threaten social ethics . . . and has rigid instructional methodology. On top of all this, it is also expensive and requires full-time attendance unsuited to a nomadic culture.

Indigenous and ethnic-minority children are continuing to be excluded because partnerships and negotiations between the community and externally oriented schools are not sufficiently effective or open. Creativity and flexibility in curriculum choices, appropriate balancing around language of instruction and use of traditional versus child-oriented teaching styles, are not common.

While a community such as the Karimojong is able to bring considerable strengths to any serious effort seeking its participation, it is rarely invited to do so. The tragedy of these communities and their children is that so many interventions assume that they have nothing on which to build, nothing to contribute to the analysis of problems or to the development of alternatives. The tragedy of education systems in dealing with these communities is that so few provide the professional competency, motivation and material resources necessary to allow such participation.

Cutting across all categories of excluded children is the situation of those who are, in fact, no longer really children. Except for those who get into trouble of some kind, capacity, knowledge and life-style issues of concern to young people in that period of transition called adolescence (usually between 11 and 18 years) have not tended to be specifically addressed in much of the EFA discussion.

The situation is changing as young people of this age are increasingly recognized as being particularly vulnerable and at risk. Maternal mortality and morbidity are higher for girls under 20; violence, delinquency and substance abuse are on the rise in this age group; 6510 of the reported cases of HIV/AIDS in Thailand are here. Most child-soldiers, labouring children and those who are sexually exploited are here.

In many African countries, over 50% of the population is under the age of 18, but youth is 'an excluded category in terms of policies, services and participation'. Adolescents are becoming a larger proportion of prison and detention centres populations, and are often those same ones who have not completed school and, while inside, remain without access to regular or good quality education programmes.

Adolescence is a period of life with a special need for supportive caring relationships, to feel respected and appreciated, to have a sense of belonging and membership in families and communities which can help young people to develop the 'inner strengths' and resilience for effectively managing themselves and acting on their environments. Unfortunately, although these are still children for whose learning families, schools and the wider community are responsible, they are the ones very often denied support.

Teachers and parents frequently do not recognize the nature of the changes they are going through, treating their confusion and testing behaviours as undisciplined, aberrant and hostile. Schools that supply little beyond custodial management and rote teaching methods are ill-prepared to provide supportive, flexible learning environments for youth struggling with the demands of an adult world. They are excluding and opening up these children to risk by failing to provide them with protection from, and opportunities to acquire skills and knowledge about, the dilemmas and threats of HIV/AIDS, drug use, early pregnancies, exploitative relationships; or how to meet the challenges of an unknown future.

As a result, these young people are becoming increasingly disaffected and discouraged, angry and sometimes hopeless. In all societies, more are coming to see themselves as not only without a sense of security and personal worth now, but as potentially without a better future. In Western countries, violence in schools and among street gangs is growing along with dropping out of school, home and community. Homelessness is becoming a permanent condition of their lives rather than a passing teenage phase.

In developing countries, whole communities of youth are living in and with marginality as their life condition. Some of UNESCO's efforts to give these people a voice are producing not only a platform for them, but a window for the adult world on how serious the situation is becoming. 'But really young guy, you won't go to school. Of course not, you're too poor; your father and your mother, they have no time; they are too busy serving for more. Days come and go until sudden death. Your life is as hard as stone; don't forget you're raw to the bone'.

Present Scenario

In situations of poverty. The vast majority of children excluded from their right to education are those living in conditions of absolute poverty. Poverty is the most persistent and inexorable of all exclusionary factors. Because of this, it is also the least dramatic and the least likely to mobilize action. The fact that whole communities of children and parents are not participating in education is a reality often unseen except in annexes of international reports. Exclusion by neglect becomes an intergenerational, effectively natural, condition for families who come to assume irregular, inadequate and dysfunctional schooling and for societies which ignore them.

Absolute poverty is also universal. In both developed and developing countries, in both rural and urban areas, it exists. On a national level, it is reflected in governments not having the resources or the willingness to meet their social development obligations, including provision of functional education systems with competent teachers and enough schools.

On a more human level, it is an all-inclusive condition of families not being able to meet their basic needs of survival, health and development. Poverty affects every dimension of a family's life and the lives of its children. In particular, it diminishes their individual and collective sense of control over immediate and long-term options, making education a less compelling value. Poverty at this level is about having few real choices and limited flexibility. From a national socio-political perspective, absolute poverty among the population is sometimes a happen stance. More typically, it is a matter of persistently failed public policy, corruption and civil or environmental trauma.

Children are excluded by poverty in countries where policies of national and local governments create and exacerbate it by cutting social expenditures in response to structural adjustment programmes, subsidizing an urban middle class, building up the armed forces or large-scale infrastructures, or sustaining corruption. All of these deny large numbers of children adequate schools, trained teachers and good curricula. They are excluded in countries or provinces where policies, by action or default, distribute resources, power and access to information inequitably and sometimes not at all. They are excluded in families and communities without the qualities of health, income security or sense of a 'future benefit' that might incline them to send their children to school – even to pay the fees, were good schools available.

Absolute poverty exists in countries where it should not exist. A growing body of US-based research on children having problems in school or dropping out points to chronic poverty, often confounded by race, as the common factor. Families in both rural and urban poverty tend to have more children with special needs; they certainly have fewer resources to address those needs, or the psychological margin, social support and self-confidence to collaborate in affirmative action with schools. Research on the state of urban education in developed countries indicates that poverty significantly reduces the likelihood of communities 'bucking' the trends of low attendance and achievement, patchy standards and dropouts. In Canada, with 20% to 25% of children considered to be living in poverty, the effects on their education are clear: poor performance, chronic stress and adjustment problems, conflicts at home and school, feelings of rage and despair and, especially among Native American communities, teenage suicide.

In situations of traumatic change. Children already made vulnerable to exclusion by living in poverty are pushed even further into crisis by being in situations of severe economic decline and traumatic changes in socio-economic governance systems. In times of such stress, already-fragile education systems push marginal children out with special harshness, usually without clear or committed strategies for protecting the gains they have made or for bringing them back. Some of the countries in South-East Asia have served as an important object lesson in recent years in how quickly this can happen. In Indonesia, entire cohorts risk being lost as children are forced to drop out of the system and do not come back. Even where some are financially able to return, and want to, schools are likely to have trouble accommodating them where classes will be full and many children over-age for their level. It is a condition becoming critically worse as the social dislocations of ethnic conflict begin to take hold.

The countries of the Commonwealth of Independent States present another version of a near-systemic exclusion of children created through abrupt economic reversal and political change. In this case, the dramatic recasting of the socio-economic paradigm of these countries has changed equally fundamentally the nature of the education system and families' relationship to it. Children are being excluded as the costs and benefits of participation lose their previous equilibrium. In a situation of 'major educational melt-down', more than 32,000 Russian pre-schools have closed, contributing to a decline of close to 20% of children in kindergarten (UNICEF, 1999a, p. 1). Fees for schooling have risen significantly. State support for teachers' salaries and training, for curriculum materials, for school meals and medical care, for subsidized clothing and other incentives have all fallen or been eliminated. Most at risk, of course, are the already vulnerable: children from the poorest, chiefly rural, families, ethnic minorities, children with disabilities. A new and very large generation of excluded children and adults is being created as stratification in access is denying 'equal education to the poorest and most marginalized children'.

In situations of structural adjustment and debt. Excluded children are also to be found where international agencies and national governments have insisted on the strict application of structural adjustment or debt repayment regimes. They are excluded further where these interventions are applied without sufficient consideration of their implications for vulnerable groups, and are not monitored for their impact on these groups. Impacts have certainly been felt, especially in Africa. Painting a quite graphic description of broad-brush, systemic, exclusion from the perspective of Senegal, for example:

> Many families were plunged into relative or absolute poverty and children of poor families paid the heaviest price: . . . between 2,000 and 3,000 children live in the streets. Around 100,000 children beg in the streets. Worse than that, the number of child beggars increases from year to year. In 1997 there were 6,300 children begging in the streets of Dakar, compared to 1,000 in 1991 ... more than 60% of these children are between 7 and 12 . . . 33% suffer from malnutrition in rural areas, and 22.4% in urban areas. If these children fall sick they have no access to either curative or preventative medicine.

Reconfirming the 'close, and incontrovertible, relationship between poverty, health and education', the crisis has had an impact on survival strategies of Senegalese families. According to a World Bank report, 70% of the income of poor families is spent on food, while only 2% is dedicated to education. The state budget for education is considered insufficient in view of population growth and educational demand, and even those children who go to school find themselves in crowded classrooms in which quality teaching is impossible.

On the Street. Children living with poverty and other conditions putting them at risk are increasingly to be found as children on the street: as beggars, scrap pickers, street sellers, prostitutes, petty thieves. This categorization is complicated by the fact that these children are not a single 'type', the label being based on where donors and society find them rather than who they are or what they are doing. While many do live on the street, alone and with other children, many others live at home.

The street is the place where they earn income and find their social networks. Most are in some risk of servitude to adults who use them in their prostitution, drug and other criminal activities, and many find themselves involved with the law as a result of direct and indirect criminal activity. Many leave the street to go to worse situations, into indentured labour and into prisons. Few are in any kind of educational programme. As with working children generally, the specific conditions under which these children come to the street, and stay there, are still not well understood. Data as to numbers, causes and conditions are limited.

There are assumed, however, to be over 100 million worldwide, chiefly young boys. It is clear, however, that while their conditions vary, they all include exclusion at other levels — lack of health care, security from violence or sexual exploitation, or sporadic access to educational opportunities.

Some choose to be on the street; the majority, however, are there because they have few other choices. They are the victims of dislocation caused by conflict or economic crisis or of parental abuse and/or abandonment. They are victims of family poverty, forced out to fend for themselves or to augment the family income. Schools also contribute to sending children into the street where, instead of serving to 'offset and even compensate for society's and parental failings, by providing a propitious environment for human growth have themselves become scenes of violence.

In Institutions. Excluded children are also found in institutions. Placing children with disabilities, in trouble with the law, or without adequate family and community support away from society's sight happens in most countries, to varying degrees and for varying reasons. Though justified in terms of serving the child's 'best interest', the underlying rationale is often one of making the management of that child, by society or the sector, easier. In not all cases, of course, do such children fall within the parameters of exclusion as used in this chapter.

Professionally managed, child-friendly and rights-based institutions, with strong links to the community, can provide precisely the kind of support at-risk or abused child needs to establish a sound intellectual and psychosocial footing, from which he or she can then move forward.

But these conditions are not the norm. Brazil is but one country where children and adolescents from the streets make up a significant proportion of the population of detention centres, children with no access to resources or to school. In Eastern Europe, the practice of institutionalizing children considered to be 'uneducatable' persists, based either on a perception that the influences of disability cannot be mitigated, or on a disinclination to try. Institutionalization is also based on inflexibility in the face of cultural or linguistic differences, especially of groups considered to be ethnically inferior. And it is based on an unwillingness to invest limited resources in children not seen as able to 'pay back' society's investment through their eventual financial independence. All of these are reasons for policy and practice decisions to put them aside.

In countries that have come through war or economic crisis, children are in institutions as a result of a breakdown in the ability of communities and social-support agencies to provide more light-handed support.

In Cambodia, for example, serious shortfalls continue in the human and fiscal resources of its social welfare sector which, when coupled with the many still-unstable communities, results in children continuing to be put into 'orphanages'. These offer little more than basic custodial care.

Not all such children are orphans; many are abandoned because of poverty or family breakdown; because they have disabilities of some kind; or because their parents are lost. Regardless of cause, few are adequately supported in these institutions. They are rarely helped to realize their full psychosocial or intellectual development. Only recently have efforts been made to facilitate linkages to the formal schools and wider community.

In War and Conflict. With increasingly horrific damage, excluded children are in situations of war, or the persistent communal conflicts and dislocations which are the precursors and aftermath of war.

Over the past decade, in addition to the estimated 2 million children in armed conflict, several times that number have been injured and permanently disabled, exploited as soldiers, starved and exposed to extreme brutality. Millions snore have been displaced, internally and into other countries.

For all these children, the entire fabric of their societies has been torn to pieces-homes, schools, health systems and religious institutions. And these social traumas have not tended to be short-term, one-off instances, but to drag on for long periods with no clear beginning or end, creating in yet another way, a cycle of serious and endemic exclusion and endless struggles for survival. Long after fighting ends, many children continue to feel its repercussions, forced on to the street or into factories as communities, governments and even their families focus on priorities other than children and education. They are further excluded where the focus of education reconstruction is on replicating previous elitist structures, or bringing in a foreign, often donor-preferred, system without considering the implications for social dislocation.

The significance of this for children and adolescents can be tragic. Facing the same trauma as adults, they often do so without the capacities they need to act in their own best interest and without the support of families, communities or opportunities for learning.

Children who suffer most from exploitation and abuse, as child soldiers or girls forced into prostitution, are likely to be those already at risk or in trouble from exclusion. Conflicts tend to grow from conditions of social disintegration, and many of these children were previously found in communities where systems failed and forced them away from support services, including school.

Even where schools exist, children may not be able to enrol because they lack proper documentation, are not considered residents of the area or are unable to pay school fees. Feelings of exclusion, and the struggle for survival and protection, may lead children to join parties to the conflict or to become street children. In the course of the ten-year Liberian civil war, the number of teachers is estimated to have dropped from 12,000 to 4,000-5,000; approximately 10,000 to 15,000 child soldiers acquired little education and no marketable skills; and 20,000 to 30,000 primary-school-age children have not attended regularly in the last seven years.

Vulnerable and excluded children are found where their government's military and civil action against domestic minorities or other perceived threats blatantly make them the weapons as well as the victims of war. Burning school, intimidating and murdering teachers and destroying books are all weapons of choice in policies to deny children both the immediate opportunity to learn and undermining any potential they might have for recapturing a life of normal development and effective participation later on. International sanctions imposed against hostile countries can also exacerbate exclusion when they are applied 'too bluntly' and where they are inadequately monitored to ensure that the impact does not fall on children.

A most critical message for education from Machel concerns the durability and scope of conflicts, and their permanent impact on the exclusion of large numbers of children. Persistent instability, unpredictability and randomness of even low-grade violence 'which never begins or ends' produces a generalized vulnerability years of lost schooling and vocational skills will take equivalent years to replace and their absence imposes a greater vulnerability on the ability of societies to recover after war.

The interdependencies of exclusion will guarantee that this 'greater vulnerability will fall most heavily on those least able to cope, already-marginal families even more hard-pressed to find financial and psychological resources for ensuring the health and emotional well-being of children, and less likely to have a future-looking faith which might make ingesting in education a sensible use of resources. Systems have fewer opportunities to provide them and those they have are 'of lower quality'. Funds are short; the supply of materials slow and erratic; fear and disruption making it difficult to create an atmosphere conducive to learning.

In Refugee Settlements and Displaced. Immediately consequent to children being excluded through war, they are being excluded in their millions in refugee camps and as the internally displaced. For many such children, this nether world is a more-or-less permanent condition. Lao and Palestinian refugees, for example, have seen several generations born in camps; Afghan refugees have been in the Islamic Republic of Iran for some twenty years. As with other social-support structures, the education available to these children and their families is precarious.

Host governments rarely allow open access to the regular school system; even when able to attend, refugee children often face exclusions of discrimination, social harassment and failed communication (cultural and/or linguistic). Motivation within refugee communities to educate their own children may be high, but their capacity to manage coherent and consistent programmes is typically not. In the Afghan case, in the few refugee schools which are run, classes in all of them are very small, overcrowded and under-equipped. Implying ongoing exclusion, they are also not formally recognized and no certification is given.

They are working. Among the most obvious causes and consequences of exclusion is the fact that children who are not in school are not sitting idle. They are at home, generating income or filling in for working parents; they are in the field, in factories, and on the street. Definitions of work vary by type, level of hazard or exploitation and the amount of time involved, making detailed figures on working children difficult to calculate with certainty. Broadly, the number of children in the developing countries estimated to be working, full- or part time, is 250 million.

Asia, reflecting conditions chiefly in South Asia, continues to have highest absolute numbers of working children. As of 19.97, 120 million children between ages-5 and 14 were 'fully at work', and there are many more for whom work is a secondary activity.

In Cambodia, 1996 statistics indicated 16% working children between ages 5 and 17, most of these in fisheries and agriculture and the rest in domestic service, scavenging and small factories or sweatshops. In some East Asian and Pacific countries, one in three households depend on their children's labour; and 2% to 16% of the region's gross national product is earned through a sex industry in which, for some Mekong countries, 33% of those involved are under 16 .

Statistics from elsewhere are no better. In the most seriously affected provinces of Brazil, over 700,000 children aged 10 to 14 are working and not attending primary school; over 2 million work and attend part time.

Another 2 million or so of 15- to 17- year-olds are similarly distributed. In addition, close to 600,000 5- to 9-year olds are 'in the work market', and while below official school starting age, are seriously risking both their future life and their eventual success in school by undermining their health and establishing patterns of family income earning which are hard to break.

Poverty statistics on working and street children relate closely to their exclusion from education. In 1993 in New Delhi, 63% of working children were illiterate; 17% completed primary school and 61% of the girls had never been to school. In Yangon, 39% had no schooling and 54% had dropped out by second grade. 64% of Cambodian street children are estimated not to attend school, most are girls; estimates for minority children in remote areas are worse.

Histories of working children with respect to exclusion from education are all too similar: rural areas with no or incomplete access to primary schools; low-income families, single parents with limited educational background; marginal urban areas with few, over-crowded schools; communities and schools with high levels of crime and violence; school failure, repetition and abuse. Two critical issues for all these children are choice and consequences. Research suggests that many want to work — to support families, have the freedom to make their own life-decisions, avoid ineffective and unfriendly schools. The fact is also that many do not.

Interviews with eighty-four Cambodian street children found that the majority aspired to go to school because they wanted to read like other people and get a job. Where children do choose to work, many of these choices are pyrrhic; the consequences serious and long term. Their jobs may give them immediate and necessary income, but little of the knowledge or skills to enable them to move to better, more flexible, stable or financially secure employment. Much of the work is informal, providing a life of limited alternatives and increasing dependency on the vagaries of uncertain economies, unscrupulous adults, political expediency and fleeting charity. It also creates a great deal of personal risk, subjecting girls especially to sexual abuse.

Working children of seasonal migrant families are probably less at risk than those who work on their own, protected for the most part within the framework of a coherent community structure. They are, however, vulnerable to exclusion on a wide range of social dimensions, including education, given families' often high levels of poverty, the unhealthy working conditions and the instability of an enforced transient lifestyle. In Mexico, over 3.5 million people are estimated to be in seasonal agricultural work, with numbers increasing 'as one of the few alternatives to survival' given the endemic poverty, lack of productive infrastructure and deteriorating natural resources of their communities. Approximately 900,000 of these are children, 50% under 14. Their contribution to family income is critical, estimated at over 30%, but at a cost: 40% illiterate; 21.5% never in school.

Globally, the number of children in this situation is again difficult to assess. The living conditions and size of such 'floating communities' are often not well monitored by governments; nor is their children's absence from school. The dilemma is in how to provide appropriate educational opportunities and facilitate learning when the children's work is so intimately woven into their lives. It is clear that there are risks to both the children and their families in forcing them into educational arrangements in ways that undercut the stability they have managed to create. But without an education, their future is unlikely to be less vulnerable than their present.

Progress and Development

On the plus side, progress has been made: the decade since Jomtien has laid a solid groundwork for action against the exclusion of children, in terms both of education as a defined sector, and of learning as a cross-cutting process necessary to all aspects of survival and development.

The World Conference on Education for All (WCEFA) was a watershed, a critical juncture in global thinking about the legitimate place of learning and education as core to all human and social development. Jomtien established an unarguable link between poverty and exclusion, for the individual and the society; exposed the failure of most nations to provide adequate basic education for all their citizens; and confirmed the inevitability of future exclusion for those children and their families who are denied access to such education. Critically, it set a new 'expanded vision' for education and declared national and global responsibilities for taking action.

The Convention on the Rights of the Child (CRC) provided the critical overarching framework for EFA in making the education of all children their right. It committed a global imperative of action to ensure all children an effective education, not simply to a seat in school and not simply for those who turn up. Governments, civil societies and donors are now compelled to give highest priority to an explicit and intensive focus on the chronically excluded: under the CRC umbrella, all children are owed an education which meets their basic learning needs and enables them to live an individual life in society in the spirit of peace, dignity, tolerance, freedom, equality and solidarity. Responsibility for providing this quality of education for all rests with everyone in world society, at global, national and — by extension — local levels. Ultimately, of course, much of the onus for children's learning and education falls on families and schools.

The Salamanca Statement and Framework for Action on Special Needs Education further refined and focused the message of EFA, committing the international community to addressing the large-scale and typically systemic exclusion of those children with special learning needs. This continues to be a problem in all countries to some degree, both by education systems omitting to identify, count or support children's special learning needs, and by their committing actively against them, declaring children who are 'different' as incapable of learning or participating. For children in either context, Salamanca was important in placing more explicitly on the global EFA agenda the imperative of recognizing, valuing and managing their learning; and doing so in ways that ensure their full participation in education, the successful realization of their learning goals and, ultimately, their independence as adults able to sustain themselves as parents, workers and citizens.

Salamanca was also the key to reinforcing and extending the EFA principle of an expanded vision of education, one in which 'ordinary schools should accommodate all children, regardless of their physical, intellectual, emotional, social, linguistic or other conditions'. 'Inclusive' schools give particular attention to enabling the learning of each child, serving to integrate all and not to segregate any. They serve to bring all children into mainstream education. Salamanca recognized that 'regular schools with this inclusive orientation are the most effective means of combating discriminatory attitudes, creating welcoming communities, building an inclusive society and achieving education for all'.

Less a formal international commitment than a global re-declaration of the central place of learning and education for all, the Delors Commission served further to under-score the role of education as a basic element of individual and societal development and peaceful co-existence. In confirming the capacity to learn as the 'treasure' everyone has within them, the task of education is to ensure all children and adults the right to life-long learning along four core dimensions or pillars: learning to know, learning to do, learning to be and learning to live together. Some have added a fifth: learning to transform oneself and the world around one.

In both general and specific terms, all these initiatives placed education at the centre of action in support of the children who are most excluded, as both a tool for their development and a place for their protection. Regional meetings in Stockholm, Oslo, Cairo, Amsterdam. Beijing and other international actions have, through the remainder of the past decade, made substantive contributions to the EFA framework. Their discussions and commitments have taken a harder look at the realities of the especially vulnerable and forgotten child and, within this framework, the special protection and development rights of girls and women.

The World Summit for Social Development (WSSD), Copenhagen, March 1995, was especially important in looking specifically across all groups and sectors to consider the interactive nature of socio-economic exclusion and development. In consequence, it stressed the need for integrative strategies and collaborative actions by domestic institutions, NGOs and international agencies to deal with them.

Suffering to some degree by not having a clear constituency to keep its 'Action Framework' on the table, the WSSD nevertheless presented a significant opportunity to push the critical role of learning as the enabling dimension of all organizational and social change aimed at social integration:

> . . . the capacity of people to live together with full respect for the dignity of each individual, the common good, pluralism and diversity, non-violence and solidarity as well as their ability to participate in social, cultural, economic and political life .... It requires the protection of the weak, as well as the right to differ, to create and to innovate.

The WSSD thus made critical distinctions between inclusion and conformity and between diversity and exclusion, distinctions and implied directives central to realizing effective and equitable education. It went further, urging specific actions to mobilize funding of the 'Agenda for Development' to which the summit participants had committed themselves: reduced military spending; enhanced transparency and accountability at all levels; better focusing on basic human needs; recognition and support to alternative financing mechanisms; open exchange of technology, knowledge and skills; application of the 7% Official Development Assistance/ODA commitment, debt relief, and action on the 20/20 initiative.

All these factors, if coupled with concerted action to address the professional quality of teachers and curricula, would clearly have gone far to ending education exclusion. The UN Development Assistance Framework (UNDAF),-though not yet as far advanced as it needs to be in mobilizing and ensuring effective collaborative and consistent action on children's exclusion, is clearly the way to go. Multilateral agencies, NGOs and bilaterals each have their own areas of comparative advantage, mandates and partners. Each, however, shares a common constituency of people who are excluded, marginalized and living in poverty, and to whom it owes action that is relevant, sustainable and of high quality.

On the other side, more is to be done. Progress in following up all of these global agreements is far from wholly positive. While enrolments and school spaces have increased, these have not been matched by gains in ensuring that pupils persist in their schooling and emerge from primary school with the knowledge and skills they need expected benefits are being undermined by significant levels of drop-out' in both developing and developed countries. The Jomtien target of 80% completion for primary school is still a very distant goal in sub-Saharan Africa, South Asia and much of Latin America. The 80% figure is no longer, of course, tenable under the CRC. In presenting this number as sufficient, Jomtien may have suggested that 'the rest' could legitimately be left to fail or not to count at all — in effect, serving to legitimize exclusion.

In focusing on UPE as an expressed goal, and defining that within the specific context of schooling, Jomtien ironically may also have served to undermine the probability of its own key concept of the 'expanded vision' taking root. Education for all has become minimized in too many countries and too many agencies as school for all. The expanded vision of basic education is inclusive of, but clearly greater than, formal schools and traditional classroom methods. Though the WCEFA strongly endorsed the place of alternative educational arrangements within the vision, the UPE-cum-schooling emphasis appears to have left them relegated to a second-class, choice-limiting status. The CRC is significant in changing the paradigm. Eight out of ten children completing primary school is no longer the issue; two out of ten not completing is.

The EFA Declaration was important in establishing the core of what effective education and learning systems should be, the 'what' of basic education. Jomtien and the succeeding decade have been less clearly successful, however, in making explicit, and putting into effect, the 'how' of mobilizing subsequent action; of stimulating demand and improving supply. The Mid-Decade Meeting of the International Consultative Forum on Education for All provided a useful, albeit justifiably modest, stocktaking of the progress made in the first five years. It, too, was unfortunately vague in analysing the 'how' of why the Framework was not being fully implemented. Where and what the implementation gaps were, and how to fill them – especially with respect to such fundamental issues as the training of teachers and mobilizing of sustained political action – remained largely unknown.

Nor has the decade finished strongly in terms of tracking the progress of EFA targets. While anecdotal evidence suggests that many innovations are showing good effects, there is little systematic assessment of them. Many of the advances reported are based either on broad averages, or narrowly focused pilot efforts, both of which have drawbacks in terms of informing wider practice.

Monitoring and tracking systems remain universally weak, not well able to determine the real quality and impact of many of the interventions on, or the deeper reasons for, continuing exclusion. Rare also are the comprehensive case studies and implementation analyses that might present the kind of integrated social development picture urged by the WSSD. Instances of serious and interactive exclusion remain without good explanations as to how to disentangle them.

Highlighted throughout the Johannesburg Sub-Saharan Africa Conference, for example, were the multiple needs of creating stronger capacities for analysis, of undertaking research, and of using results to inform policy and practice. Data throughout the continent are considered to be weak in quality, narrow in scope and limited in quantity. In particular, too little is known of patterns and trends on such key issues as participation and achievement, especially concerning the children who are at risk and excluded – girls, children with disabilities, minority groups. Analysis is often poorly carried out, not considered sufficiently reliable, and not presented with sufficient assurance, to mobilize, guide or evaluate change.

School and community-based action research is rare. Teachers, parents and students have little input to assessments made within the education sector as it affects them. What is happening in the classroom, what teachers and students are actually doing, is rarely observed let alone analysed.

While a wide range of innovations and pilot programmes are being tried through the region and may well be relevant to the excluded – on community and out reach schools, multi grade classrooms, double-shifting, use of quasi-professional resource teachers – few are being systematically assessed to determine whether or how they are making a difference, to which children, and under what conditions. Lack of analysis makes it difficult to take corrective action on the unsuccessful ideas; to strengthen and extend those that are effective; or to share lessons.

The types of study currently being promoted by the UNESCO/ UNICEF Monitoring Learning Achievement/MLA project and by regionally-based projects such as the Southern African Consortium for Monitoring Educational Quality, are steps in the right direction. They will focus particularly on the more qualitative factors impeding access and successful participation of especially vulnerable children, and on the relevance of what they are learning. These assessments also need to be persistent and participatory. The use of 'pilot' projects as the mechanism for focusing and managing action for the excluded also merits closer attention. Pilots are often undertaken because difficult for people to agree on the pace of change; they let small groups of mobilized people do it on their own.

Unfortunately, the logic of pilots often fails in application, leaving them 'outside the mainstream, threatening people in the rest of the and causing resentment. Eventually, most of these programmes collapse, not from lack of value, but from lack of support'. Where they involve marginal communities, those with few resources and little room for experimenting, they are often too demanding to be sustained. Real control over planning, design and implementation of most pilots rests with interveners rather than with the schools and communities involved; and efforts to develop local capacity are often too limited to shift the ownership. Sustaining the results of innovation requires serious, long-term attention to the change process, to organizational learning and to participation. These are the necessary conditions of 'full scale' implementation, which many EFA pilots have tended not to give.

Ministries of education need to assert their strong commitment to the excluded in this area. Although the educational innovations targeted to various excluded groups are often managed and executed by NGOs, it is essential that the Ministries are involved from the initial [stage] by, for example, assigning officials to work with the innovations or by directing some resources; and later adopting the innovation for dissemination. Separate projects which are not well incorporated in the framework of the national education system tend to be short-lived.

There are recurrent themes and common threads, principles of action which appear to characterize moves towards more effective and sustainable action, not simply against exclusion, but in support of inclusion.

These themes are not new. Broad participation and synergy, within a holistic framework and using enabling processes to ensure local relevance. These are the concepts and principles underlying all the international commitments noted above. What must be new for the next decade is that action is taken to actually implement them — by states, civil societies and the international community.

Participation at a Larger Scale

Perhaps the two most significant advances of the decade since Jomtien in reaching excluded children, indeed all children, have been (a) the increasing realization that education, like learning, is a necessarily holistic and integrated system, and (b) the persistent movement towards greater participation of communities, families and children in matters concerning learning, education and schools.

Coincident with both of these has been a more sensitive appreciation of teachers and school as critical actors; a distinct trend toward focusing the reform efforts at a level nearer to the 'action': the school itself.

None of these developments is revolutionary. All, however, are fundamental and mutually reinforcing in reaching the excluded. They recognize that no education policy will be sustainable by attempting to mandate attitudinal or behavioural change from the centre, or in one narrow aspect of the system. They acknowledge that genuine implementation of change in classrooms, families and communities that are socio-culturally and economically marginalized and at risk requires equity, transparent accountability and joint responsibility.

The Family. Participation in the context of excluded children most particularly concerns their families. The concept of the family as a place of security and support for children and as a partner of the school has been slowly emerging over the past decade as efforts are made to find better ways to address the rights and needs of all children to education. Facilitating that emergence should be happening more quickly.

The CRC in particular recognizes families and parents as the first line of intervention in, and support for, children's emotional, psychosocial and intellectual learning. The capacity, or incapacity, of families to act on behalf of the survival, protection and development of their children is especially critical in the early years, and not much less so as children become adolescents and begin to confront the confusion of uncertain and conflicting choices and demands. Families are the key in keeping children out of exploitative working conditions and in school; the opposite is equally true.

Again recognizing exclusion as a cycle, the education level of the family is the 'single best predictor of how long children will stay in school and how well they will perform'. It is much more difficult for illiterate parents and those who have been harmed by schools to see the value of education for their children, or to help them to participate even when they do. Programmes promoting parent literacy, therefore, are also likely to have positive effects on children's learning. Mobilization campaigns to get girls into school are most successful when they take place in collaboration with the family — and with community leaders, civic groups and NGOs — the bodies that are often in closest touch with the values and needs of families and so most able to influence their decisions. The particular importance of the family during times of stress is clear. Conflict, forced migration and economic crisis are periods when family stability and consistency are the child's best link to learning, adaptation and sense of identity, and when the loss of family can be especially devastating. The effectiveness of action such as that by the World Bank and the Asian Development Bank in working with Indonesian families to put in place scholarships for the children most at risk will be critical in this regard.

One area in which gains have been made in this respect is the greater attention being given to early childhood care and development interventions. Most successful where set within the context of their families, ECCD programmes recognize that only with whole-hearted parental participation can such programmes succeed.

They are critical in countries such as the Lao People's Democratic Republic where, especially among indigenous families, primary-school attendance is very low. The village based early childhood education project is concerned with children's early learning within the framework of support both for their own developing capacities, as well as the capacities of their care givers, especially mothers. The project strengthens family knowledge and practice in basic nutrition, hygiene and health and child development, including infant stimulation and ways to increase language ability. It links with women in development/WID and basic-education interventions so that there is support for increased income generation, village planning and schooling; and with the media and early childhood education sub-project to produce educational radio broadcasts, videos and print material on good parenting, nutrition and child development practices.

For seriously at-risk children, and those unlikely to have access to reasonably effective schools, ECCD interventions may be the only quality learning support that they will have. It is, therefore, especially critical that the interventions should be of high quality: learning and learner-oriented, interactive and participatory, culturally sensitive and responsive, holistic and engaged with all family members and the community agencies with which they also interact.

Programmes which are able to engage with marginalized families, to work with them in the context of the constraints and strengths of their own setting, and which bring them together to support one another, are the most effective. They impose less risk to vulnerable families, allowing them to find their own 'best way' in developing strategies of childcare and learning that they are able to sustain in collaboration with neighbouring families and local support agencies.

A main difficulty with efforts to engage such families in changing their relationship with the school is, of course, their own negative history with education — if they have had one at all. Parents who have themselves been excluded from school are less likely to have the knowledge, skills or psychological 'margin' for risk-taking which would make them feel naturally comfortable in their children's school. One example of an attempt to overcome this distance is the school-based education project in Peru. Working through activates aimed at developing a shared vision, breaking down dysfunctional perceptions and creating a partnership among parents, students and teachers, the underlying strategy of the programme has been to start a dialogue on the child as a priority for parents and for teachers in terms of their shared responsibility in the child's education. Parents and teachers work together to formulate solutions and alternatives which could help create the 'ideal' school. At the same time, teachers develop 'conversations' with students, on the assumption that they, too, are in a position to have opinions about the quality and content of their learning and have the capacity to contribute.

The task is an evolutionary and open-ended one, attempting to create a culture of inclusion where both community and school are able to bring together their expectations and priorities, evaluate options for 'translating them into reality' and developing frameworks of action they can then work to apply. Interventions such as this are critical to building on and strengthening the learning within families in ways that will help them engage with the school. It is important that schools themselves reach out to support families, especially the vulnerable ones, in doing better, to encourage them to be involved throughout their children's schooling.

The results of a large-scale study of poor inner-city schools in the United States, for example, showed clearly that effective schools were those that were able to help parents to change the ways in which they connected to the school and promoted their children's learning as they moved through the system. Beginning when children were very young, these schools helped parents to help their children in 'building the skills' they needed to do well in school.

They 'coached' parents in how to talk to teachers, helped them to monitor their children's progress and support them with their schoolwork. Effective schools helped parents to learn 'how the system works' so they could be better advocates for their children, to make decisions, about how to make the school better, and to make sure that their children were learning what they needed to know.

The Community. It is important to recognize families *per se,* their unique role in creating and raising children and the need to take them into one-to-one partnership. But most excluded families and their children live in the context of a community. Less a geographical construct than a sociological one, communities are important here as the primary reference group for families and their children (especially older ones).

Particularly in traditional societies and cultures, communities can play a major role in defining a family's available resources and support structures, its social obligations, and its core values, attitudes and expectations. The community in this sense is especially critical in addressing exclusion. No attempt to create equitable and inclusive education programmes for children and families will succeed independently of their surrounding community.

Using this broad definition of community, the learning and education of excluded children can be enhanced where families and local groups come together to support them in formal and non-formal programmes, with and without government support. Excluded children can also be supported through 'communities of interest', networks formed among them as individuals who share a common bond of vulnerability. These are child labourers or street children who form family type bonds; or support groups formed by adolescents affected by HIV/AIDS. Mutual support and exchange associations of these kinds can constitute significant forms of psychosocial 'margin'. They provide a sense of belonging, a nurturing role and guidance; often they also provide very pertinent and effective venues for learning information and skills. They can provide critical focal or entry points for education interveners, as interlocutors able to interpret between an NGO or school out reach initiative and children unable to communicate effectively or from a position of equal participation what they want and need to learn.

Communities, whether geographical or interest-based, can also play a critical role in finding and engaging 'missing' children. Informal associations of child carpet-workers in India, for example, have proved to be much better able to locate other children and convince them that it is safe to get involved in learning programmes than are officials from the ILO International Programme for the Elimination of Child Labour or from the government.

Somewhat more systematic, Lok Jumbish in Rajasthan is another example of community-based mapping of the excluded, where and as they are. Working with community members interested in educational improvement, it creates an 'inspirational group' which then undertakes to depict every household in the village visually on a simple map indicating the schooling status of every household member aged 5-14'.

Serving as an 'occasion for interacting with the community', block-based interviews help to show where special help is needed and what priorities families see as barriers to their children attending school. Leaders of the village and the local community draw up a set of proposals based on the mapping data, where new schools and NFE centres are needed and where present ones need fixing.

The methodology is intended to be empowering as well as informative, allowing even non-literate families to be involved in the analysis. The follow-up is also community-based and is critical in fostering 'continuous evaluation'. Attendance of children is locally monitored and neighbourhood blocks are free to determine and revise appropriate issues and strategies (creating residential study camps for girls, for example).

The Myanmar All Children in School (ACIS) project is concerned with fairly broad systemic reform to reduce the severe national-level exclusion. In order to achieve this it focuses on an integration of three levels: the community, engaging people in enrolment surveys and school mapping, local data management and PTA training; teachers, providing decentralized training for multi-grade and learner-centred teaching, in-class supervisory support and materials development; and school structures, through promotion of school clusters and improved monitoring and evaluation.

Significant for the potential sustainability of increased student participation, ACIS appears to be having a positive impact on the relationship between community and school: local teachers hired through community donations; a 'growing willingness' of teachers to talk with parents about their children's progress; and community-based identification and enrolment of previously 'invisible' children such as migrant workers.

The Kolondieba District community schools project in Mali aims at addressing deep-seated, poverty-based exclusion. It is a particularly cogent example of the dilemmas facing communities and their children as they try to act on the very mixed 'causes and consequences' of that exclusion. Poverty is clearly the over aching issue for the communities, which have very few resources and minimal national support. Families live at subsistence level, speak the local language with a limited capacity in French, and have little access to the few and distant government schools.

At the project's start in 1992, only 1210 of the 207 villages in the district were reached by the formal system and there was little to indicate that the situation would change. Community schools appear to be succeeding, however, as a way to shift the paradigm – from one of children trying and failing to accommodate within the formal system, to one of the community ensuring a school designed to suit them.

Based on explicit commitments by the community to ensure enrolment, regular attendance and girls' participation, and to pay salaries of locally hired teachers and monitor their work, the project has created learning environments to which children apparently want to come and in which they are, on the whole, succeeding. Teaching is in the local language, of subjects selected by the community as important to their children's current lives. Literacy, mathematics and French are also taught, as a base for children who eventually choose to move into the formal system.

The success of the schools appears to lie specifically in these efforts to localize content, process and ownership; but so, too, lie their core dilemmas. Teachers can be hired locally because they are minimally trained, and paid locally because they are paid very little. Curriculum can be relevant because it is developed locally, but it has little reference to the national system. All these characteristics are consistent with the fundamentals of creating inclusive learning, but not necessarily with inclusion beyond the community.

Critical questions must then be asked of all such community-based programmes. Whether the approaches are sustainable, and whether they should be; whether they risk confining excluded children to further exclusion in 'pockets of learning', positive but inevitably isolating. Children are learning in their community schools; in the Mali case, they are even laying a basis of French-language competency and there appears to be interest at the national level for extending the approach. Nevertheless, these communities and their supporters need continually to explore the children's long-term 'best interest': if the structures and methodologies of the education can be adapted and sustained; whether eventually the students must move out of the community to move up in the education system, and whether that system can somehow come into the community without undermining the latter's coherence and culture.

Action Plan

One example of a community-based programme which has gone a considerable way towards answering some of these questions has done so because it has developed an integrative programme for excluded children and their families. Based in a slum area of Jaipur (India), the Bodh Shiksha Samiti is a good example — in the extent to which it has become part of the very fabric of the community, in the long time scale it has allowed itself, and in its forging of a genuine two-way link to the formal system.

The effective owners of the Bodh schools are the migrant and landless labourers, disadvantaged castes and traditional artisans who live in the community. With no previous access to schools sufficiently affordable, flexible or 'welcoming' for them, the community agreed in the late 1980s to engage with a small group of social activists to create a school as a form of 'collective endeavour' for their children's education.

Seven schools have been built by the community over the past decade. A 'sense of ownership' and a bridge between school and community have also been built. The Bodh has ensured children's inclusion by becoming part of the community itself.

It has been a process through which people in 'an organized framework pool their ideas, concerns, aspirations and resources, and develop a dynamic networking of communication among students, parents, teachers and Bodh organizers'.

Together, they have worked through many of the core issues of exclusion: dealt with the absenteeism of working children and appropriate forms of discipline; negotiated teaching methodologies, balancing the benefits of active versus rote learning; selected curriculum topics appropriate to the life of the community; created relevant and affordable teaching materials; and jointly assessed children's ongoing progress. Confronting many of the barriers to the inclusion of socially marginalized children, the Bodh programme is holistic. It includes all aspects of community education, from pre-school through to adult literacy. Mothers and older children are trained as part-time resource teachers, creating another tie between school and community.

At the same time, emphasis is put on the continuous training of the full-time teachers in methodologies stressing participatory learning. The entire primary curriculum is divided into three broad ability groups, among which children can easily move as appropriate to their competencies rather than being fixed by age.

Curriculum topics are flexible, but ensure coverage of basic issues, such as hygiene and nutrition, which are immediately useful to children and their families. A core of community- agreed generic-skills training (language and mathematics, analysis and reasoning) and attitude development (independence, co-operation, motivation for learning) aims at building children's capacities for future learning.

All this is intended to give the act of learning, and the process of education, a more valued place in the community, encouraging parents and children to pursue further study in the formal system.

In preparation for this end, textbooks and written examinations are eventually introduced and, important in realizing that 'seamlessness' which is the key to inclusive education, an 'adoption programme' has recently started to work with and train teachers from the formal system in the main principles and teaching approaches of the Bodh programme. The aim is systematically to integrate aspects of the two educational approaches.

Within Schools. Reaching excluded children and encouraging their participation requires making education, and especially schools, easily accessible, physically and emotionally welcoming and oriented to each child's learning capacities and needs. This may seem a self-evident point, but both the international community and national education systems have taken a long time in coming to it. In the broadest sense, it means paying much greater attention to conceiving and organizing schools holistically.

More specifically, it means assessing schools, and acting to improve them, on the same lines as they have been using to keep out the most vulnerable children:

- quality of the environment, to create safe and girl-friendly physical facilities, policies and practices of non-violence and mutual respect;
- modes of delivery, to explore use of school clusters, multi grade teaching, double-shifting and distance technologies;
- methods of facilitating learning, to use interactive small group arrangements, peer and child-to-child tutoring, teacher-generated curriculum;
- role of the teachers, to encourage teacher-teacher support groups, peer counselling, in-service monitoring;

- partnerships with families, to develop school linkages, school-based ECCD, parent literacy and work-related programmes, PTA and school councils.

Such actions imply major shifts in thinking, in perspectives, in relationships and in ways of working. They require that those designing the innovations, and especially those delivering them, be open and ready for change, for taking risks and for reflective experimentation. This extent of support for learning is, unfortunately, not often provided in education reform efforts, especially when the targeted community is of low status or politically invisible.

However, while application of change may not have gone very far since Jomtien, and the traditional top-down, information-transfer model of schooling remains the norm, serious efforts continue to be made to cast doubt on the efficacy of that traditional model and to create a new one. The nomenclature for identifying these more holistic approaches varies among agencies and organizations. However, while problematic for the outsider trying to sort through the terminological stew, common threads are visible across most of them.

The latest education policy framework of the UK Department for International Development (DFID), for example, speaks of a whole school development approach, 'designed to bring together and integrate the many inputs and processes which constitute the learning environment and the learning experience of children'. The approach includes inter alia a focus on school-based planning, on motivating and supporting teachers, on creating safe and secure school environments, on partnerships with families and community agencies, and on setting and monitoring reachable learning goals.

The wholesome education school programme in Bhutan, supported by SC-US, has a similar point of departure. Set within the broader context of an education reform effort with community-based change as its base, it includes aspects of community development education, participatory rural appraisal/PRA and skill-development for out-of-school youth, and children's clubs. The programme's goal of increased inclusiveness is reflected in its integrative schools-based management and teacher-focused orientation. Considering 'the needs and rights of the whole child, bridges health and education', encouraging schools to 'come up with their own plans' and helping them develop 'a self-assessment tool help sensitize teachers to the concept, and show them that there are things they can do and concrete steps can take'.

One of the potentially most influential initiatives in this regard is the concept of the child-friendly school (CFS). Perhaps most energetically promoted by UNICEF, the concept is becoming increasingly reflected in similar approaches of agencies such as the World Health Organization, Save the Children and Radda Barnen, bilateral donors and a number of national governments. In essence, the CFS framework aims at creating education systems and school settings that are inclusive, effective, equitable and secure for all children.

The child-friendly school seeks to engage children and their parents in all aspects of the learning event; to be more welcoming of the diversity of children, and to keep them longer in the educational environment. It seeks to be more nurturing, academically professional and programmatically flexible. The underlying premise of the CFS is that all children must be provided positive learning opportunities, and that all must be expected to succeed no matter what their background and whether in or outside the formal school setting.

The child-friendly concept thus widens the framework. It assumes that learning, and society's commitment to supporting it encompass children from birth through adolescence, whatever capacities they bring and whatever their learning needs.

It assumes the need for partnerships with families and communities in developing facilities and programmes which are physically safe, foster a sense of security, well-being and self-confidence, and help children to respect themselves and others. It aims, at promoting responsible and collaborative citizenship through abuse-free schools, codes of conduct, anti-bullying policies and training in peer mediation for 'peaceful playgrounds'.

For teachers as well as children, it includes norms against all forms of harassment, no-tolerance policies against violence, and development of positive disciplinary alternatives to corporal punishment which are clear, consistent and provide support to teachers in their fair application. By engaging with families, the CFS seeks to become a place where children and adults can have conversations about issues of immediate concern to them and about the values, attitudes and behaviours underlying them.

While certainly applicable to all children, then, the flexibility and responsiveness inherent in the concept are especially important for reaching the excluded in the 'especially difficult circumstances' where children, adolescents and families are particularly at risk. They are important when normative social controls are breaking down-due to the rapid and unmanaged social change of communal conflict, urban stress or rural dislocation; and when families are not able to support their children because they are themselves fighting fragmentation or alienation.

Two programmes currently under way in Thailand reflect different approaches and emphasis to the child-friendly concept and give a sense of its scope.

Working under the auspices of the Office of National Primary Education, the Children's Integrated Learning and Development (CHILD) initiative in the north-east (with input from UNICEF) and the Child-Friendly Schools (CFS) programme in the north (supported by SC-US) are both intended as fairly holistic interventions.

Each involves several layers of activity, various strategies for engaging with schools and their communities and different types of content. Both deal with a range of schools and children, confronting problems of exclusion to varying degrees. Situated in the poorest region of the country, child takes a broad-brush approach to the child-friendliness concept, aiming to create a 'constructive context' in which children's learning is enhanced through the school, in collaboration with the community and in a holistic way. It begins with a 'futures search', to mobilize teachers, parents and students in thinking and talking about children's protection and development rights and agreeing to take action.

The first most concrete action, offered as an enabling incentive, is on the micro level, introducing for the school's consideration a relatively simple computer-based management information system/ MIS technology. Including computer and training, the technology helps teachers to organize and track data related to students' academic and health status. The innovation at this level is not dramatic.

It is easily accessible to teachers of even the most resource-poor schools and is, for the most part, manageable in its first stages by the expertise available. It moves previously scattered pieces of hand-noted data on each child into more visible patterns, 'whole pictures' of a student's developmental progress. In this, the key strength of the intervention is that it allows teachers to do more easily and effectively what they already do.

At the same time, the project allows for growth. Teachers and schools are becoming increasingly more interested and expert in analytical manipulation and in thinking and talking together about students in more holistic -and integrative ways. Some are looking for ways to add new and more locally important data to the MIS' on drug use, absenteeism, nutrition — and are working with students and parents on ways to address problems revealed by their analyses.

The Child-Friendly Schools project operates on the other side of the country, in a region characterized by relative wealth, the persistent social inequities and social trauma of marginalized hill-tribe communities, high rates of drug abuse and child prostitution and epidemic levels of HIV/AIDS.

The project is framed explicitly within the core themes of survival, protection and development, equity and participation. It begins with a relatively intensive Self-Assessment Process asking parents, teachers and students to define their ideal of a child-friendly school, and to contrast that with what they perceive to be the current situation. It then pursues a broadly focused intervention strategy based on a negotiation of the perceived gaps and creation of an agreed 'school charter'. Specific activities aim at strengthening home-community-school links, promoting the safe and secure psychosocial development of children, and introducing the notion of participatory active learning into classroom practice.

The logic of the child-friendly and teacher-engaged school appears to be proving intuitively sound in both regions, irrespective of social, economic and cultural differences. In large part, the positive response is a function of the holistic and non-restrictive nature of the concept, which allows each of the projects to be framed and implemented with considerable flexibility and adaptation. Each has been able to base the precise entry point, focus and evolution of its interventions on its respective schools, teachers and students as coherent organizational 'systems'.

More problematic here, and in 'piloting' initiatives generally, are the physical and psychological distance of the programmes from each other and from the national education policy centre, making communication and joint action difficult. From the perspective of articulating, managing and sustaining a nationally coherent and integrated 'child-friendly reform programme', it is obviously more difficult to promote change in a situation where each reform application and trajectory is different in approach and emphasis.

It is more complicated to create and organize training materials and action, to plan inputs, or to track outcomes jointly. If the impact is to be sufficiently national in support and scope, it is especially important for projects like these to create and maintain transparent and regular communication, horizontally between the work in the field and vertically with the policy centre. Underlying principles of action must be openly and regularly discussed and implementation must be monitored and outcomes assessed in co-operation with the communities expected to be benefiting.

Though with limited attention to teaching and learning quality and academic performance, the overlapping health promoting and healthy school initiatives of the World Health Organization are conceptually consistent with that of the child friendly school. They also are concerned with a holistic conception of children, with their lives both inside and outside the school and with building linkages between the school, family and community. Their main emphasis, however, is on mental and social health as the underpinnings of children learning to make sound choices (on factors such as nutrition, sexual behaviour, interpersonal relationships) and to protect themselves from high-risk behaviours, violence and abuse (to make better judgements, for example, and assess the veracity of advertised information).

They aim to foster healthy school environments, deliver appropriate health messages and interventions through the auspices of the school and its curriculum, and promote healthy life-style behaviours. They also project a more activist role for the school in providing input to health-promoting and violence reducing public policy; reorienting community health and referral services to ensure effective diagnostic and remedial support for vulnerable children; and mobilizing community participation around child health and protection issues.

A third variation on this same theme is that of inclusive education, introduced at Salamanca. Intended to capture the ideals of CRC and EFA commitments through schools which are welcoming of all children, irrespective of capacities, UNESCO in particular is promoting this terminology as a direct counterpoint to education which excludes. Inclusive education aims to be 'transformative'.

It includes advocacy (creating public platforms for people with disabilities), capacity development (training teachers, decision-makers, community leaders) and management strengthening activities (guidance for school staff, curriculum developers, supervisory systems).

As with child-friendly and health-promoting schools, much of the focus of 'inclusive schools' has been on networking and professional development to spread the idea in principle and ground it in practice.

It is concerned with identifying all forms of exclusion and barriers to learning within national policies, cultures, educational institutions and communities. It has implications for redirecting resources, inter-sectoral collaboration, teacher training, curriculum development, local capacity building and community involvement.

It is about developing an education within communities which is relevant to local needs and maximizes the use of community resources to overcome problems. It requires everyone involved in supporting learning at whatever level-in identifying and responding to priorities for development as they exist locally. It emphasizes the roles of communities and centres of learning in creating and sustaining each other.

All these programme approaches are, or should be, attempts to create learner-friendly schools; schools with teachers and managers who are able to recognize and build on the differences children bring to school, in gender, age, background and capacities. Simultaneously, they should be schools that actively seek out and remove the barriers to learning which might exist within their own arrangements and resources, barriers which prevent accommodating the mix of children who do come and which serve to keep others out.

As a typology, it is critical that these are schools in which ECCD programmes are given high priority, tailored to the specific learner characteristics of the young child and the active inclusion of their primary care givers. They must be schools that also give consideration to the particular learning styles and priorities of adolescents, as children in transition, to provide opportunities for genuine participation and to help them make linkages between the knowledge and skills of the school and those of the world outside. They must be schools that help students at risk to test the parameters of their values, knowledge and capacities to act by inviting input from, and collaboration with, other youth-oriented institutions and services of the community.

The recent efforts to implement a stronger life-skills orientation in and across programmes, to strengthen students' abilities to translate knowledge, attitudes and values into action' are especially critical for students in marginal communities who may have no chance other than school for guided exploration.

They are important, too, for specific at-risk children and adolescents — for child workers, young soldiers, teenage parents, those who are HIV/AIDS affected — who may be able to engage only in non-formal education settings. Again, the priority must be on forging links, on developing a porous education system, one allowing children and young people to move back and forth as their changing situations warrant.

An example of an effort to move in the direction of greater synergy among various education development initiatives is beginning in the Lao People's Democratic Republic, a country with few resources, little bureaucratic capacity and almost no civil society participation. Most of its children are indigenous and most remain vulnerable, excluded from even minimal learning opportunities.

Educational interventions, however, are beginning to happen in a number of sub-sectors. The overarching framework of all the donor interventions is important in their attempt to be explicitly integrative. One of the more important structural components of these activities is the cluster school, intended to serve as a way to increase the participation of parents in the schooling of their children, to improve access to good teaching and learning materials, to increase learning achievement and decrease wastage rates especially among remote and indigenous areas.

The cluster, an arrangement of some half-dozen schools linked administratively, serves to promote common use of materials and interaction among teachers and principals, including extended opportunities for joint training and more regular supervision.

Parents are also encouraged to use the facilities of the cluster, and to contribute to its governance.

The administrative clustering of schools and implementation of joint activities is no doubt a necessary condition of sustainable synergy; it provides the skeleton. Equally important in this case, however, are the apparent commitments to ensuring that all other educational interventions also reinforce one another in content, process and community focus; and that all are based within an essentially learning-for-implementation paradigm. Thus, clusters are located in the same communities as village-based early childhood programmes, creating and facilitating parent-teacher student associations to deal with issues of access and retention, especially for indigenous children.

Resource centres are built to train teachers from the clusters in materials production and localizing curriculum. These, in turn, complement efforts of the National Teacher Training Programme to upgrade untrained and unqualified indigenous teachers in the use of child-centred methods, increase their knowledge of the new curriculum, and help them work in multi-grade classrooms which comprise the majority of schools in ethnic areas. None of this is very dramatic in the telling; it is also labour-intensive and slow in such a vertically managed and centrally controlled country. Nevertheless, it is an approach suited to institutionalizing an inclusive system.

With out-of-school learners. Holistic education recognizes the fact and critical importance of learning beyond the school. The Jomtien Conference opened wider the door unlocked a decade or so earlier by the Faure Report to the legitimacy of non-formal education. In its potential for flexibility of out reach and interactive teaching methodologies, out-of-school learning is not only legitimate, it is necessary if all children and young people are to have access to a comprehensive and truly seamless education. Community, non-formal, literacy and adult education are all terms which, in principle at least, operationalize the EFA 'expanded vision" of all people being able to address their basic learning needs at any and all points in their lives. 'For basic education to be equitable', and for it to be useful and inclusive, 'all children, youth and adults must be given the opportunity to achieve and maintain an acceptable level of learning'. NFE is intended to do this.

Building on considerable experience from the previous half-century, the decade following Jomtien has seen an increasingly positive recognition accorded to the right and value of this kind of learning. It is often seen as the basis of marginalized and fragmented communities becoming 'empowered'. Much of this progress has been realized under the ambit of specific communities of people at risk (women, people affected by HIV/AIDS, subsistence farmers, street children) or of sectors with a strong out reach agenda (primary health care, water and sanitation, management of the environment).

Although evaluations as always tend to be somewhat anecdotal, many of these programmes appear to have been fairly effective in mobilizing change at the grassroots level, at least for the short-term benefit of those involved. Much of the change has involved children's learning, directly and indirectly through early childhood development programmes and functional literacy or job training for youth. Unfortunately, there appears to have been relatively little community-based education aimed specifically at designing NFE programmes for the long term. Nor has there been much attempt to strengthen linkages between families and the formal school; PTAs and other such mechanisms often remain little more than channels for eliciting school fees and local services.

One potentially significant impact of the increased status being accorded to non-formal education with particular relevance for excluded children, however, are programmes allowing them to come back – either to formal schools or more informally organized learning activities. Children who for whatever reason have been kept, or put, out of school are being given more opportunities to find appropriate 'learning spaces' when and as they are ready, irrespective of age or school history. Such second-chance education is especially positive where it combines curriculum elements of the formal system with more non-formal delivery arrangements: another movement towards the critical criterion of seamlessness.

The Mauritius basic education for adolescents (BEFA) programme on the island of Rodrigues addresses a situation of primary completion rates at less than 50/0, with few children who drop out having the knowledge or skills either to manage their lives or to find productive work. The BEFA programme provides a mix of life and livelihood-skills modules, delivered through a variety of venues, often facilitated by secondary school students. Participants are, in part, drawn to the programme by mobilization and out reach activities; in part also because the community and their families are active supporters of it. Unfortunately, while there is some co-operation with the formal school in BEFA management, there is less indication that the strengths of BEFA (learner-centredness, participatory approach, links with the community, peer-peer delivery) are being adopted by the formal side.

Uganda's Complementary Opportunities for Primary Education (COPE) project is in a much stronger educational environment and, while also concerned with presenting formerly excluded children with 'an alternative educational strategy', it has been able to do so with greater expectation of sustainable results.

Significantly, COPE takes cognizance 'of the fact that many of these children have stayed out of school through conscious family decisions based on the logic of their circumstances. Living in poverty, families have considered their children's ability to work as outweighing the vague potential of an education system seen as low quality. COPE is important in being a strongly community-based initiative. The community's choice of teaching times, school year and instructors gives it the power to provide an acceptable alternative to the formal system.

The project is important, too, in attempting to de-link age from grade, involving children age 8 to 14 in multi-age groupings and learner-centred methods. Classes are small enough to allow some use of participatory methods, individualized attention and continuous feedback to students on their progress. Significantly, it also emphasizes strengthening the capacity of locally recruited teacher-instructors through community-based in-service training.

COPE is understood to be a temporary solution to the problem of excluded children, one that will no longer be needed once the formal system is able to provide quality, affordable and accessible opportunities for all children. This may be an overly short-sighted perspective in situations of probably fairly chronic poverty.

Even once the formal system is better established, it seems likely that significant numbers of children and youth will continue not to enrol or to drop out early. This suggests that permanent action against exclusion requires programmes such as COPE to serve in an equally permanent role, extending the parameters of what constitutes 'legitimate' education. Non formal education, functional literacy and training programmes have long provided a recapturing role of a kind, but rarely in ways that allow learners to draw on, or integrate with, the resources and contents of formal education and more rarely do they do so in ways that may bring change in the system.

3

Non-formal Education

Recomendation regarding technical and vocational education outlines the guidelines in order to bring about improvement in such education.

Sphere and Scope

1. This Recommendation applies to all forms and aspects of education that are technical and vocational in nature, provided either in educational institutions or under their authority, by public authorities, the private sector or through other forms of organized education, formal or non-formal, aiming to ensure that all members of the community have access to the pathways of lifelong learning.
2. For the purposes of this Recommendation "technical and vocational education" is used as a comprehensive term referring to those aspects of the educational process involving, in addition to general education, the study of technologies and related sciences, and the acquisition of practical skills, attitudes, understanding and knowledge relating to occupations in various sectors of economic and social life. Technical and vocational education is further understood to be:

(a) an integral part of general education;
(b) a means of preparing for occupational fields and for effective participation in the world of work;
(c) an aspect of lifelong learning and a preparation for responsible citizenship;
(d) an instrument for promoting environmentally sound sustainable development;
(e) a method of facilitating poverty alleviation.

3. Technical and vocational education, being part of the total educational process and being a right as described in Article 26 of the Universal Declaration of Human Rights, is included in the term "education" as defined in the Convention Revised Recommendation concerning and the Recommendation against Discrimination in Education adopted by the General Conference of the United Nations Educational, Scientific and Cultural Organization at its 11th session (1960) and the Convention on Technical and Vocational Education adopted by the General Conference at its 25th session (1989). The provisions of these documents are therefore applicable to it.
4. This Recommendation should be understood as setting forth general principles, goals and guidelines to be applied by each individual country according to its socio-economic needs and available resources in a changing world, with a view also to enhancing the status of technical and vocational education. The application of the provisions and the timing of the implementation will depend upon the specific conditions, and constitutional provisions existing in a given country.

Aims and Objectives

5. Given the immense scientific, technological and socio-economic development, either in progress or envisaged, which characterizes the present era, particularly globalization and the revolution in information and communication technology, technical and vocational

education should be a vital aspect of the educational process in all countries, and in particular should:

(a) contribute to the achievement of the societal goals of greater democratization and social, cultural and economic development, while at the same time developing the potential of all individuals, both men and women, for active participation in the establishment and implementation of these goals, regardless of religion, race and age;

(b) lead to an understanding of the scientific and technological aspects of contemporary civilization in such a way that people comprehend their environment and are capable of acting upon it while taking a critical view of the social, political and environmental implications of scientific and technological change;

(c) empower people to contribute to environmentally sound sustainable development through their occupations and other areas of their lives.

6. Given the necessity for new relationships between education, the world of work and the community as a whole, technical and vocational education should exist as part of a system of lifelong learning adapted to the needs of each particular country and to worldwide technological development. This system should be directed to:

(a) abolishing barriers between levels and areas of education, between education and the world of work, and between school and society through:

   (i) the appropriate integration of technical/vocational and general education at all levels;

   (ii) the creation of open and flexible educational structures;

   (iii) the taking into account of individuals' educational needs, the evolution of occupations and jobs recognizing work experience as a part of learning;

(b) improving the quality of life by creating a learning culture that permits individuals to expand their intellectual horizons, to acquire and to constantly improve professional skills and knowledge, and to engage positively in society to utilize the fruits of economic and technological change for the general welfare.

7. Technical and vocational education should begin with a broad base which facilitates horizontal and vertical articulation within the education system and between school and the world of work, thus contributing to the elimination of all forms of discrimination, and should be designed so that it:

   (a) is an integral part of everyone's basic general education in the form of initiation to technology, the world of work, and human values and standards for responsible citizenship;

   (b) may be freely and positively chosen as the means by which people develop talents, interests and skills leading to an occupation in various sectors or to further education;

   (c) allows access to other aspects and areas of education at all levels, including institutions of higher learning, by being grounded in a solid general education and, as a result of the integration mentioned in paragraph 6 (a), containing a general education component through all stages of specialization;

   (d) allows transfers from one field to another within technical and vocational education;

   (e) is readily available to all and for all appropriate types of specialization, within and outside formal education systems, and in conjunction or in parallel with training in order to permit educational, career and job mobility at the minimum age at which the general basic education is considered to have been acquired, according to the education system in force in each country;.

   (f) is available on the above terms and on a basis of equality to women as well as men, and where the learning and working environment is made suitable for the participation of girls and women by removing overt and covert bias and discrimination and seeking, strategies for motivating girls and women to take an interest in vocational and technical education;

(g) is available to people with disabilities and to socially and economically disadvantaged groups such as immigrants, refugees, minorities (including indigenous peoples), demobilized soldiers in post-conflict situations, and underprivileged and marginalized youth in special forms adapted to their needs in order to integrate them more easily into society.

8. In terms of the needs and aspirations of individuals, technical and vocational education should:

(a) permit the harmonious development of personality and character, and foster spiritual and human values, the capacity for understanding, judgement, critical thinking and self-expression;

(b) prepare the individual for lifelong learning by developing the necessary mental tools, technical and entrepreneurial skills and attitudes;

(c) develop capacities for decision-making and the qualities necessary for active and intelligent participation, teamwork and leadership at work and in the community as a whole;

(d) enable an individual to cope with the rapid advances in information and communication technology.

Government's Role

9. Policy should be formulated and technical and vocational education administered in support of the general objectives adopted for the educational process as well as for national and, if possible, the regional social and economic requirements of the present and the future, and an appropriate legislative and financial framework adopted. Policy should be directed to both the structural and the qualitative improvement of technical and vocational education as stipulated in Article 2 of the Convention on

Technical and Vocational Education (1989) and further described in the recommendations of the Second International Congress on Technical and Vocational Education (1999):

(a) Although governments carry the primary responsibility for technical and vocational education, in a modern market economy technical and vocational education policy design and delivery should be achieved through a new partnership between government, employers, professional associations, industry, employees and their representatives, the local community and nongovernmental organizations (NGOs). This partnership must create a coherent legislative framework to enable the launching of a national strategy for change. Within this strategy the government, apart from actually providing technical and vocational education, can also provide leadership and vision, facilitate, coordinate, establish quality assurance and ensure that technical and vocational education is for all by identifying and addressing community service obligations.

(b) Technical and vocational education is best served by a diversity of public and private providers. The appropriate mix can be found in many ways, with the responsibility of governments being to facilitate choice while ensuring quality.

(c) Government and the private sector should recognize that technical and vocational education is an investment, not a cost, with significant returns, including the well-being of workers, enhanced productivity and international competitiveness. Therefore funding for technical and vocational education should be shared to the maximum extent possible between government, industry, the community and the learner, with government providing appropriate financial incentives. Furthermore, the governments of least developed countries in particular should seek bilateral and multilateral capacity-building cooperation in technical and vocational education.

(d) Within governments, there are often shared and overlapping responsibilities for various elements of technical and vocational education among departments and agencies. It is desirable that governments streamline their own public institutional framework to the maximum extent possible to coordinate the national technical and vocational education effort, create an effective partnership with the private sector, and promote technical and vocational education for the benefit of all stakeholders.

10. Particular attention should be given to planning the development and expansion of technical and vocational education by:

    (a) giving high priority to technical and vocational education in national development agendas as well as in plans for educational reform;
    (b) evaluating national short-term and long-term needs;
    (c) providing appropriate current and future allocations of financial resources;
    (d) establishing a national body responsible for coordinating planning in technical and vocational education based on analysis of statistical data and projections to facilitate complementarity between educational policy planning and employment policy.

11. Planning should respond to national and; if possible, regional, economic and social trends, to projected changes in demand for different classes of goods and services, and for different types of skills and knowledge in such a way that technical and vocational education may easily adapt to the evolving scientific, technological and socio-economic changes. This planning should also be coordinated with current and projected training action and the evolution of the world of work in both urban and rural areas.

12. While the education authorities should have primary responsibility, the following groups of relevant stakeholders should be actively associated in polity formulation and in the planning process; corresponding structures, both

national and local, taking the form of public agencies or consultative or advisory bodies, should be created to permit this:

(a) public authorities responsible for planning economic and social policy, labour and employment, and for the manufacturing and service sectors;

(b) representatives of non-governmental organizations within each occupation sector from among employer; and workers as well as of the informal economy, small enterprise owners and entrepreneurs;

(c) authorities or bodies responsible for out-of-school education and training;

(d) representatives of those responsible — both in public education and in State-recognized private education - for executing educational policy, including teachers, examining bodies and administrators;

(e) parents', former pupils', students' and youth's organizations;

(f) representatives from the community at large.

13. Policies for the structural improvement of technical and vocational education should be established within the framework of broad policies designed to implement the principle of lifelong education through the creation of open, flexible and complementary structures for education, training and educational and vocational guidance, considering the provisions of modern information technology in education regardless of whether these activities take place within the system of formal education or outside it. In this respect consideration should he given to the following:

(a) multipurpose secondary education offering diversified curricula linking education to the world of work;

(b) having institutions of higher learning offering flexible admission and programmes ranging from short specialized ones to longer full-time programmes of integrated studies and professional specialization;

(c) establishing a system of equivalencies whereby credit is given for completion of any approved programme and recognition is granted to educational and/or professional qualifications and work experience;

(d) providing articulation and pathways between technical and vocational education and programmes of higher education for the benefit of those learners who may wish to continue their education.

14. Policy should be directed to ensuring high quality so as to exclude discrimination between the different educational streams. In this respect, special efforts should be made to ensure that national technical and vocational education seeks to meet international standards.

15. In order to ensure quality, responsible national authorities should establish criteria and standards, subject to periodic review and evaluation, applying to all aspects of technical and vocational education, including, to the greatest extent possible, non-formal education for:

(a) all forms of recognition of achievement and consequent qualification;

(b) staff qualifications:

(c) ratios of teaching and training staff to learners;

(d) the quality of curricula and teaching materials;

(e) safety precautions for all learning and training environments;

(f) physical facilities, buildings, libraries, workshop layouts, quality and type of equipment.

16. National policy should foster research related to technical and vocational education, with particular emphasis on its potential within lifelong learning, and directed to its improvement and relevance to the prevailing socioeconomic context. This research should be carried out at national and institutional levels, as well as through individual initiative. To this end:

(a) special emphasis should be placed on curriculum development, research concerning teaching and learning methods and materials, and, where the need exists, on technologies and techniques applied to development problems;

(b) financial resources and physical facilities from public or private sources should be made available to institutions of higher education, specialized research institutions and professional organizations for applying the results of this research on an experimental basis in representatively selected institutions for technical and vocational education;

(c) the positive results of research and experimentation should be widely disseminated using all available media, especially information and communication technology;

(d) the effectiveness of technical and vocational education should be evaluated using, among other data, relevant statistics including those concerning part-time enrolment, dropout rates and placement in wage and self-employment;

(e) research efforts to humanize working conditions should be emphasized.

17. Administrative structures should provide for evaluation, supervisory and accreditation services to ensure the rapid application of new research findings and to maintain standards:

(a) evaluation services as a whole should ensure the quality and smooth operation of technical and vocational education by continuous review and action directed to monitoring progress and maintaining standards through constant improvement of staff, facilities, programmes and, most importantly, student achievement;

(b) supervisory services for the staff should encourage improvement in the quality of teaching by providing guidance and advice and recommending continuing education;

(c) all technical and vocational education programmes, including those offered by private bodies, should be subject to approval by the public authorities;

(d) individual institutions should have the autonomy to design their programmes with the involvement of business and industry to suit local needs.

18. Particular attention should be given to the material resources required for technical and vocational education. Priorities should be carefully established with due regard for immediate needs and the probable directions of future expansion in consultation with representatives from the world of work:

(a) institutional planning should be directed to ensuring maximum efficiency and flexibility in use;

(b) the planning, construction and equipping of facilities should be carried out in collaboration with specialists from industry, teachers and educational architects, and with due regard for the purpose of the facilities, prevailing local factors and relevant research;

(c) adequate funds should be allocated for recurrent expenditure for supplies and maintenance and repair of equipment;

(d) institutions should be given greater autonomy in their administration and financial management.

General Education : Various Aspects

19. An initiation to technology and to the world of work should be an essential component of general education. An understanding of the technological nature of modern culture and an appreciation of work requiring practical skills should thereby be acquired.

This initiation should be a major concern in educational reform and democratization. It should be a required element in the curriculum, beginning in primary education and continuing through the early years of secondary education.

20. Opportunities for general technical and vocational initiation should continue to be available to those who wish to avail themselves of it within the education system and outside it ire places of work or the community at large.

21. Technical and vocational initiation in the general education of youth should fulfil the educational requirements of all spheres of interest and ability. It should mainly perform three functions:

    (a) to broaden educational horizons by serving as an introduction to the world of work, and the world of technology and its products through the exploration of materials, tools, techniques, and the process of production, distribution and management as a whole, and to enrich the learning process through practical experience;

    (b) to orient those with the interest and ability in technical and vocational education towards preparation for an occupational field or training outside the formal education system;

    (c) to promote in those who will leave formal education with no specific occupational aims or skills, attitudes and thought processes likely to enhance their aptitudes and potential, to facilitate the choice of an occupation and access to a first job, and to permit them to continue their vocational training and personal development.

22. General technical and vocational studies in schools, having great importance for the orientation and education of youth programmes, should include an appropriate balance between theoretical and practical work. Such programme of studies should be drawn up in collaboration with the professional community and with those responsible for technical and vocational education. These programmes should:

    (a) be based upon a problem-solving and experimental approach, and involve experience in punning method and decision-making;

    (b) introduce the learner to a broad spectrum of technological fields and to productive work situations;

    (c) develop a certain command of valuable practical skills such as tool use, repair and maintenance and safety procedures, and a respect for their value;

(d) develop an appreciation of good design, craftsmanship and quality;

(e) develop the ability to function as a team member and to communicate technical information;

(f) be closely related to the local environment without, however, being limited to it.

23. Technical and vocational initiation programmes in general educational enrichment for youth and adults should be directed to enabling those engaged in working life to:

(a) understand the general implications of technical change, its impact on their professional and private lives, and how to adapt to these changes;

(b) use practical skills for improving the home and community environment, and thus the quality of life and productive leisure-time activities;

(c) inculcate an awareness of the possible impact of technology on the environment, and of the concept of sustainable development.

Education for Professional Purpose

24. Given the disparities that may exist between formal education, whether secondary or tertiary, and the employment and career opportunities available, the highest priority should be given to technical and vocational education. Consequently the structure and content of traditional education, whether general or technical and vocational, should be adapted accordingly through:

(a) the diversification of secondary education in the later stages so that it may be pursued in conjunction with employment or training, or may lead to employment or to higher education, thereby offering to all youth educational options corresponding to their needs and abilities;

(b) the development of educational structures and programmes on all levels centred on organized and flexible interchange between educational institutions (including universities), training institutions and the world of work.

25. Technical and vocational education as preparation for an occupational field should provide the foundation for productive and satisfying careers and should:
    (a) lead to the acquisition of broad knowledge and generic skills applicable to a number of occupations within a given field so that the individual is not limited in his/her choice of occupation and is able to transfer from one field to another during his/her working life;
    (b) at the same time offer both a thorough and specialized preparation for initial employment, including self-employment, and also training within employment;
    (c) provide the background in terms of knowledge, skills and attitudes for continuing education at any point in the individual's working life.
26. Premature and narrow specialization should be avoided:
    (a) in principle, the age of 15 should be considered the lower limit for beginning specialization;
    (b) a period of common studies providing basic knowledge and generic skills should be required for each broad occupational sector before a special branch is chosen.
27. Technical and vocational education programmes should be designed as comprehensive and inclusive systems to accommodate the needs of all learners with special emphasis on motivating girls and women. Their equal access and participation should be ensured by:
    (a) appropriate legislative measures;
    (b) widespread dissemination of information concerning opportunities;
    (c) gender-sensitive guidance and counselling;
    (d) other incentives relevant to the local context.
28. Special provision should be made for out-of-school and unemployed youth and children of socially disadvantaged groups such as minorities, migrant workers, refugees, etc. with little or no primary education, as well as for those not entering education or training programmes after completion

of compulsory schooling, in order that they may acquire skills for wage or self-employment.

29. Given the necessity of integrating people who are disadvantaged due to physical and intellectual disabilities into society and its occupations, the same educational opportunities should be available to them as to those without disabilities in order that they may achieve qualification for an occupation to realize their potential and optimize their participation in the work force; special measures or special institutions may be required.

The Setup

30. Technical and vocational education as preparation for an occupational field should be organized on a national or provincial/local basis, so as to respond positively to overall social, economic and educational requirements and to the needs of different groups of the population without discrimination.

31. Several organizational patterns of technical and vocational education, including full-time, part-time, open and distance learning options, could exist within each country. The following patterns should be considered:

   (a) full-time programmes including general education and practical training, provided in an educational establishment, either comprehensive or specialized;

   (b) part-time programmes such as the following, in which general education and theoretical and broad practical aspects of the occupational field are given in an educational establishment, while specialized practical training is acquired during work in the chosen occupation:

      (i) the day-release system, providing for workers and apprentices to attend an educational establishment one or two days a week;

      (ii) the sandwich system, under which periods in an educational institution alternate with training periods in a factory, farm, business establishment or other undertaking;

(iii) the block-release system, whereby workers are released to attend courses of 10 to 15 weeks per year;

(c) open and distance education programmes provided through:

(i) correspondence;

(ii) special radio and television broadcasting;

(iii) the Internet and other computer-based media.

32. The responsible authorities should encourage part-time education; therefore:

(a) these programmes could be available after completion of minimum compulsory or required schooling, and should continue to be available throughout life;

(b) the qualifications acquired by this means should be equivalent to those acquired by full-time education:

(c) the practical training conducted by employers should be as broad as possible, and should aim to meet international standards.

33. In view of the increasing requirement for qualified middle-level personnel and the increasing numbers completing secondary education or its equivalent, the development of technical and vocational programmes at a tertiary level should be given high priority, by both public and private providers. The following patterns should be considered:

(a) a period of one to two years of guided work experience followed by part-time or full-time programmes of specialization;

(b) part-time and/or evening programmes;

(c) full-time programmes as an extension to those given in specialized secondary or tertiary institutions;

(d) programmes offered through open and distance learning.

34. In view of the high cost of equipment, its usage should be organized to yield optimum benefit. This could be achieved as follows:

(a) centralized or mobile workshops and libraries could be used to serve several educational institutions;

(b) when educational institutions close for the evenings and vacations, their classrooms and workshops should be utilized for continuing education and non-formal training programmes;

(c) workshops and laboratories should also be used to instal the culture of maintenance and respect for safety standards;

(d) enterprises should be encouraged to make their equipment and facilities available for practical training.

35. Enterprises should be actively involved in the theoretical and practical training of those preparing for occupations in their particular sector, and should interact with educational institutions regarding the organization of such training.

Different Schemes

36. All programmes of technical and vocational education as preparation for an occupational field should:

(a) aim at providing scientific knowledge, technical versatility and a cluster of core competencies and generic skills required for rapid adaptation to new ideas and procedures and for steady career development;

(b) be based on analyses and forecasts of occupational requirements by national education authorities, employment authorities, occupational organizations and other stakeholders;

(c) include an appropriate balance between general subjects, science and technology, as well as subjects such as computer literacy, information and communication technology, the environment and studies of both the theoretical and practical aspects of the occupational field;

(d) stress developing a sense of values, ethics and attitudes to prepare the learner for self-reliance and responsible citizenship.

37. In particular, programmes should:
    (a) be interdisciplinary in character, as many occupations now require two or more traditional areas of study;
    (b) be based on curricula designed around core knowledge, competencies and skills;
    (c) include studies of the social and economic aspects of the occupational field as a whole;
    (d) include an interdisciplinary perspective to equip students to work in the changing employment environment, and incorporate a multicultural perspective, which may include the study of a foreign language as preparation for international employment;
    (e) include the study of at least one foreign language of international use, which, while conducive to a higher cultural level, will give special emphasis to the requirements of communication, the acquisition of a scientific and technical vocabulary, and the need to prepare for international employment and multicultural working environments;
    (f) include an introduction to organizational, planning and entrepreneurial skills;
    (g) emphasize instruction in safe and environmentally sound procedures relative to the materials and equipment used in a given occupational field, the importance of safe working conditions, and the health aspects relative to the occupation as a whole, including emergency and first-aid training.
38. While based on the above general principles and components, and thus pursuing in all cases broader educational aims, programmes in their practical aspect should be designed taking into account special occupational requirements, especially in "new" professions and those undergoing change, and particularly the use of the new information and communication technology as a tool for enhancing the effectiveness of all vocations, including those considered traditional.

39. Technical and vocational education programmes leading to university qualification, while encouraging research and offering high-level specialization, should be developed with particular attention to:
    (a) the inclusion of components directed to developing attitudes whereby those with broad responsibilities in technological fields constantly relate their professional tasks to broader social and ethical goals;
    (b) preparing the learner more generally for life and the world of work bearing in mind that technical and vocational education is for economic, personal and social benefit.
40. Programmes of technical and vocational education as preparation for occupations within the agricultural sector should be designed in accordance with the overall social and economic requirements of sustainable development in rural areas.
41. Where lack of resources is a serious constraint, priority should be given to developing programmes for areas experiencing skilled human resource shortages, taking into consideration the projected needs for national economic development and the corresponding labour market growth.
42. Programmes preparing for occupations in small industry, individual farming or the artisan trades, particularly for self-employment, should include entrepreneurship and elementary information and communication technology studies to enable those engaged in such occupations to take responsibility for production, marketing, competent management and the rational organization of the enterprise.
43. Programmes leading to occupations in the business, commercial and service sector, including the tourism and hospitality industries, should consist of:
    (a) training in the methods and skills developed as a result of the application of computer-based technology to business and office management, and particularly to the acquisition and processing of information:

(b) training in the organizational and management skills required for the smooth operation of enterprises:
(c) an introduction to marketing and distribution procedures.

44. Special attention should be given to developing programmes for preparing personnel at all levels for the social services system (e.g. community and family work, nursing and paramedical occupations, nutrition and food technology, home economics and environmental improvement). Those programmes should:

(a) orientate the special occupational field to raising standards of living in terms of nutrition, clothing, housing, medical services, the quality of family life and that of the environment:
(b) be adapted to the special requirements of local conditions, in particular those of climate and geography, materials available, community organization, and social and cultural patterns.

4

Continuing Education

1. The development and expansion of technical and vocational education as continuing education, both within and outside the formal education system, with either public or private funding, and within the framework of lifelong learning, should be a priority objective of all educational strategies. Broad provision should be made for allowing everyone, whatever their prior qualifications, to continue both their professional and general education by facilitating seamless pathways for learners through articulation, accreditation and recognition of all prior learning and relevant work experience. Technical and vocational education should develop close interfaces with all other education sectors to facilitate seamless pathways for learners with an emphasis on articulation, accreditation and recognition of prior learning. Within this spectrum, technical and vocational education has a responsibility to ensure a sound initial education and training aimed at learning to learn, the most precious skill for all citizens, both young and adult. In addition to permitting adults to make up deficiencies in general or vocational education, which has often been its sole objective, continuing education should now:

(a) offer possibilities for personal development and professional advancement by providing flexibility in programme administration and curriculum design to facilitate smooth lifelong learning and ensure continuous entry, exit and re-entry points;
(b) permit the updating and renewal of knowledge and practical abilities and skills in the occupational field;
(c) enable individuals to adapt to technological changes in their occupation or to enter another occupation;
(d) be available throughout the individuals' working life without restriction with regard to age, sex, prior education and training or position, recognizing work experience as a substitute for prior learning;
(e) be available to the increasing numbers of the aged population;
(f) be broad in scope, including general education elements and contemporary cross-cutting areas.

2. The appropriate authorities should be encouraged to provide the basic conditions for continuing technical and vocational education, such as providing for paid educational leave and other forms of financial aid.
3. Continuing technical and vocational education should be actively encouraged through:
   (a) widespread dissemination of information concerning, the programmes available and ways of taking advantage of existing opportunities, including full use of the mass media and the Internet;
   (b) recognition of successful completion of programmes by increased remuneration and professional advancement, with the involvement of employers and professional associations.
4. Organizers of continuing technical and vocational education should consider the following flexible forms of delivery:
   (a) courses and training offered during working hours at the workable;

   (b) part-time courses utilizing existing secondary and tertiary technical and vocational education institutions:
   (c) evening and weekend courses;
   (d) correspondence courses;
   (e) courses on educational radio and television and the Internet;
   (f) short professional "refresher" courses.

5. The following forms of study/training leave from work should be considered:
   (a) day release;
   (b) block release of varying lengths;
   (c) release for one or more hours during the working day.
6. Programmes of continuing technical and vocational education should:
   (a) be designed and delivered to suit the special requirements of adults using flexible teaching methods that recognize already acquired expertise;
   (b) be designed for individually paced learning:
   (c) be programmed to accommodate the potential that information and communication technology has to offer.
7. Provision should be made for the particular requirements of special groups:
   (a) to enable women completing maternity leave to update their knowledge and professional skills for re-entering the workhorse;
   (b) to enable older workers and the unemployed to adapt to new occupations:
   (c) to provide minorities, foreign workers, migrants, refugees, indigenous people and people with disabilities with training programmes to help them to adapt to working life;
   (d) to enable other marginalized and excluded groups, such as early school leaves, out-of-school youth and demobilized soldiers in post-conflict situations to re-enter the mainstream of society.

8. Continuing technical and vocational education programmes through the distance learning mode should be promoted for the benefit of those disadvantaged by distance and location, such as individuals in rural communities and those engaged in seasonal work.

Essential Measures

9. Guidance should be viewed as a continuous process spanning the entire education system, and should be directed towards aiding all to make conscious and positive educational and occupational choices. It should ensure that individuals are provided with the prerequisites:
   (a) to become aware of their interests, abilities and special talents, and to help them frame a plan for life;
   (b) to pursue courses of education and training designed to realize their potential and fulfil their life plans;
   (c) to acquire flexibility in decision-making concerning their occupations, in the initial and later stages, for developing a satisfying career;
   (d) to facilitate transitions back and forth as needed, between education, training and the world of work.
10. Guidance should take into account the needs of industry, the individual and the family while preparing students and adults for the real possibility of frequent career changes, which could include periods of unemployment and employment in the informal sector, to be achieved through:
   (a) close liaison and coordination between lifelong learning, training, the wordplay and placement services:
   (b) ensuring that all necessary information concerning the world of work and career opportunities is available, and actively disseminated using all available forms of communication;
   (c) ensuring that those engaged in work have access to information concerning continuing education and training as well as other work opportunities.

11. While emphasizing the needs of individuals, guidance should be accompanied by information that gives them a realistic view of the opportunities available, including trends in the labour market and employment structures, the environmental impact of various occupations, and what may be expected in terms of remuneration, career advancement and occupational mobility.

12. Particular attention should be given to guidance for girls and women to ensure that:

    (a) guidance is gender-inclusive and covers the whole range of education, training and employment opportunities:

    (b) girls and women are encouraged and motivated to take advantage of the opportunities available;

    (c) girls and women are encouraged to pursue subjects such as mathematics and science, which are prerequisites for vocational education and training programmes.

13. Guidance in the formal schooling context should promote technical and vocational education as a viable and attractive choice for young people. It should:

    (a) cover a broad range of occupations, include supplementary visits to workaholics, and make the student aware of the eventual necessity of choosing an occupation and the importance of ensuring that this choice is made as rationally as possible;

    (b) assist students and their parents/guardians in making a positive choice concerning educational streams, and encourage learners to keep open a wide range of options so as to increase their learning and occupational flexibility.

14. Guidance in technical and vocational education as preparation for an occupational field should:

    (a) inform students of the various possibilities open in the particular field of interest, the educational background required, and the subsequent possibilities for continuing education and further training;

(b) encourage students to choose educational programmes that will not limit their later employment options;
(c) follow the students' progress through their educational programmes;
(d) supplement the programmes by short periods of work experience and study of real work situations.

15. For individuals engaged in continuing technical and vocational education as a part of their lifelong learning, guidance should:
    (a) help them to choose the programme best suited to their needs;
    (b) enable them to make effective choices regarding their entry into suitable levels of specialization.
16. Guidance should take into account:
    (a) economic, social, technological, cultural and family factors influencing the learners' attitudes, expectations and choice of career;
    (b) results of testing, including aptitude tests;
    (c) educational achievements and/or work experience;
    (d) opportunities and prospects in the occupational sector of interest;
    (e) individual preferences and special needs, including medical conditions, physical limitations and disabilities.
17. Guidance systems need to be accountable to the beneficiaries and sponsors of the service. Quality assurance and long-term results should be continually monitored at national and institutional levels through:
    (a) accurate records of clients, needs addressed, programmes and interventions used and resultant employment including self-employment;
    (b) a system of evaluation both of staff performance and of the methods used to determine the long-term effects of guidance and the degree of self-reliance of beneficiaries.

Process of Learning

18. The challenges facing technical and vocational education in the twenty-first century demand learner-centred

innovative and flexible approaches including a rearranged curriculum to take account of new subjects and issues such as technology, the environment, foreign languages and cultures, entrepreneurship and the requirements of rapidly growing service industries.

19. Theory and practice should form an integrated whole and be presented in a manner that motivates the learners. Experience in the laboratory, workshop and/or enterprises should be linked to mathematical and scientific foundations, and conversely, technical theory, as well as the mathematics and science underlying it, should be illustrated through their practical applications.
20. Full use should he made of contemporary educational technology particularly the Internet, interactive multimedia materials, audiovisual aids and mass media, to enhance the reach, cost-effectiveness, quality and richness of programmes, especially in the promotion of self-learning.
21. The methods and materials used in technical and vocational education should be carefully adapted to the learners' needs. In this respect:
    (a) where the language of instruction differs from the native language, teaching materials should make maximum use of numerical and graphical representation, written material being kept to a minimum;
    (b) where materials developed in one country are adapted for use in another, this adaptation should be carefully made with due regard to local factors;
    (c) considering, however, the increasing mobility of labour, the acquisition of foreign language skills should be considered a vital aspect of the curriculum.
22. Machines and equipment used in workshops in educational institutions should be geared to the needs of the workable, and should simulate it as closely as possible. Learners should be capable of operating and maintaining the equipment.

23. Evaluation/assessment should be an integral part of the teaching and learning process, and its major function should be to ensure the availability of appropriate programmes for the development of learners in accordance with their interests and capacities, and competence in the world of work.

24. The learners' performance should be evaluated/assessed on an overall basis that considers class participation, interests and attitude, aptitude for acquiring practical skills and competencies, and relative progress, allowance being made for aptitudes and examinations and other tests.

25. Learners should participate in the evaluation/assessment of their own progress, and this system should have an inbuilt feedback mechanism to identify and correct learning problems.

26. Continuous evaluation of the teaching and learning process, including formative assessment, should be undertaken with the participation of teachers, supervisors, learners and representatives from the occupational fields concerned to ensure that the programme is effective and that the knowledge and skills imparted meet the needs of the work place, and include recent developments in the field of study.

Organisation

27. To ensure the high quality of technical and vocational education, priority should be given to the recruitment and initial preparation of adequate numbers of well-qualified teachers, instructors/trainers, administrators and guidance staff, and to the provision of continuous professional upgrading throughout their career, and other facilities to enable them to function effectively.

28. The emoluments and conditions of service which are offered should compare favourably with those enjoyed by persons with similar qualifications and experience in other occupational sectors. In particular, promotions, salaries and

pension scales for technical and vocational education staff should take into account any relevant experience acquired in employment outside the educational sector.

Role of Teachers

29. All teachers in technical and vocational education, including instructors/trainers who teach practical skills, should be considered an integral part of the teaching profession, and should be recognized as having the same status as their colleagues in general education. In this regard:
    (a) the Recommendation concerning the Status of Teachers adopted by the Special Intergovernmental Conference on the Status of Teachers on 5 October 1966 is applicable to them especially as regards the provisions concerning preparation for a profession, continuing education, employment and career, the rights and responsibilities of teachers, conditions for effective teaching and learning, teachers' salaries, and social security;
    (b) arbitrary distinctions between teachers in specialized technical and vocational institutions and those in general education institutions should be eliminated.
30. Technical and vocational education teachers, on a full-time or part-time basis, should possess the appropriate personal, ethical, professional and teaching qualities, and a strong initial preparation that will enable them to operate in and adapt to an ever-changing scientific, technological and social environment.
31. Teachers of technical and vocational subjects in general education should:
    (a) be familiar with a broad range of specialities;
    (b) develop the ability to relate these to each other as well as to the larger social, economic, environmental historical and cultural context;

(c) where these subjects serve primarily an occupation or educational orientation function, be able to give guidance.

32. Teachers of technical and vocational education for occupational fields should have relevant qualifications so that:

    (a) if the occupational field requires primarily practical skills, they should have significant experience in the exercise of these skills;

    (b) if learners are to be prepared for technician or middle management positions, teachers should have a thorough knowledge, preferably acquired through appropriate practical experience, of the special requirements of this type of position;

    (c) if the occupational field requires research and theoretical analysis, e.g. an engineering field, teachers should have a background in research methods.

33. Teachers in technical and vocational education as continuing education should, in addition to the special preparation for teaching adults, have an adequate knowledge of the working environment of the learners, and be able to provide distance and individually paced education and training.

34. Skilled professionals working outside education should be invited to teach in schools, universities or other educational institutions in order to link the world of work more closely to the classroom.

35. Teachers of general subjects in technical and vocational education institutions in addition to qualifications in their own field, should have an appreciation of the nature of the learners' specialized technical and vocational education programme.

36. Preparation for technical and vocational teaching should preferably be offered as a tertiary programme, requiring completion of secondary education or its equivalent for

entrance. All programmes should be designed with the following objectives in mind:

(a) to maintain standards of education and professional preparation in effect for the teaching profession as a whole and to contribute to raising these overall standards;

(b) to develop in future teachers the ability to teach both the theoretical and the practical aspects of their field, with special emphasis on the need to use, whenever possible, the information and communication technologies;

(c) to develop in future teachers the responsibility for keeping up to date with trends in their field, as well as with the related work opportunities;

(d) to develop in future teachers the ability to guide learners with special needs;

(e) to ensure that future teachers are equipped, by means of supplementary training, to teach other subjects related to their primary subject.

37. Flexible training and retraining programmes, combining instruction on the campus and in the work place, must be adapted to suit the concerned subjects and the needs of the learners and the work place by developing new and appropriate instruments of assessment, accreditation and articulation, and certification standards.

38. When local conditions prevent future teachers from receiving practical work experience in their training, the teacher-training institution should attempt to simulate work place conditions as part of the curriculum.

39. The professional preparation of all technical and vocational teachers should include the following elements in pre-service training and in-service upgrading programmes:

(a) educational theory in general and particularly as it applies to technical and vocational education;

(b) educational psychology and sociology relevant to the subjects/fields to be taught by the future teachers;

(c) classroom management, special teaching methods appropriate to the subjects/fields of the future teachers and methods of evaluating/ assessing the students' work;

(d) training in the choice and use of contemporary teaching technique and aids, including information/ communication technologies;

(e) training in how to create and produce appropriate teaching materials, including modular and computer aided instructional materials, whenever such materials are in short supply;

(f) a period of supervised practice teaching before appointment to a post;

(g) an introduction to educational and occupational guidance methods as well as to educational administration;.

(h) planning the instructional environment of practical classes and laboratories and managing/maintaining these facilities;

(i) a sound training in safety, with emphasis on teaching safe working practice and setting a good working example.

40. Staff responsible for the preparation of technical and vocational teachers should have obtained advanced qualifications in their field:

(a) teacher-educators responsible for special technical and vocational fields should have qualifications in their field equivalent to those of special subjects staff in other higher education institutions and programmes, including advanced degrees and employment experience in related occupational fields;

(b) teacher-educators responsible for the pedagogical aspect of teacher preparation should themselves be experienced teachers in technical and vocational education, and should possess advanced qualifications in education.

41. Staff responsible for the preparation of technical and vocational teachers should be actively engaged in technical research and analyses of work opportunities in their field. Provision should be made for this in terms of a reasonable teaching load, and access to appropriate facilities.
42. Teaching staff should be encouraged to continue their education and training, whatever their specialized field, and should have the necessary means to do so. Lifelong learning should be made available in a wide range of facilities, and should include:
    (a) continuous review and updating of knowledge, competencies and skills;
    (b) continuous updating of specialized professional skills and knowledge;
    (c) periodic work experience in the relevant occupational sector.
43. When questions of promotion, seniority and status sire considered, teachers' achievements in continuing education and training as well as relevant work experience should be taken into account.

The Administration

44. Administrators of technical and vocational education programmes should be equipped with the following qualifications:
    (a) teaching experience in a field of technical and vocational education;
    (b) some work experience in one of the fields taught in the programme;
    (c) a broad vision of technical and vocational education as a vital element in personal, social and economic development;
    (d) knowledge of administrative techniques and procedures.
45. The heads of technical and vocational education establishments should devote a significant portion of their

time to the educational and scientific aspects of their work. Sufficient staff should be available to provide the following services:

(a) counselling and guidance for candidates and students:

(b) the preparation, supervision and coordination of all practical work and experiments;

(c) the maintenance of instruments apparatus and tools in workshops and laboratories;

(d) academic support services such as libraries, information and communication technology centres and information resource centres.

46. Administrators should keep up to date with new administrative techniques and trends, especially through relevant lifelong learning programmes. They should receive special training in the methods and problem associated with the specific features of technical and vocational education programmes, such as flexible entry and re-entry patterns, continuous training in the work place, and relevance to the needs of the world of work. This preparation should include:

(a) management methods appropriate to educational administration, including techniques that utilize information and communication technologies;

(b) financial planning methods that facilitate the allocation of available resources, given the objectives and priorities of the various programmes, and ensure their efficient utilization:

(c) contemporary human resources management and development methods.

47. Guidance staff should receive special preparation for their tasks. They should be equipped to make objective assessments of aptitude, interest and motivation, and have up-to-date information concerning education and work opportunities. They should acquire a direct knowledge of the economy and the world of work through systematically organized visits to enterprises and training periods in enterprises. Guidance staff should be provided with

facilities – including the opportunity for practical experience – to keep up with new information and methods of guidance. Most importantly, they should bear in mind the concept that technical and vocational education must be available to all as part of the lifelong learning process. It must contribute to personal and economic development and responsible citizenship.

Cooperation at Global Level

48. Member States should give priority to international cooperation between the North and South, as well as between countries of the South, with the assistance of concerned international organizations, to renovate and sustain technical and vocational education systems, with particular emphasis on the following:
    (a) the need for developing countries to take ownership of technical and vocational education and to increase their budget for this sector of education;
    (b) the efficient coordination, within any given country, of international assistance activities;
    (c) enhancing the sharing of intellectual property, including through research and development, for the benefit of learners in all countries and situations;
    (d) recognition by all stakeholders, including international financial authorities, of the contribution of technical and vocational education to the maintenance of peace and stability and to the prevention of social dysfunction, and the need to incorporate support for this sector of education in their assistance to recipient countries.
49. Member States should take special measures to make technical and vocations education accessible to foreigners (in particular migrants and refugees) and their children living within their territory. Such measures should take into account the special needs of such persons in the host country, as well as in the event of their return to their country of origin.

50. There is significant scope for countries to share their experience in technical and vocational education. There is a need for mutual cooperative assistance between all countries, regardless of their state of development. Provision should be made at the national, regional and international levels for the regular exchange, making use of contemporary information and communication technologies, of information, documentation, and materials obtained from research and development, in particular:
    (a) publications concerning comparative education, psychological and pedagogical problems affecting general and technical and vocational education, and current trends;
    (b) information and documentation concerning curriculum development, methods and materials, study opportunities abroad, and employment opportunities, including human resource requirements, working conditions and social benefits;
    (c) ideas, innovations and new teaching/learning/training materials;
    (d) mass media programmes of an informational or pedagogical character.
51. Regional cooperation should be encouraged among countries having a common cultural heritage and/or facing common problems in the development or extension of technical and vocational education through:
    (a) periodic meetings at the ministerial level and the establishment of a mechanism to review policies formulated and actions taken;
    (b) the creation of joint facilities for higher level research, the development of prototype materials and equipment, and the preparation of staff for the training of teachers where the costs of such facilities are too high to be sustained by any one country.
52. The development of teaching and learning materials which use the information and communication technologies and

are suitable for international or regional use should be considered a priority area. These materials should contribute to the progressive establishment and recognition of common standards for professional competencies/qualifications acquired through technical and vocational education. Moreover, such teaching and learning materials should encourage deliberate international collaborative teaching and learning among institutions.

53. Member States should encourage the creation of a climate favourable to international cooperation with a view to capacity-building in developing countries, especially in the areas of acquisition, adaptation and application of technology, through:

   (a) fellowship and exchange programmes for teachers/ trainers, students and administrators/managers;
   (b) establishing sustained cooperation between similar institutions in different countries, such as through twinning arrangements;
   (c) provision of work experience abroad, particularly when opportunities at home are limited;
   (d) encouraging countries to present and make known their educational programmes outside their national boundaries.

54. To facilitate international cooperation, Member States should, through the exchange of good practices and methods, aim to apply relevant and appropriate internationally recommended standards and norms relating in particular to:

   (a) systems of assessment/evaluation;
   (b) scientific and technical symbols;
   (c) occupational qualifications and certification:
   (d) equipment and technical standards;
   (e) information processing;
   (f) equivalencies of qualifications implying standardization of curricula and testing, including aptitude tests;

(g) occupational safety and security through testing of materials, products and processes;

(h) environmental protection and conservation.

55. Internationally recommended standards and norms should be continuously evaluated through sustained research on and monitoring of the effectiveness of their application in each country, with a view to enabling countries to use lifelong technical and vocational education as a means of narrowing the disparities between the North and the South and as a bridge to a more prosperous and peaceful future in the twenty-first century.

Practical Training

1. A critical challenge that faces human society at the start of the twenty-first century is to attain full employment and sustained economic growth in the global economy and social inclusively. The ILO's framework of decent work addresses both the quality and quantity of employment and provides a basis for new education and training policies and strategies. Human resources development, education and training contribute significantly to promoting the interests of individuals, enterprises, economy and society. By making individuals employable and informed citizens, human resources development and training contribute to economic development and to achieving full employment and promoting social inclusion. They also help individuals to gain access to decent work and good jobs, and escape poverty and marginalization. Education and skills formation could lead to less unemployment and to more equity in employment. The economy and society at large, like individuals and enterprises, benefit from human resources development and training. The economy becomes more productive, innovative and competitive through the existence of more skilled human potential. Human resources development and training also underpin the fundamental values of society-equity, justice, gender equality, nondiscrimination, social responsibility, and participation.

2. Technological changes, changes in financial markets, the emergence of global markets for products and services, international competition, dramatic increases in foreign direct investment, new business strategies, new management practices, new forms of business organization and of the organization of work are among the more significant developments that are transforming the world of work. Many of these developments are also components of globalization which is the name given to the various processes producing the dramatically increased integration of economic activity in the world today. These developments offer both opportunities and challenges for enterprises, workers and countries. For enterprises increased competition has meant more winners and losers. For countries globalization has increased both national development and disadvantages as globalization has exacerbated differences in the relative advantages of countries. For some workers these developments have resulted in career opportunities or successful self employment, improved living standards and prosperity but for other workers they have resulted in job insecurity or unemployment, declining living standards and poverty. Many of these developments are dramatically increasing the importance of the application of human knowledge and skills to economic activity. Human resources development, education and training are necessary and essential elements required to take both full advantage of the opportunities and to rise to the challenges of these developments for enterprises, workers and countries. There is a growing recognition that globalization has a social dimension that requires a social response. Education and training are components to both the economic and social response to globalization.
3. Education and training cannot alone address this challenge, but should go hand-in-hand with economic, employment and other policies to establish, in an equitable manner, the new knowledge and skills-based society in the

global economy. Education and training have distinct but converging outcomes as society is changing. They have both a dual rationale: develop skills and knowledge that will help countries, enterprises and individuals utilize the new opportunities and enhance the employability, productivity and income-earning capacity of many population groups that have been adversely affected by globalization and changes in society at large. Education and training are necessary for economic and employment growth and social development. They also contribute to personal growth and provide the foundation of an informed citizens. Education and training are a means to empower people, improve the quality and organization of work, enhance citizens' productivity, raise workers' incomes, improve enterprise competitiveness, promote job security and social equity and inclusion. Education and training are therefore a central pillar of decent work. Education and training help individuals become more employable in rapidly changing internal and external labour markets.

4. Human resources training and development are fundamental, but are by themselves insufficient to ensure sustainable economic and social development, or resolve the aggregate employment challenge. They should be coherent and form an integrated part of comprehensive economic, labour market and social policies and programmes that promote economic and employment growth. Policies that expand aggregate demand in the economy such as macrocosmic and other measures must be combined with supply-side policies, e.g. science and technology, education and training, and industrial and enterprise policies. Appropriate fiscal policies, social security and collective bargaining are among the means to distribute these economic gains on a fair and equitable basis, and constitute basic incentives to invest in training. Pursuing these integrated policies requires consideration of a new financial and social architecture for the global economy, a subject for ILO research.

5. It is the task of basic education to ensure to each individual the full development of the human personality and citizenship; and to lay the foundation for employability. Initial training develops further his or her employability by providing general core work skills, and the underpinning knowledge, and industry-based and professional competencies which are portable and facilitate the transition into the world of work. Lifelong learning ensures that the individual's skills and competencies are maintained and improved as work, technology and skill requirements change; ensures the personal and career development of workers; results in increases in aggregate productivity and income; and improves social equity. Both in developed countries as well as in developing countries there are many workers without the basic skills for literacy and numeracy. National and international strategies have to be developed to eliminate illiteracy, based on concrete targets, benchmarks and quality assessment.
6. Education and training of high quality are major instruments to improve overall socio-economic conditions and to prevent and combat social exclusion and discrimination, particularly in employment. In order to be effective they must cover everyone, including disadvantaged groups. Therefore, they must be carefully targeted at women and persons with special needs, including rural workers; people with disabilities; older workers; the long-term unemployed, including low-skilled workers; young people; migrant workers; and workers laid off as a result of economic reform programmes, or industrial and enterprise restructuring. In addressing the needs of these groups, particularly of young people, access to a combination of formal, off-the-job, and work place learning should be systematically offered and developed as it provides for effective learning outcomes and increases the chance of entering the labour market.

7. Training can be one of the instruments that, together with other measures, address the challenge of the informal sector. The informal sector is not a sector in the traditional sense of economic classification but a name given to the economic activity of persons in a variety of situations, most of which are survival activities. Informal sector work is unprotected work that is, for the most part, characterized by low earnings and low productivity. The role of training is not to prepare people for the informal sector and keep them in the informal sector; or to expand the informal sector; but rather it should go in conjunction with other instruments, such as fiscal policies, provision of credit, and extension of social protection and labour laws, to improve the performance of enterprises and the employability of workers in order to transform what are often marginal, survival activities into decent work fully integrated into mainstream economic life. Prior learning and skills gained in the sector should be validated, as they will help the said workers gain access to the formal labour market. The social partners should be fully involved in developing these programmes.
8. Education and training are a right for all. Governments, in cooperation with the social partners, should ensure that this right is universally accessible. It is the responsibility of all persons to make use of the opportunities offered. Free universal, quality public primary and secondary education must be made available to all children, and they should not be denied sustained access to education through child labour. Education cannot be separated from training. Basic and secondary education is the foundation on which an effective vocational education and training system should be built. Good quality basic education and initial training, availability of adult and second chance education, together with a learning culture, ensure high levels of participation in continuous education and training. Qualified teachers and trainers are the fundamental key to providing quality education for helping children and adults reach high

standards in academic and vocational competencies. Their recruitment, remuneration, education, training and retraining, assignment and provision of adequate facilities are critical elements of any successful educational system. In addition to education and training, career guidance and job placement services (career development services) embracing career education, career counselling, employment counselling and educational, vocational and labour market information, all have a crucial role to play in human resources development. The fostering of a career development culture throughout education, training systems as well as employment services is a means to promote continuous learning. The development of this culture among youth and adults will be of particular importance for ensuring their employability and facilitating their transition from education and training to work or further training.

9. Employability is defined broadly. It is a key outcome of education and training of high quality, as well as a range of other policies. It encompasses the skills, knowledge and competencies that enhance a worker's ability to secure and retain a job, progress at work and cope with change, secure another job if she/he so wishes or has been laid off, and enter more easily into the labour market at different periods of the life cycle. Individuals are most employable when they have broad-based education and training, basic and portable high-level skills, including teamwork, problem solving, information and communications technology (ICT) and communication and language skills, learning to learn skills, and competencies to protect themselves and their colleagues against occupational hazards and diseases. This combination of skills enables them to adapt to changes in the world of work. Employability also covers multiple skills that are essential to secure and retain decent work. Entrepreneurship can contribute to creating opportunities for employment and hence to employability. Employability is, however, not a function only of training — it requires a

range of other instruments which results in the existence of jobs, the enhancement of quality jobs, and sustainable employment. Workers' employability can only be sustained in an economic environment that promotes job growth and rewards individual and collective investments in human resources training and development.

10. There is tripartite and international consensus about guaranteeing universal access of all to, and increasing and optimizing overall investment in, basic education, initial training and continuous training. Discrimination which limits access to training should be combated both by anti-discrimination regulations as well as by common action of social partners. These principles have been endorsed already in the Tripartite Declaration of Principles concerning Multinational Enterprises and Social Policy adopted by the Governing Body, 1977. The Committee endorsed the core commitments made in the Cologne Charter of the Group of Eight leading industrialized nations (G8) in 1999 calling for renewed commitment of all partners to lifelong learning: ' ... by governments, investing to enhance education and training at all levels; by the private sector, training existing and future employees; by individuals, developing their own abilities and careers". However, structural adjustment programmes, restrictive fiscal policies, low wages, debt repayment obligations, decline of development assistance flows, competitive price pressures on enterprises and lack of resources of large sections of the population in a number of cases induce governments, enterprises and individuals to under-invest in education and training. Furthermore, market uncertainties, poaching of skills by other enterprises and the growth of insecure forms of work and consequential high turnover of staff may reduce enterprises' incentives to invest in training. This is especially true for the least developed countries, most of which are in Africa, given their dire socio-economic situation. The culture of developing, on a continuous basis, individual and collective skills for

enhanced productivity and employability in a rapidly changing environment has to be improved further.

11. The cost of education and training should be seen as an investment. Increasing this investment can be fostered by recognizing that investing in education and training can be a shared responsibility of both the public and private sector. Government must always assume the primary responsibility for investing in basic education and initial training, and it should also invest in other forms of training. Government must also share the greatest responsibility for investments directed at groups where combating social exclusion or discrimination is an important objective. With respect to the responsibility of individuals, the government must also share responsibility in order that access not be denied on financial grounds and to the detriment of the broader interest of society. Government as an employer, must also assume responsibility to invest in training. With respect to the private sector, the responsibilities of both enterprises and individuals should be recognized and, where appropriate, encouraged. These responsibilities are especially appropriate with respect to investment in work place-based and continuous education, which can raise workers' efficiency and the competitiveness of enterprises. The organization and implementation of private sector responsibilities in this area can best be accomplished through partnerships between the government and enterprises, between government and the social partners or between the social partners. Ensuring increased investment for SMEs is especially suitable to a partnership approach.
12. There is no universal model of investing in training. Government should create a general economic environment and incentives conducive to encourage individuals and enterprises to invest individually or jointly in education and training. This investment and the responsibility for it should generally be determined by the objectives of training, e.g. individual, enterprise or social objectives. Countries can

use different ways and means to foster investment in training and increase resources or training. Enterprises have a critical role to play in investment in training. A number of mechanisms used in combination to further investment in training and to guarantee access are required. These may include levy systems on enterprises accompanied by public grants, establishment of training funds, various incentives for training and learning, e.g. tax rebates, training credits, training awards, individual training accounts, collective and individual training rights, sabbatical leave, collective training agreements and emulation of national and international best practices of investing in training. The chosen mechanisms should take into account the special needs of the SMEs. Where levies are the chosen mechanism for funding training, the governance of funding distribution should be tripartite, or where these are agreed by the social partners, such governance should be bipartite. Decisions regarding government policies on education and training should be based on genuine tripartite dialogue and give the tripartite partners the opportunity to develop the best ways and means to increase investments in training. Measures such as the provision of childcare facilities are needed to facilitate access to training. One means of encouraging countries and companies to increase current efforts possibly differentiated for different regions of the world, size of companies or sector of industry, as a mirror and point of orientation for countries, sectors, and companies.

13. Flatter hierarchical structures, and devolved decision making, initiative and control, also widen the need for higher-level skills and training, and result in increased responsibility for workers. ICT is accelerating these management trends and changes in the world of work in general. ICT has the potential to improve enormously people's access to quality education and training, including in the work place. There is however a danger that these

technologies may create a "digital divide" and worsen existing inequalities in education and training between urban and rural areas, between rich and poor, between those who possess and those who lack literacy and numeracy skills and between developed and developing countries. Countries should expand their investment in the infrastructure needed for use of ICT, in education and training hardware and software, and in the training of teachers and trainers. Such investments should be undertaken by both the public and private sectors and make use of collaborative local, national and international networks. Governments may also provide incentives for the private sector and individuals to encourage computer literacy and to develop new communication skills. New modes and methods need to be deployed for training and learning when using ICT. Distance-learning methods can be used to make training available at convenient times, at accessible places or at reduced costs. Distance learning should not replace all other learning or teaching methods but can be a valuable part of the total teaching tools available. Distance learning should, as far as possible, be combined with traditional training methods in order to avoid a sense of isolation of the learner. The social framework for training needs to be adapted to these new forms of training.

14. The many driving forces, have a significant impact on organization and working methods of companies. Also, new sectors are emerging, many of them based on the use of ICT products and services, including the Internet. All this increases demand for new skills and competencies, including personal skills and ICT competencies. Education and training need to respond to these new demands, both those related to ICT and those related to changing work organization.

15. Electronic networking provides opportunities for learners to assist each other more actively, for learners to be more

active in the training and education process, and for formal and non-conventional teaching methods to be utilized. In order to apply ICT in training, trainers must master these technologies and be systematically trained. Teaching methods need to be updated to accommodate the teaching of new developments in ICT, new types of organization of schools should be devised to take full advantage of ICT; and the individual needs to learn self-iearning methods. New training is needed to provide trainers and individuals with these skills. Enterprises may provide ICT facilities or support schemes for workers for the use of ICT at home or in general, and to schools or other training providers, in order to promote the diffusion of ICT skills and access in society. Appropriate government incentives could facilitate this development.

16. For many developing countries, the challenges are much more basic. Societies with huge and growing levels of adult illiteracy, and massive debt crises, will not be able to design, fund or implement the modern education and training policies which are prerequisites for development and economic growth. In the age of the knowledge society, 884 million adults are illiterate, unable to operate effectively even with the intellectual tools of the "old economy". UNESCO estimates that, in the least developed countries, while 144 million adults were illiterate in 1985 by 2005 this will rise to 188 million – in other words, the number of illiterate adults will grow by 30 per cent in the least developed countries. Additionally, structural adjustment programmes have in specific instances operated to reduce public investment in education, thus, further weakening the longer term capacity for economic' growth and development.

Much of the developing world lacks access to the physical infrastructure through which much of the new knowledge is pulsing. The lack of electricity and telephones, the cost of computers and Internet access, all contribute to deprive citizens, enterprises and workers in developing countries from benefiting from the ICT revolution, and create the conditions for a "digital divide" to grow between countries. Developing countries should make greater efforts to invest in ICT and to develop ICT-appropriate methods of teaching rather than simply adding computers to existing teaching methods. The international community should, as part of creating the conditions for skills formation in the least developed economies, undertake bold and substantial debt relief, or, where appropriate, debt cancellation; help mobilize resources for programmes to secure basic literacy and numeracy and the development of communication and information infrastructure; and assist with training in the new information and communication technologies. This is a direct challenge to the ILO and international development agencies.

Multinational corporations should be encouraged to agree fair technology transfer agreements, to develop local high-level skills in developing countries, and to help create the infrastructure for the new knowledge economy. The contributions to development that multinational companies can make through training as elaborated in the Tripartite Declaration of Principles concerning Multinational Enterprises and Social Policy should be recalled. These measures, taken together, contribute to developing the economies and societies of the poorest parts of the world. They provide a ladder through which developing countries can move up the value chain in production, making goods and providing services which add significant economic value, and which receive significant economic return in the global economy. Education and training is one of the packages of measures to leapfrog from underdevelopment to the information society.

In developing an education and training base in developing countries, the existence of new technology can open up new possibilities and possibly save costs on more traditional methods. This is a major challenge for the developing countries to invest in ICT and develop appropriate policies.

Closer collaboration is needed between the ILO, UNESCO and other international organizations; regional organizations, such as the EU and MERCOSUR; and donor countries that place high priority on human resources development and training. It should also work more closely with international financial institutions such as the International Monetary Fund, the World Bank, and regional development banks, to ensure that structural adjustment programmes do not inhibit investments in education and training. Greater national and international efforts also should be made to eradicate illiteracy worldwide. All of these measures and support can only be effective if the developing countries make efforts to set up policies and programmes to promote economic growth and develop their human talent.

17. The development of a national qualifications framework is in the interest of enterprises and workers as it facilitates lifelong learning, helps enterprises and employment agencies match skill demand with supply, and guides individuals in their choice of training and career. The framework should consist of a number of elements: appropriate, transferable, broad and industry-based and professional competency standards, established by the social partners, that reflect the skills required in the economy and public institutions, and vocational and academic qualifications; and a credible, fair and transparent system of assessment of skills learned and competencies gained, irrespective of how and where they have been learned, e.g. through formal and non-formal education and training, work experience and on-the-job learning. Every person should have the opportunity to have his or her experiences and skills gained through work, through society or through formal and non-formal training assessed, recognized and certified. Programmes to compensate for skill deficits by individuals through increased access to education and training should be made available as part of recognition of prior learning programmes. Assessment should identify skill gaps, he transparent, and provide a guide to the learner and training provider. The framework should also include a credible system of certification of skills that are portable and recognized across enterprises, sectors,

industries and educational institutions, whether public or private.

The assessment methodology should be fair, linked to standards, and be non-discriminatory. Potential hidden discrimination should be actively guarded against. For example, the shift to the service sector, with an overall stronger female component, often relies on greater communication and problem-solving skills, which are not always explicitly recognized. Similarly, testing systems conducted in an individual's second language sometimes distort results of technical and other skills possessed. New forms of work organization often shift the skills requirements within an enterprise. For example, flatter managerial structures are predicated on shifting certain responsibilities from management to the work force. These should result in explicit recognition of the new competencies required by the work force under these circumstances; and reward systems have to take these into account.

The vocational qualifications system should be tripartite, offer access to workers and anybody wanting to learn, should cover public and private training providers and be updated on a continuous basis. It should ensure multiple entry and exit points in the education and training system during a worker's career. The ILO should develop a database on best practices in developing a national qualifications framework, conduct a general study on the comparability of different national qualifications frameworks based on this database, and undertake research into recognition of prior learning.

18. Trade unions and employer associations may also contribute to training by managing their own training institutions and providing education for their members. Particularly at the sector and enterprise levels, collective bargaining can set appropriate conditions for the organization and implementation of training. Such collective bargaining could encompass issues such as:

- skills required by the enterprise and the economy;
- training necessary for workers;

- assessment of basic skills and skills gained either in the work place or during individual or associative activities;
- development of career paths for workers;
- personal training and development plans for workers:
- facilities needed to allow the maximum benefits from training;
- recognition and reward schemes, including remuneration structuring.

19. The social partners should strengthen social dialogue on training, share responsibility in formulating education and training policies, and engage in partnerships with each other or with governments for investing in, planning and implementing training. In training, networks of cooperation also include regional and local government, various ministries, sector and professional bodies, training institutions and providers, non-governmental organizations, etc. Government should establish a framework for effective social dialogue and partnerships in training and employment. This should result in a coordinated education and training policy at national level, and long-term strategies, which are formulated in consultation with the social partners and are integrated with economic and employment policies. It should also include tripartite, national and sector training arrangements, and provide for a transparent and comprehensive training and labour market information system. Enterprises are primarily responsible for training their employees and apprentices, but also share responsibility in initial vocational training of young people to meet their future needs.

20. The scope and effectiveness of social dialogue and partnerships in training is currently limited by the capacity and resources of actors. It varies between countries, sectors and large and small enterprises. Recent regional economic integration also brings a new dimension to social dialogue on training and the need for capacity building. There is a

pressing need to raise this capacity by various means such as technical cooperation, public grants to trade union and employer organizations, and exchanging experience and best practices between countries. Education and training in industrial relations and on trade union education, business administration and the social contribution by the work and the organization of the social partners, should also be an integral part of capacity building and a part of initial and vocational training. Being a tripartite organization, the ILO should lead international cooperation to build up capacities for social dialogue and partnership building in training. Additional efforts should be made for the benefit of developing countries.

21. Terms of reference for a review of the Human Resources Development Recommendation, 1975, (No. 150), should be based on the present conclusions, adopted by the International Labour Conference at its 88th Session, 2000, the conclusions of the Cologne Charter 1999, and the statements on this subject jointly made by international employer and trade union organizations; and should include the following:

    (1) address training and education needs in the modern world of work in both developing and developed countries, and promote social equity in the global economy;
    (2) advance the decent work concept through defining the role of education and training;
    (3) promote lifelong learning, enhance employability of the world's workers, and address the economic challenges;
    (4) recognize the various responsibilities for investment and funding of education and training;.
    (5) promote national, regional and international qualifications frameworks which include provisions for prior learning;
    (6) improve access and equity of opportunity for all workers to education and training;

(7) build the capacity of the social partners for partnerships in education and training;
(8) address the need for increased technical and financial assistance for the less advantaged countries and societies.

Recommendation No. 150 should be revised in order to reflect the new approach to training. Although some aspects of the recommendation are still valid, others have lost their relevance. There is a need for a more dynamic instrument that is more applicable and used by member States and the social partners in formulating and implementing human resources development policies, integrated with other economic and social policies, particularly employment policies. A new recommendation should be complemented by a practical guide and database prepared and updated by the office from time to time as a matter of routine.

5

The Achievements

Role of DPEP

In order to assess the level of success in realising the DPEP objectives after lapse of three years, a Mid-term Learning Assessment Survey (MAS) covering all the 42 districts of Phase I States was conducted by the NCERT in 1997. Except two districts in language and four in mathematics in the State of Madhya Pradesh, all other districts have crossed 50 per cent level of achievement in both the subjects in class I. While student performance in classes III-IV has touched 60 per cent marks in some of the districts, in some others it has stood below 40 per cent mark.

A comparative analysis of Class I students' achievement on Baseline Assessment Survey (BAS) tests conducted in 1994 with that of the same set of tests re-administered in 1997 under MAS has shown positive trends in 28 out of 42 districts in language with 19 districts showing statistically significant improvement. In mathematics 33 out of 42 districts have significant improvement. The hike in achievement in language and mathematics varies widely ranging from 1 per cent to 44 per cent for Class I.

Similar analysis of Classes III-IV students' achievement on BAS tests in 1994 vs 1997 shows positive trends in 31 out of 42 districts in language with 27 showing significant improvement, and in 29 out of 42 in mathematics with 23 showing significant improvement. The hike in achievement in these classes varies from 10-25 per cent.

The goal of reducing the differences between gender groups to less than 5 per cent has been realised in almost all the districts across the classes in both the subjects. The results, however, are not so encouraging in regard to social groups.

EFA Strategy

The goals of EFA in India are to be viewed in relation to the stage of educational development that obtained in 1990 ¾ the year of World Declaration on EFA. By then, fairly large expansion of primary schooling and the teaching force had already taken place in all parts of the country. Other sectors of education like adult education and non-formal education had also developed fairly well. Therefore, the main challenges in education in 1990s related to EFA have been the following:

- access to basic education for the unreached segments and uncovered habitations.
- qualitative improvement in content and processes of education; to make them more responsive to learning needs of individuals-children, youth and adults, families, community and development in different sectors of social and economic life.
- consolidation and newer orientation wherever required in different areas of education through innovative programmes and changed role of educational personnel.
- community participation in education; making education a people's movement.
- evolving effective and efficient management structures in education.

All goals and targets of EFA to be fulfilled in 1990s have to be assessed in terms of the nature of the programmes, the degree to which they have led to achievement of the goals of EFA, and the promise they hold for making the processes and supportive structures sustainable.

Thus, when EFA programmes were implemented in 1990s, a new framework for development of basic education in the country was emerging which had the following broad features.

Holistic Approach

The approach adopted for planning and implementation of EFA programmes is characterised by:

- a holistic view of basic education with greater linkages and integration between pre-school, primary education, non-formal education and adult education;
- relating programmes of education with national concerns such as nutrition and health care, environment, small family norm and life skills education.
- collaboration of different departments and sectors of development with primary education.

Process of Decentralisation

Decentralisation has been one of the major strategies for designing different programmes for EFA and implementing them. Operationally, this can be characterized in terms of:

- shift from taking 'state' as the unit of planning to 'district' as the unit for programmes of basic education; and to move further to 'sub-district' levels wherever found necessary and feasible;
- increasing community involvement in implementation and monitoring of programmes; and
- participation of panchayati raj institutions (local self-government bodies in rural areas) and urban local bodies in planning and management of education.

Welfare of the Deprived

Some remotely placed areas and several social and cultural groups still remain outside the fold of basic education. Therefore, in order to ensure full accessibility not only in terms of availability of school but also in terms of facilitating conditions for participation of children, the strategy adopted for EFA involve the following:

- household surveys
- surveys of educational status of specific social and cultural groups
- school mapping and micro-planning
- alternative schooling
- support to community based innovative and experimental projects by voluntary agencies.

Campaign Approach

It is recognized that mobilizing civil society to participate in the programmes of basic education is essential for achieving the goals of EFA. It is with this perspective that major efforts are being made to use all means including mass media for advocacy and promotion of EFA activities. Further, in order to reach the common stakeholders, mass campaigns have been launched for creating awareness about educational needs of children, youth and adults, and help them to develop proper appreciation of the role of education in improving the quality of life. It is also evident that programmes in basic education have to be implemented in a mission mode involving the community in an effective manner through mechanisms such as District Literacy Committees, Village Education Committees and Parent-Teacher Associations. Literacy campaigns have made big strides in this direction and efforts are on to implement other basic education programmes in a mission mode.

Relevant Laws

A significant change in the perspective towards basic education is that it is not viewed merely as a service provided by the state but as a right of every individual. The Supreme Court of India has recognized education as a fundamental right flowing from the right to life and liberty. It is with this in view that attempts are being made to incorporate education as a fundamental right of all children upto 14 years of age in the Indian Constitution so that participation in education by all children becomes obligatory for the state as well as the parents as a legal requirement.

Several state governments are moving forward with new legislation in this regard. For instance, the State of Tamil Nadu has enacted afresh legislation for providing free and compulsory primary education.

Participation by all members of the community in basic education is considered as the main plank on which the whole effort towards EFA is to be orchestrated. Several strategies such as school mapping and micro planning are being adopted to ensure participation of people in bringing all children to school and to articulate their demand for improved school services. Community participation is also seen as an essential prerequisite for ensuring long term sustainability of the initiatives. It is with this in view that Andhra Pradesh Government has passed an Act providing for School Management Committees with community participation for overseeing the functioning of schools.

Though considerable progress has been achieved in recent years, the magnitude of the task ahead is so gigantic that government alone cannot achieve the goal of EFA. Recognizing this, participation of non-government organizations (NGOs) and voluntary agencies has been given an important place in the implementation of basic education programmes. It is envisaged that involvement of NGOs will on the— one hand, enlarge the network of agencies and individuals for implementation of basic education programmes and on the other hand, it will bring greater flexibility and innovation into basic education programmes.

It is visualized that quality programmes of EFA will cost more money than what has been available to the education sector in the past. Programmes of educational development, especially basic education, are therefore being planned keeping the expectation that larger allocations to education would be available in future. The Government stands committed to raise the allocation to education to 6 percent of GDP as recommended in various national policy documents. Receiving international assistance for basic education is seen as part of the larger effort to mobilize more resources for education.

Management and Decision Making

Basic education in India is a shared responsibility of the central and state governments. Decision making for EFA is, therefore, done at both the levels. Central government essentially deals with national policy and programme formulation as guided by the Central Advisory Board of Education, Parliament and expert committee and commissions.

Within the framework and guidance provided by these bodies, long term plans for education development are drawn by the Planning Commission with the help of specialized working groups involving educationists, educational administrators and representatives of NGOs. Keeping in view the parameters specified in the long-term (five year cycle) plans, specific programmes and projects are formulated for central funding to states usually on a matching basis.

Following the National Policy on Education — 1986, a number of centrally sponsored schemes to strengthen basic education were initiated through mutual consultation among the central government and the various state governments. The scope of such specific programmes got further enhanced during the 90's with the availability of external assistance for area based basic education projects. In addition to these, some of the states have also launched their own programmes for expanding the out reach of primary education.

The last decade has witnessed the emergence of a variety of models management of basic education, mainly with the aim of decentralizing decision making, promoting community participation and rigorous monitoring of programme implementation. As was mentioned earlier, management of school education is essentially a subject with the state governments. In order to simplify and accelerate the process of decision making autonomous bodies with expertise, delegated authority and representation of civil society have been created for management different projects/programmes. Some of these are as follows.

Societies at District Level

Launching of literacy campaigns demanded a decentralized arrangement for mobilizing people within a district, involving local volunteers, and evolving locally relevant strategies. With this in view, the National Literacy Mission promoted the setting up of autonomous committees in each district involving administrators, local activists and NGOs. The district literacy committees (DLC) are vested with powers to decide on the course of action with respect to literacy and continuing education. The DLCs receive funds directly from the NLM as well as state governments and utilise the money within the broad parameters set by the NLM.

Societies at State Level

Major programmes with external financial assistance brought with them a new framework of management and decision making in States. While broad policy decisions are made by Government of India, detailed plan of action for the EFA is designed, implemented and monitored through a state level autonomous body set up for the purpose.

This model of management decision making and monitoring is being adopted under the District Programme of Primary Education (DPEP) which currently covers more than 200 districts as well as in Lok Jumbish and Shiksha Karmi Projects in Rajasthan.

Government of Rajasthan has gone further down from the district to sub-district level under Lok Jumbish with regard to important decision making on primary education development. Under this, a block level committee is set up in each block, with representation from the block level administration, Lok Jumbish project team at the block level, NGO representatives and other educationists. The Committee is authorized to take decisions on such vital matters as opening of new schools, sanctioning additional teachers, sanctioning additional classrooms and buildings, and opening of non-formal education centres.

In fact, the strategy has been to facilitate local level decision making and monitoring processes. It is expected that the rejuvenation of panchayati raj institutions in most States following the Constitutional Amendment recognizing these as the third tier of governance would lead to institutionalization of the decentralized management framework for basic education. Major nationally funded projects such as National Literacy Mission, Operation Blackboard, Non-Formal Education and those funded by international agencies such as the DPEP and Lok Jumbish have devised their own monitoring systems.

Apart from these project specific arrangements, progress towards meeting learning needs get continually assessed and articulated in different forums. Specifically, periodical survey of educational facilities conducted by the NCERT has been a major exercise to generate a data base on basic education. Besides, annual statistics are collected and collated every year for planning and monitoring purposes.

Selected Statistics published annually by MHRD is another source of data on education at all levels. These have been utilised in different ways to assess the progress of UEE. Currently a specially designed package (District Information System for Education-DISE) is being implemented with UNICEF assistance to create a computer based information system which provides for ready access to district level information on basic education.

With evolution of EFA programmes, it is increasingly recognized that people from different areas of development and social life ought to be involved in decision-making on educational issues.

The need is also recognized equally for the co-operation and collaboration required between different ministries and allied sectors of development. It is with this in view that gradually, the decision-making and management structures for EFA programmes and their operational aspects are taking shape with the local community at the centre and the local self government as an important organ of management for basic education.

The Cooperation

Cooperation for EFA has to be seen from different perspectives. Seen from the angle of implementing national programmes one can refer to the partnership between central and state governments as well as between government and non-government organizations. One has also to view this in terms of the contributions being made to EFA by the NGOs. And finally, one can also observe an expanding relationship between government and international funding agencies.

One should also mention the role played by national organizations such as NCERT and NIEPA as well as many higher education institutions in providing technical support in the implementation of major initiatives in the area of EFA.

Government and Private Bodies

The Central Government and the State Governments, which have the joint responsibility to provide basic education services, are committed by the constitutional mandate to providing free education to all children upto the age of 14 years.

However, situation with respect to actual provision varies from one state to another. Overall, there are four arrangements for provision and management of primary schools education. In the first category are those which are fully funded and managed by the state governments. Majority of the formal primary education institutions fall in this category.

A second category of schools which are also fairly large in number of those managed by the local self-government bodies such as the panchayat raj bodies in rural areas and municipalities/ corporations in urban areas. These are also almost fully financed by the state government sources. The third category of institutions are those managed by private/ voluntary bodies but with substantial grants from the government. The fourth category consists of a small proportion of schools that are established and managed by private/ voluntary bodies without any monetary grants from the government.

Funds are mobilized mainly through student fees and voluntary contributions. In the recent years, a few corporate houses have also begun contributing to primary education development programmes, particularly in urban areas.

Non-Government Organizations in Action

Non-government organizations, commonly referred to as voluntary agencies in India, also participate in EFA programmes. For instance, a large number of voluntary agencies are implementing non-formal education programmes to meet the educational needs of out-of-school children. Many of them focus on socially and economically backward areas and marginalised sections of the society and on education of girls.

A large number of voluntary agencies are providing education, health and nutrition to children in urban slums and for working children. The Central Government provide grants for meeting their expenditure on basic education programmes. Some NGOs conduct innovative programmes for formal primary schooling also. There has been, a remarkable involvement of NGOs in the adult literacy programmes. Ever since its inception, the National Literacy Mission has taken measures to strengthen its partnership with NGOs.

The current decade has seen the emergence of a number of EFA programmes supported by international agencies. These include support multi-lateral agencies including UN bodies, the World Bank and the ADB.

Bilateral grants have been obtained from a number of donors such as the European Commission, DFID, SIDA, NORAD, HIVOS Netherlands and Japan. In fact, large programmes such as the DPEP are being supported and funded jointly by several of these agencies.

Five UN agencies have supported the development of a joint initiative with the Government of India and State Governments on community based primary education. Assistance from UN agencies and bilateral donors is in the form of grants, while the World Bank provides concessional loan assistance through IDA. Matching contributions in cash and kind are provided by Central and State Governments for such projects.

The statement made in the National Policy on Education – 1986 and 1992 that from the Eighth Five Year Plan (1992-1997) onwards the outlay on education would uniformly exceed 6 per cent of the national income is yet to materialise.

At present (1996-97), 3.8 per cent of GNP is being invested in education. The share of elementary education in GNP in India has been relatively low, even though this has also increased by three times, from 0.48 per cent to about 1.7 per cent during the last five decades. The expenditure by education departments as a percentage of GNP at current prices has increased from 0.68 per cent in 1951-52 to 3.14 per cent in 1995-96. The central expenditure on education has increased substantially over the last ten years. The central plan expenditure increased from Rs. 30,360 million in the Seventh Five Year Plan (1985-90) to Rs. 74,430 million in the Eighth Five Year Plan (1992-97).

The Government is committed to raise the expenditure on education to six percent of GDP, as against the level of 3.9, by the end of the Ninth Plan. Fifty per cent of the enhanced allocation is expected to be spent on primary education. This increasing financial participation of the Central Government through Central and Centrally Sponsored schemes for promotion of primary education is in keeping with the spirit of partnership between the Central and the State Governments.

One of the most significant factors related to change in the pattern of expenditure on education in recent years is the gradual increase in the proportion of funds spent on elementary education in comparison to secondary and higher education sectors.

The last three Five Year Plans have witnessed significant shift in the expenditure of the Department of Education in the Central Government towards primary and adult education and away from tertiary education. That the central government is paying serious attention towards achievement of the goal of EFA is brought out by this actions of government.

6

Current Scene

The EFA imperative of an expanded vision of education finds reaffirmation in the Convention on the Rights of the Child (CRC) that all children have the right to learn at all stages of their development, and to do so in ways that are appropriate and easily accessible. It reconfirms that this learning must be such that it contributes to children's physical, psycho-social, emotional and intellectual development. Under the umbrella of the CRC and the EFA, children's right to education cannot be played off against their rights to health, protection or participation. Nor can it take second place to the environment, defence or structural adjustment in determining national priorities.

National and international policies, development analyses and planning, advocacy and interventions -each must take a holistic and inclusive focus in ensuring that all children realize all their rights, including the right to education.

Moreover, as reiterated at the EFA Sub-Saharan Africa Conference, not just any kind of education will do. Education must be such that it enhances the potential of children and young people to respect themselves and others, participate in the decisions of their society, live in peace and dignity, and earn a living. Increases in the percentage of children reached are important, but are no longer sufficient. Quality counts. All children have the right of access to effective opportunities for learning. Exceptions cannot simply be argued away on the basis of 'especially difficult circumstances'. There should be no excluded children.

Exclusion from education is part of an intricate web of human rights violations. It reflects a complex, progressive and sustained process of 'being excluded'. Millions of children are, of course, excluded from education, largely because they are excluded from development benefits in general. Exclusion is interactive and comprehensive. It touches all aspects of the lives of affected children. It results either in their having no access to education or in their being poorly served when they are there. Exclusion is a broad-brush phenomenon. Children who do not go to school are also children living in conditions of poverty, socio-cultural marginalization, geographical isolation, racial and/or gender bias. They are children living with the corollary burdens of disease and disability, sexual exploitation, indentured and injurious labour, or forced involvement in civil and military conflict. Their exclusion from education is simply one more manifestation of a web of rights violations.

Without access to good quality education, children are denied the opportunity to acquire the knowledge, capacities and self-confidence necessary, as children and later as adults, to act on their own behalf in changing the circumstances which are excluding them. Within the context of the CRC, then, the education of children whose rights are being denied must be considered in two respects: how their situation is affecting their access to education and learning achievement; and how education can better serve to end their broader exclusion, or at least mitigate its harm.

Exclusion from education, then, is not a single 'one-off' event in the lives of the children affected. Having no access to school, or access only to those that are ineffectual and harmful, needs to be understood as part of a pattern of systemic exclusion, one linked to other social, economic and political conditions which can, in effect, serve as proxy.

The child who consistently does not go to school is also the child who consistently suffers from poor nutrition and health care, from inadequate water, sanitation and shelter; who lives in a family with an unstable income and limited opportunities to participate; whose community is in conflict. Exclusion from education must therefore be understood in context; in the complex of conditions and factors which together act to keep a child from participating in effective, relevant and well-organized learning experiences. For example:

Children within the family and the community: The way children are treated in school, and the way in which they participate with the learning opportunities and relationships they experience there, are influenced by the particular intellectual, physical and personality characteristics they bring with them. The family influences these characteristics by its form (nuclear, extended, single-parent) and its members. The family influences the way a child develops by its beliefs about the place of children in the social structure and the importance of facilitating learning; by how and to whom its resources are allocated; by how it deals with gender.

The values, knowledge and skills present within a family have a profound impact on its ability and willingness to meet its child's basic needs: health care and nutrition, psycho-social nurturing and cognitive stimulation. The community in which a family lives also has a determining role in the life of a child by how it treats its citizens: by the range of socio-economic, and cultural diversity it accepts; by its mechanisms for resolving conflicts; by its economy and infrastructure; and by whether it is rural or urban, geographically isolated or nationally and internationally 'connected'.

The school within the education system: The school exacerbates or mitigates exclusion by how it interacts with the children, families and communities it serves. It also does so by how it relates to its own bureaucracy and manages the resources and policies it receives. Related to both of these, the school influences exclusion by its physical safety, the professionalism and commitment of its leadership and teachers, and the quality and range of materials it has available.

It creates and mitigates exclusion by how it welcomes children; by its flexibility in matching each child's learning style with its teaching methods; and by its capacity to value -and build learning opportunities around – the diversity of cultures, talents and interests each child brings. The education bureaucracy, in turn, plays a part in all of this by its policies and competencies in curriculum development and teacher training, its decisions on language of instruction, its level of decentralization, and the quality and consistency of its monitoring and supervision.

National education policy within the society and international community. Education policies are influenced most notably by the overall national political regime of the country, its socio-economic environment and its propensity to countenance violence and make war. Some governments lack the resources to educate all children; others choose not to use their resources for this purpose. The development status and culture of the society at large, and its relations with the international financial, professional and technical-assistance community also influence the level and quality of attention given to education. National education policies influence exclusion through their budget allocation and distribution decisions; by the attention they give to displaced, hard-to-reach and culturally 'different' families and children; and by their broad education philosophy and the weighting of programme alternatives therein.

The reality of these multiple exclusionary factors is particularly invidious. It makes finding entry points and facilitating change difficult, and it injures children in multiple, interactive ways over the long term. It is a reality of deficit for children which goes far beyond schools and education systems, while having a profound impact on both of these in their capacity to be inclusive. It is in the specific mix of characteristics and interactions of any one context that the scope, causes, consequences, severity and dynamics of exclusion for each child will be found. So, too, its resolution.

Without families, communities and societies which can provide protection and nurturing for children, and which can support their establishing a broad capacity to learn, these children are less likely to be able to make fully effective use of any learning opportunities that are available.

They will be less able to acquire the knowledge, skills and sense of empowerment necessary for their continued development or for living effectively and co-operatively. They will be less likely to pass these capacities on to their children. For both individuals and societies, exclusion is a tragedy because its impact is now and in the future. It is intergenerational and all-pervasive.

The key, of course, is in breaking the cycle, and this involves a consideration of education beyond children and beyond schooling. It involves a vision of education – its policies, planning and actions – which does not assume narrow and linear definitions of who and what 'counts'. It is clear, for example, that children are unlikely to move out of poverty, create healthy living conditions or confront their marginalization – or go to good schools – on their own.

The Jomtien Conference recognized this in affirming within the ambit of EFA the importance of adults learning to earn a living and to participate effectively, and of families learning to care for, protect and educate their children. It recognized adult literacy and out-of-school education as legitimate and core elements of basic education for all. Further, the conference recognized that children do not only begin to learn at 6 years of age. Nor do they learn only in classrooms or by rote. It made the early development and education of children also a necessary part of the EFA dynamic.

So, too, are teaching strategies promoting problem solving, critical thinking, values clarification and life-skills; and learning which takes place both in the school as well as in less formal settings. Education for all means considering the child as a whole and unique learning person, one who needs to live in a similarly learning environment. It means, therefore, designing education contents and programmes suited to each child, in the context of families and communities. The CRC and EFA, therefore, commit societies to 'seamless' education systems, ensuring equity in learning for all. Beyond the specific social values and economic- priorities a society wishes to express through its education system, the global commitments to education it has made through the EFA Declaration and the CRC require it to ensure that every person-child, youth and adult shall be able to benefit from educational opportunities designed to meet their basic learning needs.

These needs are actually tools, of course: the knowledge, skills, attitudes and values to live, develop and participate. Helping excluded children to acquire them implies a commitment to reconsidering what constitutes the legitimate playing field of education. At a basic level, all children must have access to education programmes or schools with competent teachers, relevant curricula, and safe, secure and healthy physical and social environments.

Unfortunately, education systems are complex and traditionally staid social institutions. In most societies, formal schools have been the principal, in most cases the only, socially sanctioned means of providing such education. As such, they have realized significant results for many children, but not for all. As loosely linked and administratively ponderous systems, they have been limited in their capacity to respond and reach out to diversity. They are rarely able to act with speed or flexibility in ways beneficial to large segments of their constituencies, especially to those children and families who do not fit the mainstream.

Traditional schooling has not been, and will never be, 'enough' to reach all children with sustainable and relevant learning opportunities. In many societies, it creates exclusion both by failing to reach significant numbers of children, and by defining others as unreachable and unteachable, as drop-outs and repeaters.

The 'problem' of excluded children rests, then, with those who are failing to include them. Education for all is not schooling for all. The CRC and EFA require a movement away from the narrow paradigm distinguishing formal schooling from 'the rest'. They require societies to push the parameters, to recognize and provide for alternative means of supporting children's learning that are equal in quality, status and availability. They require changing the paradigm that has been allowing systemic discrimination to persist and become more widespread.

Exclusion of children happens at every point within education systems. Inclusion also needs to happen at all points. Inclusion in this sense becomes very much a dynamic phenomenon. A country's formal education system presents the official expression of what that society accepts as the values and activities appropriate for children's learning through the human and financial resources it allocates and the way it manages these. Through policies and resources, it determines who gets in, what they learn and in what way.

The CRC and EFA, however, require that all children 'get in' and that they learn. This requires education provision to be set within an interactive and broadly based framework; no single factor can on its own create or solve exclusion, nor can any one be dismissed as irrelevant. Serious policy commitment from the top of the national hierarchy, and sustained and integrated action throughout the whole of the education system and in association with all who touch the lives of children, are fundamental.

Prevalent Conditions

Ultimately, it is the children themselves who suffer the problem of exclusion. It is the individual child who does not have a chance to experience effective and relevant education and whose present situation and future options are consequently put at risk. But while children suffer the problem, they neither create nor maintain their exclusion. They are denied education, or decline to participate, almost always as a consequence of exclusionary conditions not of their own making.

Within the framework of the CRC, neither these conditions nor the decision not to participate can mitigate the obligation of their families, communities and governments, or of international agencies, to ensure them access and quality. The 'problem', therefore, rests in these hands, as those with the responsibility and power to take actions that make education readily available to children in forms appropriate to their learning, and to avoid actions that do not.

System of Education

Exclusion is interactive. Non-enrolment, passivity, absenteeism, repetition and eventually dropping out are the signs and symptoms of an intricate web of education-related factors that play out in a process of being and becoming excluded on an individual and social level. When schools push some children out and fail to draw others in, they are functioning as part of both an education system and a wider social, economic and political context which exclude. It is not sufficient, therefore, to focus at the micro level of the school and forget the politics of its macro environment, or vice versa.

If genuine change is to come about in creating inclusive learning environments for vulnerable and marginalized children, it is critical to keep in mind that each child as an individual is at risk and being harmed by exclusionary forces. It is easy to talk about 'the poor', 'street children' or 'girls'. But talking in the aggregate leads to thinking in the abstract and taking little relevant action. Ultimately, it is a specific young girl who is kept at home to care for siblings, or an adolescent boy from a slum who avoids school because the teacher abuses him. It is insufficient to talk about, analyse and plan on the basis solely of excluded children in the generic.

It is also necessary to talk, analyse and plan with the specific children who are being affected: to understand who they are, why they are there, what they are doing and under what circumstances they would be willing to participate in education. All children living in poverty may not be in school for broadly similar reasons. Because of this, macro policies and education systems matter. But the specific conditions under which each child and their family will decide, or be able, to participate, and the actions they take, will be unique.

They will depend on the comparative advantage they see in the alternatives, the costs and benefits they perceive and the stress caused to them by lost options.

While self-evident, both the macro and micro perspectives are the reality of exclusion, and complicate significantly any discussion of causes, consequences, who is affected and how to address it. They force consideration of a multiplicity of individual, community and situational factors, and the interactions among them, in trying to understand why exclusion is happening and the interventions needed to reverse it.

Macro-level poverty alleviation and better curricula will go some way towards getting children into school; they will not get all children there or help them learn effectively when they are. The following section attempts to untangle some of the strands of the exclusionary knot by considering ways in which it happens at the three systems levels of school, bureaucracy and national policy. The aim is to begin to create a better analytical tool for looking at the dynamics keeping children from effective learning, factors which might then serve as proxy indicators for finding those children and as more precise levers for effecting change.

Micro-level Exclusion

Schools exclude at the micro level by what they are and what they do and do not do. They exclude when they are not learner friendly, do not support their teachers as professionals and do not welcome families as partners. They exclude by their inability to provide competent and learner-appropriate teaching methods, relevant curriculum materials, or health and safety promoting facilities. They exclude because they are often places of 'pervasive grimness', overcrowded and dark, with 'little to engage the students' or encourage teachers who, in turn, escort to rigid discipline and corporal punishment or fail to turn up.

Schools exclude when they fail to create a culture of peace; when they fail to take affirmative and uncompromising action to end all forms of harassment, abuse and violence. In and around schools, between teachers and students and among students themselves, psychological and physical threats, abuse and actual violence are globally becoming matters of serious, sometimes tragic, concern. Girls are especially vulnerable in schools that fail to serve as 'safe havens' from sexual harassment, physical attack or abusive corporal punishment. often by teachers. But boys, too, are at risk. While more often the perpetrators of violence, many come to that role as the victims of earlier abuse.

Schools in remote areas and inner-city slums, those serving communities the least able to demand better, may be unmotivated or unable to apply behaviours which ensure the safety and protection of children. They are often assigned principals and teachers who are not happy to be there, especially if they are from a better-off community outside. Where the community itself is deprived or marginalized, even local staff may be less than effective: poorly trained, largely unsupervised, with few teaching resources. There is little in this to allow or encourage the kind of teaching which creates an inclusive, effective classroom.

With few teachers able to use responsive, interactive teaching strategies, these schools are more likely to use power rather than participation as a means of managing behaviour, and less likely to have positive disciplinary alternatives to corporal punishment. Exclusionary factors are interdependent. Where such methods do not actually push children out, they can generate an increasingly dysfunctional school climate leading to antagonistic, abusive or violent responses in some children, or passive resistance and truancy in others. They can also produce bum-out, inertia and abuse on the part of teachers themselves.

Schools exclude when they apply narrow paradigms of what children are and how they learn; when they are unable to deal with diversity. Children from 'different cultures, environments, and social classes are exposed to different materials, experiences and informal teaching by their families and neighbours, and this results in the appearance of different competencies at different times'.

Schools which recognize only one kind of intelligence, one notion of what a child of a certain age and characteristics (ability, background, gender) can do, and one way of transferring information, exclude. They fail to recognize, and so to accommodate, what each child brings as learning capacities and interests. These individual characteristics play a significant part in how children 'make the transition to schooling, how they make use of what school offers and how long they stay at school and with what success'.

The professionally weak, narrowly traditional or simply uncaring school risks excluding all children, but especially those from already marginalized backgrounds, by being pedagogically inflexible; by controlling, telling and punishing children rather than understanding them and facilitating their active participation in their own learning. In this same vein, an inner-city school excludes when, with students from a broad mix of racial, ethnic and language groups, it allows children from various backgrounds to be overlooked and denies them the potential of shared and mutual learning. Where teachers and curricula are unable to build on the diversity, they leave minority, second-language and culturally different children a drift, neither understanding nor understood. Though from a different cause, many schools in post-colonial countries leave children similarly excluded from their learning environment.

As 'islands of foreignness', such schools exclude when they present – and represent – urban, Western or elite values, behaviours and expectations, those with which indigenous, migrant or nomadic children have little in common and from which they have little to gain beyond a sense of failure and confusion.

Schools exclude when they do not reach out proactively to the families of children who are most vulnerable. These are the children whose culture or social background, language, customs or sense of self-identity, interfere with their ability to communicate and interact effectively in a traditional classroom. They are children living in poverty who have suffered a history of poor nutrition, limited psychosocial stimulation or emotional and physical trauma. They are children with physical or learning disabilities for whom there has been no support, or children affected by HIV/AIDS.

Broadly, these are children whose circumstances have either impeded their ability to learn, or limited the range of positive experienced they have had in engaging with the learning process. They are children who are, therefore, less likely to be resilient and able to adapt successfully to the particular culture (expectations, roles, norms, approved behaviours, etc.) of the school. They are the children most likely to give up or drop out. Beyond what happens in the classroom itself, schools exclude these children by not taking their families into account; by not creating programmes expressly to link families into the educational processes their children are experiencing. Schools foster exclusion, for example, by not instituting parent-teacher association (PTA) or other home/community programmes where parents can openly discuss, in a language they understand, the strengths and weaknesses of their children's learning and behaviour.

They exclude by not facilitating, alone or with other agencies, early childhood care and development (ECCD) and parenting programmes, or day-care services to take pressure off working parents who might otherwise need their school-age daughters at home. They fail by not developing cross-cultural learning programmes for children and their families; and by not forming literacy, second-language or vocational training classes for parents who are themselves excluded or vulnerable.

Schools exclude when they fail to concern themselves with those children who do not turn up. Schools are often isolated from, and sometimes actively in opposition to, the families and communities whose children they are supposed to be serving.

They fail children by not looking for those who are missing, and by not working with other agencies that might know who and where they are (churches, health centres, drop in youth clubs). 'Heads of schools and teachers focus their attention on those who are enrolled and seldom work directly with families whose children are out of school . . . local administrators, community leaders . . . even assistant township education officers do not promote and facilitate participation'.

Schools contribute to exclusion by not putting systems in place for formally noticing and tracking the non-attender or truant: the child who has not yet officially dropped out, but who is regularly 'just not there'. In some cases, these are children who are not unduly missed because they are seen as poor or disruptive learners. In many cases, it is more simply a problem of no one feeling, or being held, accountable for them. In their broader circle of responsibility, schools exclude when they do not take account of children during their out-of-class hours. Poorly managed shift systems in some African schools, for example, 'leave children idle for much of the day' and open to involvement in street gangs and other forms of violence.

In all of these cases, exclusion happens to both individuals alone and to individuals as members of groups or categories of children. A single child may be regularly missing who has to care for HIV-affected parents, has to work, is being bullied at school or is suffering from mental or physical illness. But also a particular type of child may be regularly missing -children characterized by their race, gender, place of residence (urban slum) or provenance (hill-tribe community).

The first is a problem of uncaring and unprofessional schools; the second a reflection of this same problem exacerbated by systemic discrimination. In either case, 'absence from school is a symptom and not a causal factor'. To the extent schools do not monitor absenteeism, do not look for and assess patterns and do not work with families and community leaders in understanding the reasons for it, they are helping to create exclusion.

Schools exclude by costing too much directly and by implication. Universal primary education (UPE) notwithstanding, schools are rarely free, or even financially reasonable, for families living at the margin. Costs of schooling can be many and subtle.

Over the past decade in rural China, fees have multiplied significantly with the decline in central government subsidies to primary education. In Lijiagou, for example, with female/male enrolment rates of 20% and 40% respectively, school costs over $7 per five-month semester -a huge sum in a region where per capita income is 550 a year and the pay back for literacy seems faraway.

Despite the official elimination of tuition, the same is true in Uganda, where the burden is falling especially hard on families affected by HIV/AIDS. Similarly in India, 'the cash costs of education play a major role in discouraging poor families from sending children to school', costing a labourer in Bihar, for example, forty days of labour per year to send three children to the 'free' primary school. Timing of expenditures can also be a problem. Parents on subsistence incomes cannot always produce the immediate lump-sum payment that their child's school calls for.

There are also the hidden or imputed costs. In Indian communities where higher dowries are charged for educated girls, there is 'a clear disincentive to parents' to pay for daughters to go to school. In very poor rural families, any child at all going to school requires 'an exacting struggle'. Even where the miscellaneous charges are objectively small, cruel choices may have to be made between schooling and other opportunities.

Sending a child to school may mean less money to buy seeds or medicine, more backbreaking work for her mother at home or fewer resources for another child's education. In situations of high infant mortality, a mother who has to ask if she should 'worry about the survival of my children; or their schooling', makes it clear that education may not always be the expenditure of choice for parents. Families are forced to assess their situation, balance priorities and manage shifts of income and expenditure with very little room to manoeuvre. Even where they are prepared to make the effort to pay, they are less likely to come down on the side of education when the school experience is negative, learning is minimal and future benefits uncertain or unlikely. Reflecting the cycle of exclusion, the difficulties families face in financing their children's school attendance are leading to a situation of 'stuttering education'.

This is a problem for the child who makes little progress over an extended period, and for the school that finds itself dealing with classrooms full of children of many ages who come and go as finances at home permit.

Schools and their teachers, exclude by not being sufficiently accountable to their students and parents. PROBE's analysis of four poverty-burdened states in India found that 'the deterioration of teaching standards has gone much tc far to be explained by the disempowerment factor alone'. Though the specifics may not be generalizable to all situations of exclusion, the generic issues are probably fairly common. 'Plain negligence', for example, must explain teachers keeping a school locked for months, their drunkenness, asking children to do their domestic chores, or their seeking work elsewhere. All these factors, however, may be less devastating than the quiet inertia of the majority of teachers has become a way of life in the profession. These are situations where teachers simply do nothing, leaving children to play or go home. Without accountability mechanisms, managed by school leaders and teacher groups in collaboration with the community, there is little 'to protect the work culture of the teaching profession' and little to mobilize and guide teachers to help them to do better.

Role of Bureaucracy

The education bureaucracy excludes by failing to recognize the diversity of learners within its purview. It excludes when, in consequence, it fails to provide the education programmes and schools under its responsibility with the human and financial resources and discretionary authority they, in turn, need to support, build on and strengthen that diversity. As primary interpreter and implementer of national education policy, and venue of a country's core educational expertise and power, it is largely at this meso level where systems-based factors excluding children are officially created and operationally sustained.

The bureaucracy excludes by producing incapable teachers and irrelevant curricula. It excludes by ignoring or dismissing alternative education delivery channels and methods, especially non-formal education (NFE), as legitimate and necessary modalities for reaching hard-to-reach children. It excludes by allowing and not actively combating the kind of educational triage which supports high-quality learning opportunities for the few, mediocre programmes for the general society, and poor or no facilities for the rest. It excludes by not creating and enforcing policies of transparency, accountability acid 'no tolerance' for any kind of corruption, at any level.

The education bureaucracy excludes children when it fails to provide their teachers with the learning and professional status they need to be effectively competent, responsible and motivated. In the Lao People's Democratic Republic 35% of teachers are considered under qualified, with an even higher figure in the poorer provinces.

Teacher education in Pakistan has remained apparently unchanged since a 1988 review found that such 'a variety of authorities control different aspects of the system' that, in effect, no agency in particular is in charge no single body or institution is accountable for progress in teacher education for quality control and development. Research on classrooms in Namibia paints a sobering picture of poorly trained teachers. Hardly dramatic, but none the less clear, there is very little reason for children to go to school or engage in learning when the little that their teachers are doing is nevertheless the best they can do.

When choral repetition is the primary method of teaching in the languages, and even in maths in some cases, in the majority of cases, it was clear that the learner, were not reading, but were just looking at the teacher and repeating, children are being excluded.

Education systems exclude when they fail to provide teachers with regular in-service professional training and moral support, through learning-oriented supervisors. Failure to support teachers inside the classroom, especially those in marginal, poor or isolated schools, excludes students by giving them teachers with typically no or little pre-service training, often coming into the system as teacher aids — little more than child minders — to flounder and fail. Even where they are trained the unsupervised teacher excludes when confronted with a significant culture gap between what was expected and what those children from ethnically or resource-poor communities are able to do.

In any event, no pre-service training can prepare teachers for all they will find in the classroom, especially where the school environment has few materials and children come to school malnourished, abused, having experienced little intellectual stimulation, or reflecting a different language or culture base.

Also, teachers burn out. Especially in circumstances where they are under-prepared, where students are reluctant learners, and where families can focus simply on the day's next meal, teachers can and do fall into patterns of inaction or absenteeism. Working in a 'demotivating environment which saps their morale day after day' and where 'there is a deep lack of accountability in the schooling system', education systems most seriously exclude by diminishing the value of teaching and of its teachers. Their message says, in effect, 'conscientious teaching is the least prominent and most thankless of the activities they can be expected to perform'.

Without a regular connection to new ideas and knowledge, and the chance to regenerate their sense of curiosity about teaching and learning, teachers are less likely to be creative in their interaction with children. There will be less to motivate them to consider individual learner capacities; to attend to their varying needs for protection or to the development of the whole child. They are less likely to take the risk or make the effort of moving beyond transferring knowledge, to teach in ways which engage learners, to guide the development of critical thinking or promote problem solving. They are less likely to have the professional confidence or ability to reach out to parents concerning their children's strengths and problems as learners. All this makes it especially difficult for teachers to interact effectively with children who are emotionally or physically vulnerable or culturally and linguistically different.

Education bureaucracies exclude by being "predicated on the achievement of the 'successful', rather than on an inclusive education which aims to improve the problem-solving and critical learning skills of all pupils and not just a select few".

A narrowly focused achievement- oriented paradigm defines some children out, and defines them out with greater regularity when they are poor, marginal or in some way out of the norm. Testing procedures exclude when they act solely on a summative basis to screen out, or keep back, children who fail to meet certain criteria, rather than formatively to 'support their continuous progress'. When education systems manage by the bell curve, assume that certain children cannot learn, or maintain classrooms which do not integrate the child who is linguistically different, they not only put the validity of their assessments at risk. They also act directly to exclude those children whose learning capacities and needs the tests fail to recognize or to 'count'.

Children already at risk are made more vulnerable to exclusion when the system's assessment procedures fail to reflect the individual learning characteristics, gender or home background of each child and to accommodate itself to them.

Assessment excludes when it forces adaptations by the child rather than by the system, especially when that child does not automatically or easily 'fit in'. There is little evidence to show that children who repeat learn any more or any better through re-exposure to the same content and teaching methods, especially when there is no remedial support for filling in learning gaps.

On the contrary, the family, health, psychosocial and development factors which negatively affected the ability to succeed in the first place are likely to be exacerbated for a child who may be punished by parents for failing, or punished by the fact of now being older than classmates, probably bored and labelled with the stigma of failure. Ironically, the continued presence of such a child in the same limited class space may widen the circle of exclusion further by keeping a younger one from moving up.

The education bureaucracy excludes children when it persists in creating inappropriate and irrelevant curricula and materials of poor pedagogical quality. Curricula which are gender-biased and degrading, which are incomprehensible to specific groups of children, or which do not allow any local adaptation, force children away. An education system which causes 'alienation of the individual from the culture and community of origin', drawing children away from traditional forms, contents and philosophies of learning, excludes. African educators talk of their not yet decolonized systems 'divorcing children from their roots'.

But the problem is not just in the South. In one region of the north-west United States, for example, although the majority of students were from Hispanic, Indian and other cultures, the schools continued to present a culture based on the white, Anglo-Saxon culture. Although students seemed gifted in their drawing abilities, the entry tests were based solely on understanding print-based concepts with which they had more limited experience.

Education systems and their curricula and methods exclude when, in their wake, schools produce national assessment results that essentially relegate whole segments of children to the status of failures. They exclude by forcing a conclusion that 'very few children in a given population attained mastery in any subject they did better on subjects requiring rote memory, poorly on basic literacy skills such as reading with comprehension and writing a letter and lacked knowledge of health and hygiene principles and general knowledge'. These children are excluded by a system which not only does not let them learn, but then forces on them the lasting stereotype and implications of being 'failures'.

National Policy on Education

Government and education policies exclude in two broad ways. By commission, they actively deny children's right to education through the regulations they apply — restrictive enrolment criteria, segregating children with disabilities, denying NFE an effective co-ordination with the formal system. They also exclude by omission – failing to make 'education for all' a broad societal philosophy and articulated priority or to implement any pro-child policies which do exist in serious, systematic ways.

Numbers count. Policies at the macro level can cause exclusion so extensive as to be considered a national phenomenon. Burma, with an estimated 25% of its children never enrolling in school, and of those who do only about 34% completing the first cycle, Pakistan, with an estimated 44% of children in primary school, and the Lao People's Democratic Republic, with a drop-out rate of 60% and an average attendance of about three years must be seen as countries of exclusion.

Policies are also selective in impact, affecting specifically marginalized communities in large or smaller pockets of exclusion. Rajasthan, for example, a state of India with a large nomadic, scheduled caste and tribal population, is one among ten states with literacy rates well below the 52% national level, and with primary-school completion rates even lower. Exclusionary policies, or policy inaction, also affect generalized and scattered classes of children such as the 'urban poor'. In east St Louis, Illinois, for example, some 70% of the students fail to meet state standards; 52% drop out of high school. Sixth graders have been known to teach classes due to teacher absenteeism.

National government and education policy-making bodies exclude by rot seriously or comprehensively identifying barriers to education for families and children at risk; by not creating opportunities to allow their participation. Ethnic minorities, forced migrants and refugees, nomadic children, girls as a class in many cultures, are all communities where children vulnerable to exclusion are found, and for whom the failure of macro policy to be pro-active in support of their education is exclusionary. National education bodies exclude when they locate schools far from ethnic or poor communities, for example.

They exclude when they fail to urge colleagues in ministries of transport, industry or rural development to consider isolated, impoverished communities and education access and quality in making their decisions on road, rail or communication networks, on industrial expansion or support to small and medium-sized enterprise development. They exclude by not calling health and social development ministries to account for families with inadequate nutrition, disease- prevention interventions or HIV/AIDS counselling services. Education ministers exclude by failing to emphasize on the policy agenda that all sectors are obligated under the CRC to ensure education for all children, and therefore that considerable resources need to be equitably and efficiently allocated to that end.

National systems exclude when they purposely segregate children with special learning needs. They exclude when they determine that a child's persistent failures or problems in school arise, not from the nature of the teaching or the environment of the school, but from deficiencies in the child. They exclude when they 'deflect attention from the more general changes in curricula and teaching methods that might minimize the creation of difficulties for learners and put the onus instead on the child and family to act – often by withdrawing the child from the system. Children are further excluded when the system does not provide them schools and teachers with the knowledge, skills and resources to diagnose and 'scaffold' them, i.e. to give them the level and kind of support which will facilitate their learning.

These children are excluded when they are ignored in the class-room, left to try to survive on their own. They have often little option but to drop out. They are excluded when their ability to explore, test and adapt is removed by placements in restrictive remedial classes.

They are excluded by being removed to institutions without professional competence. Systems exclude when they discriminate 'behind an apparently benign' labelling of children as different and effectively unteachable. Macro policies exclude when 'learners are expected to aspire to a single standard of culture or educational fitness and those who cannot shed their difference are seen as having an enhanced distinctiveness and may be subject to increasing rejection'.

Macro levels exclude by failing systematically to assess variation in learning achievement across the country, or to seek patterns of factors causing them. As noted above, student assessments can exclude. National-level policy excludes by not knowing precisely what is being assessed and the quality of the results; not knowing the validity and reliability of the instruments or how they are administered.

Children, can be unfairly put out of a programme or denied progress to the next level by standardized tests which do not account for differences in linguistic or cultural background, or in school quality. Systemic exclusion is missed when certain groups of students are not regularly enough at school to take a test or pass it. Improvements in classroom-level test scores at higher grades may mean better-quality teaching and curriculum.

They may also mean that weaker, culturally less well integrated students, have dropped out. Exclusion is created at the macro level when policy-makers and evaluators are unclear, inconsistent and ineffective in ensuring accurate and well implemented assessments; and when they fail to interpret results in ways that reveal where children with persistently low achievement and non-participation are and the contextual and school factors associated with that exclusion.

Education policies exclude when they segregate the formal 'legitimate' school system from the less-worthy 'rest'. Education policies which accredit for academic advancement and social recognition only one learning channel and which designate non-formal alternatives as second-class and merely for subsistence, exclude almost all children living at the social and economic margins.

They create chronic exclusion when they fail to enable and recognize the creation of an integrated learning system, one in which a wide range of education modalities is given status, and the resources to go with that.

Policies foster exclusion by not working in collaboration with the non-governmental organizations, community-based organizations and indigenous institutions which are well-placed to deliver these other modalities, promoting instead dysfunctional competition for funds, duplication of services, inequities in educational quality and irregularity of access.

Through programmes they support themselves, and those they fund others to deliver, education systems exclude when they act on the assumption that second-class is good enough; that the education deficit faced by children who are working, marginalized and living in poverty can be made up by programmes which are under-resourced, inadequately staffed, often non-functional and, in all of this, equally marginal.

Macro policies exclude by insisting on centralized and inflexible control over standards, approaches and methods that are not relevant to vulnerable communities. The brief excerpt below describing the situation of Tanzanian children and their absence from school illustrates well the idea that EFA goals perhaps fail less often in the dramatic than in the mundane. Exclusion is essentially a matter of education systems focusing on their own priorities rather than accommodating and adapting to the real lives of children:

> . . . children stated they could not come to school because of work at home, some of which, for both boys and girls, was caring for younger siblings, but most of which (70% for boys and 65% for girls) was to 'guard the farm' . . . . In savannah cultivation the crops are under constant threat. At seed time, birds and monkeys eat the seeds; during the period when the crops are growing, monkeys, baboons and pigs may raid the crops and an entire year's harvest can be lost in a single night. Thus all family members are needed

> to protect the crop, and children are kept away from school particularly at those periods when crops are at greatest risk .... In a second area ... subject to flooding, the government solution had been to move people to the higher ground and create villages where none had been before, including schools and dispensaries. Yet, after the end of the Nyerere period of government, villagers moved back to lowland areas and became transhumant in order to cope with the seasonal periods of flooding. As schools were only available in the new villages on higher ground, children were absent from school on a seasonal basis, with attendance varying between 40% and 85%.

Undifferentiated, nationally set education policies exclude when they act independently of communities to enforce a national (often international) language of instruction. In many countries, this produces a 'schooling that cuts the young child off from the home language and is a major cause of drop-out and repetition'. An estimated 90% of people living in sub-Saharan Africa, for example, do not understand the colonial language used as the medium of formal school learning. Macro policy, supported by some donors, which insists on the use of such languages, excludes significant numbers of children both from effective learning and success on nationally set primary leaving examinations.

This issue is not straightforward, of course. Policies also risk excluding children by limiting them to local languages that are given no status or credit beyond the community, thus preventing them from engaging with, and moving into, the wider world. 'It is not in the best interests of the child to grow up in isolation from the language, culture and society of the majority population of the country'.

National systems fail on both counts where they make the decisions from the centre; when they do not collaborate with families to negotiate approaches based on local priorities, sound pedagogical experience and a range of options. Current wisdom suggests use of the first language in early years, adding others later.

An equally well-articulated position suggests that national governments in regions such as Africa need, together, to rethink their language policies and to co-operate in support of local languages whose populations cut across their national boundaries. Both positions have a certain logic. Both require solid research and evaluation, well-prepared teachers and materials, and mobilized national support for whichever strategy is adopted. National systems exclude in rarely making the effort on behalf of, or providing such resources to, the hard-to- reach.

Social and Political Factors

The major danger is that of a gulf opening up between a minority of people who are capable of finding their way successfully about this new world that is coming into being and the majority who feel that they are at the mercy of events and have no say in the future of society. Education, by providing access to knowledge for all, has precisely this universal task of helping people to understand the world and to understand others.

Exclusion is about the 'majority who have no say', and about the failure of societies to provide the education which gives them the opportunity to change that situation. It is created by social, economic and political environments that diminish and destroy the power of families to act on behalf of their children's education, or of children and young people to act for themselves.

Globally and nationally, societies are creating excluded children by allowing the emergence of a 'two-tier global order characterized by growing economic polarization, and social exclusion'.

The preceding discussion of how education systems exclude children potentially concerns all children to some degree. The concern of this chapter, and critical for the focus of global action in support of education during the next fifteen years, however, are those children who are affected in a major way by exclusionary forces. They are children, chiefly (though not solely) in developing countries, living in conditions of extreme poverty and social marginalization.

They are children who, whether on their own or through their families, are unlikely to break the exclusionary downward cycle. They are, therefore, the children for whole national systems and the international community must take significant affirmative and persistent action both to change the basic conditions of poverty and exclusion in their lives overall, and to design and implement inclusive, effective education.

More specifically, excluded children are those who are not considered to 'fit' into majority-based classrooms: ethnic minority and scheduled caste children; of different cultures, speaking other than a national language; or whose dysfunctional or broken family or life on the street lead them to be stereotyped as children incapable or unworthy of learning and appropriately kept out of school.

- contradict accepted norms of who can or should learn: girls in general and pregnant girls in particular; children with disabilities or affected by HIV/AIDS.
- cannot afford the cost or the time of schooling: children from chronically poor urban and rural families or for whom economic crises have created newly jobless families; working and street children; children who are the fall-out of structural adjustment programmes.
- are not free or available to participate: geographically isolated children in coastal fishing communities or remote mountain areas; child soldiers; unregistered migrants; children of transients, seasonal workers and nomadic communities.
- are living in the context of disaster: children in war, refugee children and children displaced by destruction of their physical environment.

The following discussion elaborates some of these circumstances, towards creating a more operational picture of what exclusion looks like. Somewhat arbitrarily, these have been grouped according to who the children are, where they are, and what they are doing. These categories are not mutually exclusive. The excluded child is, for example, a girl working as a flower seller on the street of an impoverished Brazilian slum; an adolescent boy from a hill-tribe community forced to serve in one of the drug militias of the Golden Triangle.

The differentiation into the who, where and what of exclusion is intended to provide perspective; to make the concept more accessible and actionable in terms of determining specific focus, constraints and entry points for intervention. In other words, if the conditions of exclusion exist, the existence of excluded children must be assumed.

Who these children are concerns those characteristics that are effectively 'given', the essence of the child: gender, ethnicity and race; age; basic intellectual and physical capacities; background experience and personal history. These are the bases which cannot be changed and on which the child must be accepted as a learner. They are the bases around which the society, education system and school must organize to ensure a relevant and effective learning experience. These characteristics cannot be used as justification for exclusion.

Where concerns the context in which the child lives, or has been placed. It concerns the surrounding conditions which exclude children by failing to allow for their basic rights and needs, including access to good education. The 'where' shifts the focus from the child who is struggling to those responsible for ensuring the protection and development of this and all children, pursuant to the commitments of the CRC — no matter where he or she is. The right to a good education of a child living on the street is no less than that of a child living in luxury; the obligation of a society to ensure such a child gets that education is as firm.

The 'where' forces consideration not of how the child must change to fit into school, but of how the barriers presented by the school and the wider socioeconomic, cultural and political environment can be removed, or their negative impacts mitigated, so as to ensure that the child does indeed 'fit'.

What concerns both the who and where of exclusion. It concerns how the child, based on his or her individual and social resources and personal interests, is managing or coping with the conditions of life. It includes consideration of how ready the child is to engage in learning and/or to participate in education, given the other activities and concerns he or she faces.

The focus here is on collaboration with the child concerned. It involves those responsible for the child's well being, and how they can most effectively know, and co-operate with, that child to design and implement action appropriate to ensuring effective and relevant education.

A perspective on what the excluded child is doing forces situation analyses and interventions to be more refined and tailored; to consider, for example, what working children are working at and where, with what risk and how much 'space' they have for learning. It forces interventions to consider specifically what a child is doing on the street, in a conflict zone or in an isolated rural school. It forces consideration of how education can be made to suit each child as they are now, and to help them move forward.

7

World Scenario

Today all nations lay stress on primary education and in most of them textbooks are provided free of charge. Yet 38 per cent of South Asia's children do not reach Grade 5, despite high primary-level enrolments. In Bangladesh, universal primary education is free and compulsory, and textbooks are supplied to pupils free of charge. Work books, teachers' guides, and other learning materials are, however, reported to be in short supply. Textbooks are written by staff of the National Curriculum and Textbook Board, which also contracts their production and sells them to government.

South Asian Region

Bangladesh is the only country in South Asia with a national book policy, but the committee entrusted to implement it has never met and the plan remains a blueprint. Books are produced in substantial numbers some 9,300 textbooks and other educational materials at all levels in 1996 but the quality is poor and most publishers concentrate on the higher secondary and tertiary levels and on cheap guides to passing examinations. Professional skills are not highly developed. Many books are published by the authors themselves. There is no copyright protection and few libraries. Voluntary organizations and civil society organizations promote readership and non-formal education.

Bhutan, the least developed country in South Asia, provides free education to Grade 10. The traditional monastic education is based largely on oral communication and does not support a reading/writing culture, and the fact that English is the official language impedes writing and publishing in the national language, Dzongkha. Bhutan is reported to have published only thirty-two books in 1998. Most of the people who can read are first-generation literates. The Ministry of Health and Education has developed textbooks up to Grade 8: for higher grades textbooks are imported from India.

Supplies of textbooks, work books and teachers' guides are adequate but their printing costs are high and delivery is difficult to remote areas. The government has been providing textbooks free of charge, but in an effort to reduce costs is gradually withdrawing its support for them and stationery from schools in urban and better-off areas. To encourage post literacy and continuing education, the government has produced readers in English and Dzongkha and, with UNICEF support, sponsors an annual National Reading Week and Book Fair.

Nepal, which also has free compulsory primary education, provides free textbooks' in general, for boys to Grade 3 and for girls to Grade 5. Parents must first buy the books, however, and then obtain reimbursement. The system penalizes poor families and some prescribed books do not qualify for reimbursement. The curriculum and textbooks are in Nepali, which presents difficulties for the 48 per cent of the population for whom it is not the first language. Textbooks for the public system are produced and distributed by state agencies. Private schools may use commercially published textbooks as reference materials. Some private publishers and social organizations, including the Nepalese Society for Children's Literature, are publishing children's books, but the country depends largely on book imports. The Copyright Act, introduced in 1965, is ineffective and outdated, and the National Book Development Board has never met.

India is second only to the United States and the United Kingdom in the production of English-language books and has a vigorous publishing industry in seventeen other languages. The education system that must be supplied with learning materials is massive 227 universities, 9,278 colleges, 98,134 high schools, 171,216 middle schools and 590,421 primary schools. Enrolment at the primary level alone is 100 million. A process of devolution from the central government to the states is almost complete.

Under it, the state governments will produce nearly all the textbooks, work books and teachers' guides for primary schools and the majority of textbooks for secondary and senior secondary schools. The goal is to provide the books at an affordable price, which the private sector has failed to do. Private schools draw on both locally produced and imported books. Tertiary-level texts are for the most part published locally, but postgraduate and research needs are met mainly by importation.

Maldives has a total population of well under 300,000 persons, living on 199 coral islands with a land area of about 300 km 2 . The only bookstores are in the capital, and transportation between the islands is poor. None the less, the overall literacy rate is 98.8 per cent, and 99.3 per cent for females. Book production is expensive as a result of the small market and dependence on imported materials. Textbooks are produced and subsidized by the government. There is a serious shortage of learning materials in the local languages. There are few local writers, especially in the national language, Dhivehi, and to encourage them the government holds writing competitions, including some for children's literature. Most of the libraries are concentrated in Male but some atolls have school libraries and community reading centres.

Pakistan's textbooks have long been produced by the four provincial textbook boards, but the market has recently been opened to competition from private sources. Other categories of learning materials have been neglected. There is a shortage of school and public libraries, and an imbalance between educational and general publishing: textbooks account for some 70 per cent of the total book production. Special efforts are being made, with the UNESCO office in Pakistan, to educate the children of refugees from Afghanistan, where the education system is in disarray.

In Sri Lanka, the government is responsible for supplying free textbooks for Grades 1 to 11, but does so in collaboration with the private sector. Some thirty-five commercial publishing houses are active as well as the state's Educational Publications Department. The National Book Development Council is a permanent body attached to the Ministry of Education and Higher Education and the industry enjoys an approved undertaking status that secures for it special benefits. A World Bank/International Development Association Book Development Project, just under way, includes the rewriting of some 220 textbooks, the establishment of 2,000 new school libraries and the improvement of 1,000 existing ones, and the training of authors, illustrators, book designers, librarians and other personnel.

Central Asian Region

The countries of Central Asia and the Caucasus are in the midst of a major transition from one social/political/economic system to another on an unprecedented scale. Although the transformation seems frustratingly slow, it is happening at breakneck speed compared to most other historical change. Economic decline, inflation, shortage or under-use of national resources and lack of finances are often accompanied by armed political disputes over territorial possession within or amongst countries. Deteriorating social conditions and poverty are widespread. The system of education that prevailed under communism was hierarchical and facts-based, and discouraged innovative teaching, individual questioning and critical thinking. There is no longer consensus on what aspects of education, and in particular textbooks, are required.

The countries are having difficulty breaking away from the old system in which, typically, a pedagogical institute within the Ministry of Education wrote the textbooks, evaluated them and approved them. Systems of open and fair competition, encouraging good new authors, have been difficult to introduce. Independent, objective evaluation has also proved difficult to establish. The financing of textbooks in countries that are no longer able to supply them free of charge has presented a challenge for ministries and funding agencies. Previously books were produced with low grade paper and binding, which was considered adequate because they were given new to pupils each year. Funding agencies are urging the adoption of loan or rental schemes, which are more economical but require better-quality books, and there is not enough experience to know how well they will work in these countries.

The process of dismantling state-owned monopolies in textbook publishing is incomplete. In most countries the state owned company still occupies a preferred position and benefits from the advantages of hidden subsidies. In some countries the state company has been privatized or has built up a parallel private company into which it has tipped all its resources thereby maintaining an advantage over the smaller publishers.

Fewer than 10 per cent of schools have computers. Supplementary materials such as maps, atlases and reference works are in short supply, not only from lack of funds but because of needed change in content. For example, there is still no widely accepted history of Central Asia; the facts, not to mention interpretation, are still the subject of heated debate. The introduction of new materials is further hampered by the legacy of an ideology that stressed the existence of one truth. More traditional educators are still searching for the definitive textbook that will replace the old one that is now in disrepute.

Although the situation varies from country to country, and more so from rural to urban areas within each country, financing of education in all the republics has been reduced a result of economic collapse together with the transition to a market-based economy (Table). Salaries absorb most of what is available at the expense of other recurring expenses. All schools are under funded with resulting deterioration of facilities, lack of materials and underpaid teachers. Rural schools are suffering much more than urban schools.

Public Expenditure on Education in Central Asia

	% of GNP		% of govt expenditure	
	1989	1996	1989	1996
Armenia	6.5	2.0	13.2	10.3
Azerbaijan	6.1	3.3	27.6	21.3
Kazakhstan	3.4	6.0	18.0	–
Kyrgyzstan	8.8	5.7	24.0	23.5
Mongolia	9.0	6.4	–	19.3
Tajikistan	9.7	22	28.0	11.5
Turkmenistan	4.2	–	27.1	–
Uzbekistan	9.0	8.1	23.9	21 1

Their provision has been affected by bureaucratic inertia and inexperience in operating under the new economic conditions, the abrupt interruption of economic and cultural contacts with the former. USSR, a continuing dependence upon books published and printed in the Russian Federation, state monopolies in educational publishing and printing, outdated and unreliable printing equipment, and the need to import all the paper and most of the materials required to manufacture books.

Education in *Armenia* and *Azerbaijan* suffered further from the war between the two countries and, in Armenia, from a devastating earthquake in 1988. Both Armenia and Georgia are facing an energy crisis, which paralyses Georgia for six months each year. Kazakhstan, the second largest of the former soviet republics, must deal with the problems of a vast country with an ethnically mixed population, mostly rural. Uzbekistan, Turkmenistan and Tajikistan were left isolated and socially impoverished by the break-up of the USSR, compounded in Tajikistan by civil war.

Even in *Uzbekistan,* where the proportional decline in funding may not seem substantial, the public system of education, enrolling approximately 5 million students in more than 9,300 public schools, is under stress. The situation is especially critical in rural areas. Very little equipment can be found, except in the specialized schools and selective and almost no books, maps, atlases, or reference books. The textbook situation is particularly critical in Turkmenistan, which has stopped all co-operation with the Russian Federation in this area and, consequently, all import and sale of Russian textbooks. State publishing and printing houses have reduced the amount and the quality of their production.

Armenia, which, with Georgia, was in the first rank among former soviet republics in educational achievement, has managed to renew more than half the textbooks planned for primary and secondary schools, but further provision has been blocked by lack of funds. Georgia has also revised more than half its school books in the last five years, but the new materials are rather scarce and some subjects are still taught with soviet manuals. Kyrgyzstan has met the present need for textbooks in almost half its schools, but lacks manuals and other training materials. Kazakhstan and Kyrgyzstan are unable to meet the textbook needs covered until recently from Moscow and continue to use some of the old soviet textbooks. In Mongolia, new textbooks are being produced only for Grade 1.

In Uzbekistan schools are still using textbooks published in 1989-90. Schools there have libraries, sometimes with one or two librarians; however, few students use them and the majority of the collections are class sets of textbooks. A recent decision to remove some of the soviet books from libraries has exacerbated the situation. In Tajikistan, as a consequence of civil war, schools have been destroyed, damaged and closed; new textbooks have been prepared but have not been published.

Families are required to buy secondary-level textbooks in Georgia, but students prefer to use old books and, according to unofficial data, about 30 per cent of new school books remained unsold in 1997. Armenia and Azerbaijan distribute some books for free, but some estimates suggest that only one third of the Azerbaijani students in Grades 1 to 4 who are entitled to receive free books actually do so and such books, marked 'free of charge' on the back cover, are readily for sale on the street. Kazakhstan, Kyrgyzstan, Mongolia and Uzbekistan provide textbooks free for the year, on the understanding that they will be returned.

In *Tajikistan*, secondary school text-books, which were previously given free to students, are sold in bookshops and markets at high prices. Almost all countries in the region have attempted major curriculum reforms over the past several years but there has been little actual change. Education systems, inherited from the soviet period, remain highly centralized. Many textbooks published during the soviet period are still used even when they are at odds with new curricula.

Nevertheless, because many teachers are more fluent in Russian, and because it has not yet been possible to publish and distribute enough instructional materials in many local languages, Russian remains a major vehicle of instruction. Many of the new textbooks that have been published are simply translated literally from the original Russian. The change in language in many cases involves a change in alphabet, further complicating production of new titles. In general, book publication in the region has decreased significantly over the last few years. Separation from the former Soviet Union has disrupted the supply of printing materials and equipment, and increased costs. Only Mongolia and Kyrgyzstan produce their own paper, and that in limited quantities.

Those countries close to the Russian Federation still import many textbooks from there, although that source has been reduced by a serious drop within the Russian Federation of book production. Private publishers are small and short of capital. In some countries they are impeded by complex systems for ordering and distribution, restrictions on the mark-up they are permitted and slow payment of government accounts. The physical quality of learning materials is often low. Textbooks do not last long; illustrations are often unclear and diagrams unreadable. The people involved in planning and managing textbook provision are basically the same today as they were before independence, and the same old way of management and work prevail. Training in writing, translating, publishing, printing and distribution is badly needed.

Funding agencies and donors are working to relieve the publishing crisis, among them the World Bank, the Asian Development Bank, UNESCO, the Council of Europe, the Soros Foundation, the Open Society Institute, USAID and the British Know How Fund. Programmes vary from pilot to extensive in nature, from textbook provision to training, from national to sub-national. In Armenia, for example, the World Bank has a three-year, $8 million programme that involves the publication of about 120 new textbooks, in all subjects and levels, alongside a new textbook rental scheme. In Azerbaijan, the Bank's programme is addressed to refugee resettlement and concentrates on damaged areas.

In *Mongolia*, the Asian Development Bank is funding curriculum development at the secondary level; that country has also received printing equipment from Denmark, Germany, the Republic of Korea and Japan. In Kazakhstan, the Soros Foundation is running various regional programs alongside World Bank activities, including school grants and training of authors and publishers. In Uzbekistan the Asian Development Bank is supporting a major project for curriculum and textbook development at the primary level.

Pacific Region

Most of the thirteen countries of the Pacific Islands report that they do not have enough textbooks, work books and teachers' guides, particularly in vernacular languages. Availability varies from country to country and within countries. There are significant differences in provision of books between urban and non-urban areas, capital city islands and outer islands. Photo-copying of books is common where the machines are available, which is not generally the case. All countries practise central procurement of textbooks and learning materials, but the cost of bidding documents effectively precludes participation by local booksellers.

Geography, population and economics all impede the provision of textbooks and learning materials, and particularly materials developed to meet local needs and produced locally. With the exception of Papua New Guinea, the countries are small, even minuscule. Nauru and Niue consist of one island each, comprising 21 km 2 and 259 km 2 respectively. Papua New Guinea has a population of nearly 4.8 million, but the populations of Niue and Tokelau are only 2,100 and 1,500. Those two small countries have negative growth rates because of high migration.

The countries are geographically isolated and communication within them is onerous. Kiribati consists of thirty-three islands totalling 719 km 2 scattered across three time zones and two days. In Papua New Guinea, mountain ranges make air the only practical means of transport to the interior. Throughout the region, air freight is expensive. Incomes in the area are generally low and, even where they are higher, as in Papua New Guinea, there are vast disparities. Low levels of income result in small tax bases for schools and libraries, and limited financing for publishing ventures. External aid often favours expatriate authors, editors, illustrators, typesetters, printers and publishers.

All the countries have been colonies, except Tonga which was a protectorate of Great Britain. Samoa became independent in 1962 and was followed by the other countries except Tokelau, which is a territory of New Zealand. The Cook Islands and Niue remain politically associated with New Zealand and the Marshal Islands with the United States. The long period of colonization followed by continuing relationships with large metropolitan countries have resulted in the use of foreign languages, foreign priorities in education, foreign agenda-setting backed by foreign economic power and a shortage of books in local languages.

Tokelau and Niue have enough English books but not enough books in Tokelauan or Niuean. Fiji has enough teachers' guides for English, but not always enough textbooks and work books, nor does it have enough books in vernacular languages. Locally produced books in Fiji Baat, a form of Hindi, are rare because Hindi books can be imported inexpensively from India. In Vanuatu, the official languages of instruction are English and French (a legacy of two colonial rulers) but in practice Bislama' a pidgin and the national language' is often used, although there is little material available in it.

Kiribati, the Marshall Islands, Nauru, Niue, Samoa, Tokelau and Tonga have 1 vernacular language. The Cook Islands have 2 (Maori and Pukapukan) as does Tuvalu (Tuvaluan and Kiri-bati). Fiji has 4: Fijian, Hindi, Rotuman and Chinese. Solomon Islands, Vanuatu and Papua New Guinea have 64, 108 and 869 respectively. For some of these languages, the only reading material is religious in nature.

Under a new curriculum in Papua New Guinea, the first three years of school must be taught in the vernacular language of the particular area. Some of these languages do not yet have an orthography. The publication of books in vernacular languages by nationals of the countries concerned has been encouraged by, among others, the Institute of Pacific Studies at the University of the South Pacific.

The majority of schools in the Cook Islands, Kiribati and Niue have libraries. Some schools in the other countries have libraries. The vast majority of schools in Papua New Guinea do not. The countries generally have established networks of public libraries, but access to them varies between and within countries: the three main libraries of the Cook Islands, for example, are within 200 m of one another. Supplementary reading materials are available in the market and in some schools. Children's fiction, especially for very young children, is improving in quantity and quality, but most is in English or, in Vanuatu, French. Books in vernacular languages are less common, though ministries of education, the Institute of Education at the University of the South Pacific and religious groups such as the Summer Institute of Linguistics produce books in local languages. Costs remain high, particularly for low-income countries. Nonfiction for children is increasing in quantity and quality very slowly.

Educational audio and video tapes are scarce, and many schools in the region lack power. Multimedia learning packages and science kits are available in some schools but in general there is a great shortage, with significant differences between schools, and between urban and rural areas. Fiji, however, has placed science kits in 500 elementary schools and plans to do so in its remaining 198 schools in the next two years.

Posters, wall charts and maps are donated by international and regional organizations and national governments but in insufficient numbers and, as with book provision, there are marked differences in availability between urban and rural areas and between capital and outer islands. All aspects of the book chain need attention. A considerable number of training workshops have been held in writing and editing, but little attention has been paid to distribution. Representatives of the thirteen countries undertook to promote book policies and councils during the Biennial Meeting of the Directors of Education and the UNESCO Office for the Pacific States held in November 1998.

However the only country with a book policy is Papua New Guinea, which faces by far the greatest challenges in book provision. Its National Policy on Information and Communication strives to develop a national distribution system, a national clearing house for domestically published books, publicity for government books, support for all aspects of the book chain, a subsidy on air freight to publishers and printers, and strategies for co-operation. Its Book Week and Literacy Week promote writing competitions book sales and public readings.

The difficulties of small populations and limited resources are being overcome in some countries through regional cooperation in the production of early literary resources. Fiji and New Zealand are involved in much of what is happening, often in close co-operation. New Zealand's involvement is the result, in no small measure, of its own indigenous and immigrant Polynesian populations. About one-third of children in New Zealand are Polynesian' New Zealand Maori, Samoan, Cook Islands Maori, Tongan, Niuean or Tokelauan. More Tokelauans, Niueans and Cook Islanders live in New Zealand than in Tokelau, Niue or the Cook Islands, and for every two children at school in Samoa another Samoan child lives in New Zealand. It is estimated that by about 2050 New Zealanders of Polynesian ancestry will form a majority of the population.

Teachers' guides and learning materials in the languages of these countries are still in seriously short supply within New

Zealand. In 1989, however, the country began a period of curriculum reform that allows Pacific Islands children the right to use their language as an integral part of their schooling and all children the right to learn Pacific Islands languages if they wish. Bilingual education became a school-by-school decision.

The Ministry of Education began publishing in Pacific Islands languages for early childhood centres and schools in 1976, and in large numbers from 1989 through contracts with a parastatal, Learning Media. At present a new title is added, on average, about every eleven days. The books, in early reading and in some other subjects at the primary level, are not but what might elsewhere be called supplementary readers, scarcely different from the children's books to be found in stores. This approach lends itself particularly well to multilingual publication.

Samoa, Tokelau, Niue and the Cook Islands all currently use Pacific Islands language resources developed by the New Zealand Ministry of Education and Tonga is considering doing so. New Zealand, in turn, uses resources in its schools originally developed by the Departments of Education in Samoa, Tuvalu and Tokelau, and has purchased resource development services from the Departments of Education in Niue, the Cook Islands and Tonga.

As a result, five small island states have gained access to the full-colour books normally associated with more developed countries and New Zealand has gained a level of language expertise that immigrant communities cannot always provide on their own. There are only 6,000 Tokelauans in the world, yet the New Zealand government publishes a new book for children, in full -colour, in Tokelauan about every eight weeks. Learning Media was created in 1989 when the School Publications Branch of the New Zealand Ministry of Education was transformed into a government-owned but commercially oriented educational publishing company which bids for work from its own and other ministries of education. It also publishes works in its own right.

Since 1989 it has won contracts to publish Pacific Islands language resources for the ministries or institutes of education in Tokelau, Tuvalu, Niue, Fiji and Samoa, and has recently quoted on work for the ministries of education in Vanuatu, the Marshall Islands, Tonga and Hawaii. With the Institute of Education at the University of the South Pacific, a regional institution, it has run workshops and publishes Pacific Literacy, a thirty-book series which forms the basis for the first three years in primary school literacy programmes in a growing number of church and state school systems. With UNESCO support, the partners will publish Pacific Science, a forty-two book early science series, in 2000.

The full-colour but low-cost literacy series is printed on rugged paper with rust-resistant staples to survive tropical island conditions. By printing the same book in several languages, with only the black plates for text changed for each edition, print runs can be high and costs per copy accordingly low. A full-colour book in a local language costs no more than what some countries in the region would pay per copy for black and white, poorly illustrated books printed on nondurable grades of paper.

Each book is accompanied by teachers' materials that typically include an English translation, notes on cultural elements in the story, information about the author and illustrator, an explanation of where the material fits in the curriculum, and some suggested teaching activities. Competing books from the United States, the United Kingdom and Australia have no Pacific content or authorship and their guides do not reflect the realities of classroom conditions in the Pacific.

African Continent

The countries of Africa have appeared many times in the ADEA survey as examples and over the years that continent has attracted more donor interest than any other and more documentation of its textbook shortage and attempts to alleviate that shortage. Rather than repeat themes from Parts II and 111, here is a snapshot of Africa as it seemed in 1999 to educators, publishers and consultants familiar with its education system. The information is based on 126 responses, from the 26 countries listed above, to the ADEA/ UNESCO survey. Not all the respondents answered all the questions. The opinions do not always coincide with trends identified in Part III (ADEA, 1999).

Some 103 of those responding to a question about book shortage in their country considered it serious. The 9 who did not regard it as serious overall said it was serious in rural areas or for pre-primary and tertiary-level books that had to be imported; 36 said the book shortage was a result of poverty.

The same number blamed inadequate government funding and planning in the light of increased school enrolments a weak local publishing industry was described as responsible by 30 while 20 blamed government policies' monopoly publishing of text-books, lack of co-ordination with funding agencies, and taxes on printing materials. Others cited high levels of illiteracy, lack of a book-buying culture, high costs of production, inadequate book distribution systems and the scarcity of bookshops, especially in rural areas. Some suggested that teaching styles perpetuated the book famine by focusing on a single textbook and examinations.

More than 90 per cent of respondents identified serious shortages in textbooks and learning materials of one kind or another (Table). The overwhelming majority believed that decentralization was a positive move, although a number seemed to be talking about the theoretical benefits rather than from experience. The advantages mentioned were largely related to school empowerment in the selection of books and the encouragement of bookselling if books were bought locally.

Most respondents favoured a centralized approval process, but thought there should be a wide selection of approved titles from which schools could select. Many were concerned about the means of distribution, which some regarded as so inadequate as to outweigh the benefits of local selection; 85 considered the distribution system in their country as very weak or nonexistent. Others were worried that school officials would be unprepared to select books and that corruption would simply move from the central to the local level.

Proportion of Respondents who said there was a Serious Shortage in Textbooks and Learning Materials

Textbooks	87%
Work books	89%
Teachers guides	78%
Reading programmes or schemes	90%
Children's fiction	89%
Children's non-fiction	93%
Audio tapes	98%
Video tapes	97%
Multimedia learning packages, science kits	97%
Reference books	93%
Magazine, comics	91%
Posters, wall charts, maps	98%

Only about three-quarters of the respondents answered, a question about training, but of those who did more than 95 per cent felt that all aspects of the book chain had been neglected and needed attention. The training of teachers in the use of textbooks was given a high priority. Most respondents agreed that the printing industry in their countries was better developed than book publishing, but that more training was needed.

Almost all the respondents rejected free provision of textbooks. The major reasons were: (1) there is no such thing as a 'free' book because someone has to pay; (2) the provision of free books has no place in a free-market environment; (3) free textbooks undermine the bookselling component of the book chain; and (4) free books are not properly valued or cared for. Most people, however, recognized that poor families would not be able to afford to pay the full cost of books. The following remedies were suggested: subsidies to reduce the price; tax benefits, removal of duties and other national strategies to reduce the cost of publishing; book loan or rental schemes: targeted supply of free books to those most in need; community participation in the establishment of community libraries; and community education in the value and care of books. A question about the use of local languages drew 106 responses; 8 people questioned the need for reading material in local languages, which in some countries are regarded as inferior and of little practical use for educational and economic advancement.

There was also concern that the favouring of one language over others would be seen as a political statement. About 20% of respondents said that there would be no demand for books in local languages unless the languages were officially recognized in the education system. Several recommended mother-tongue education in the lower grades, however, and several more insisted that it should be possible to take examinations in local languages in secondary school.

Respondents suggested that demand for reading materials in local languages could be generated through literacy and reading campaigns, local language supplements in newspapers, local language programmes on radio, story-writing competitions in local languages and promotion of local language materials in village and community libraries.

A large number of respondents said it would be necessary to train authors and teachers in writing and teaching the local language, and a few pointed out that for some languages it was first necessary to standardize the orthography. Several suggested that community members and members of literacy classes be encouraged to write folk tales or stories. Many respondents suggested translating existing books. Several suggested that subsidies or other incentives should be offered to publishers willing to take the risks of publishing small editions in local languages and others suggested electronic publishing as an economic means of dealing with short runs.

Respondents thought that reading programmes and campaigns possibly involving television and radio, book fairs, competitions and prizes would do most to foster a more favourable reading culture for children in particular and adults in general. Many stressed the importance of making reading part of the school curriculum, training teachers in the value of reading at school and using project-based learning as means of instilling the reading habit in children. A large number called for the development of school libraries and mobile libraries as a foundation upon which reading and literacy campaigns might be built. Several mentioned the need for more attractive, affordable books for children, published locally and using local languages. Responses to other parts of the questionnaire are incorporated in other parts of this survey.

In 1990s there was a significant improvement in the provision of learning materials in most of the twelve English speaking countries in the Caribbean region surveyed. As the decade comes to a close, no country could be described as experiencing a book famine. Nevertheless there remain significant barriers to the adequate provision of learning materials. Most countries report no serious shortage of textbooks or work books. A study made in 1991 of the countries of the Organization of Eastern Caribbean States, Barbados, Jamaica, and Trinidad and Tobago found a proliferation of high quality texts written by Caribbean educators and published by international and regional publishers.

Indeed, in many countries of the region people feel that there is too great a choice, and that parents and students are being asked to spend unnecessarily on a variety of textbooks. Ministries of education throughout the region are introducing prescribed lists of books at the primary and lower secondary levels. There is concern about unequal access within countries. Individual governments have implemented a variety of schemes aimed at improving access and reducing cost. The Jamaican Primary Textbook Project, which has been operating since 1984, provides some 350,000 students per year with more than 2.5 million textbooks and workbooks in science, mathematics, language arts, social studies and family life.

The Jamaican Secondary School Textbook Project (originally funded by the British government in 1985) rents the core textbooks to students for US$25 per year. The Barbados Rental Scheme, which is among the oldest in the region, provides every secondary schoolchild with his or her full textbook needs for an annual fee of US$37. Saint Vincent and the Grenadines will introduce a rental scheme at the secondary level in the 1999/2000 academic year. Dominica and the Bahamas provide free textbooks. The government of Trinidad and Tobago is targeting needy students under a World

Bank funded project that provides free textbooks in mathematics, English and science to 35 per cent of the country's school population since the year 2000.

Clare observed that the system of distribution of textbooks common to all countries of the Caribbean was one of the most expensive conceivable. Little has changed since 1991 and even the government rental schemes retain elements of that inefficient system. Under the Jamaica Secondary Textbooks Rental Scheme, for example, each secondary school not only selected the textbooks to be used in each subject but placed the order directly with its supplier of choice. The Ministry of Education, in theory, oversaw the process but largely confined itself to ensuring that the school had funds to pay for the order. Both ordering and shipping were inefficient, and deliveries were often late.

In 1999, the Ministry limited choice by issuing a list of approved texts, created a centralized pool of rental funds under its control and encouraged importers to consolidate textbook provision. In 2000, the government took a step further and centralized purchasing and distribution.

Jamaica has followed this principle since the 1970s. Barbados has consistently bought schoolbooks through private sector booksellers. Trinidad and Tobago, despite regular shifts in policy, has generally supported both local printing and distribution. In Guyana, however, the Ministry of Education remains the largest publisher of educational materials through the National Centre for Educational Resource Development. Most countries offer some choice, but in June 1999 the government of Trinidad and Tobago changed policy abruptly in the name of economy and opted for a single textbook in each subject/ level. It had previously accepted a recommendation of its own textbook evaluation committee that school principals be allowed to choose from two approved titles in mathematics and science, and from six in language arts.

The sudden change left local publishers with tens of thousands of books produced for the previous policy and may reinforce the dominance of metropolitan publishers in the country's textbook trade. The Jamaican Ministry of Education, in contrast, is unique regionally in its support of local publishers. The Ministry has responded positively, by adoption and purchase, to the increasing number of locally published books designed for its curricula. At the primary level, for example, of the four subject areas in which the Ministry provides books only the mathematics texts are published outside Jamaica. All the language arts, science and social studies texts are locally published. The approved textbook list for secondary schools also includes a significant number of locally published texts in English language, social studies, mathematics and science.

All countries of the region reported serious significant shortages in other categories of learning materials. With limited resources, governments have had to place a priority, on satisfying the needs of the core curriculum. Government budgets for libraries are being reduced or a greater proportion of them is being absorbed by administrative expenses, at the same time as prices of books rise. As a result, fewer books are bought. Money, however, is not the only concern. Smaller countries, such as the British Virgin Islands and Belize, which have no indigenous publishing, have difficulty in gaining access to regionally produced reading material.

Some attempts have been made to provide more supplementary reading materials in schools. In 1996 Trinidad and Tobago began establishing classroom libraries in all its 486 primary schools under a basic education project funded by the International Development Bank (IDB). The books were intended to support a new curriculum integrating reading and language. In Jamaica, 120 secondary schools received library books between 1996 and 1998 under a US$1.2 million project funded by IDB, while primary schools will also receive books some 250,000 of them in the year 2000 under a British-funded project.

In Trinidad and Tobago, teachers and librarians were given a chance to inspect and select books for their schools through a series of regional exhibitions; nevertheless, many lacked information about the range of available materials. There was also a shortage of culturally relevant material from other countries in the region and beyond. Jamaica has had difficulty in getting basic information from publishers and other sources about regionally produced materials that might be relevant for its primary school library project. As a result the first list compiled for tendering included no locally produced books or books that were culturally relevant to the country.

Barbados, with one of the highest literacy rates in the region, has opted for non-print technology. Its Edutec 2000 project, which has been declared a national priority, is focused on providing multimedia facilities in all the nation's schools. Barbados has also created an educational software review centre and is considering including software among the materials available under its well-established textbooks rental programme.

In Guyana, where the government is unable to provide for the country's reading needs, a local non-governmental organization has undertaken the task. CODE, has established 271 community libraries in the last five years and distributed some 240,000 books to schools, libraries and other educational institutions.

As a result of conferences in Saint Lucia and Jamaica, a regional association of publishers is forming, encompassing all the language areas of the Caribbean' English, French, Spanish and Dutch. Its immediate concerns are expected to include problems of distribution, training and public/private sector cooperation. None of the countries in the region has a national book policy. In mid-1999 the National Book Development Council of Jamaica, with funding from UNESCO, convened a regional consultation on national book policies.

Delegates representing all the Caribbean Community (CARICOM) member countries participated. Their reports provided a mixed picture of the state of the book in the countries of the region, ranging from virtual inertia to vitality. Positive trends included the general absence of taxes or duties on imported books, moves by several countries to enact modern copyright legislation and increasing government intervention to provide textbooks to disadvantaged sections of the population.

The book chain is best developed in Jamaica, Trinidad and Tobago, and Barbados, but no country can be said to have a publishing industry and even in Jamaica there now is only one textbook publisher of substance.

The book industry in the rest of the Caribbean region remains in a state of chronic underdevelopment which is unlikely to be changed by occasional book provision schemes. The region remains the one geographical area in the English speaking world where there is little or no initiative in book development.

Non-Western Europe

The political change in Central and Eastern Europe has brought widespread initiatives for economic and social reform. For almost a decade, the post-communist countries of this region have been attempting to lay the foundations of their future democracies and to introduce market economies a painful transition accompanied at times by economic stagnation, high inflation, unemployment, social disillusion and, in southeastern Europe, armed disputes. The production, dissemination, and use of instructional materials, like the education systems, have been affected by the transition. Fragile economies, insufficient budget allocation, and lack of legislative measures contributed to the deterioration of the publishing industry during the first half of the 1990s.

In every country there is more than one educational publisher, although often one (usually the state or former state company) is distinguished by the Ministry of Education as the leading company. In such cases, it is difficult for newly formed companies to obtain a share in the market because of tradition. In some countries the Ministry of Education helps the former monopolist through subsidies or large purchases. In Hungary and some other countries, the private publishers found it in their interest to maintain the public status of the state text-book company out of fear that, privatized and free from public obligations, it would be even more dangerous a competitor.

Planned educational reforms still have to be implemented. In every country new curricula are either under development or under implementation. The major presumption, inherited from the socialist system of education, is that the textbook is the most important item in the education system and, when you have a textbook, all other materials are significantly less necessary. Work books and teachers' guides are also recognized, but interactive materials are rare.

Textbook shortages vary, as do the availability and range of learning materials. Although market-oriented changes have been introduced in some countries, examples remain of state control of prices, textbook subsidies and deep-rooted expectations that the government will provide free or cheap text-books. Curriculum development and textbook provision have been assisted by international civil society organizations and by agencies such as the World Bank and European Union.

In the Czech Republic, Hungary, Poland and Slovakia, the transition towards a democratic order and market economy is progressing and, although the financial situation is still difficult, textbooks suffer more in quality than in quantity. The total number of textbook titles published in the Czech Republic, Hungary and Poland rose slightly between 1994 and 1997.

In the largest market, Poland, the publication of instructional materials has been turned into a profitable, competitive activity. Comprehensive educational reforms aim to replace the old fact-based, textbook-oriented learning with alternative methods and curricula. New textbooks are being developed primarily with the help of international funding agencies and experts.

Estonia, Latvia and Lithuania undertook economic, political and social reforms after their separation from the former USSR and all have achieved political stability and progress in commercial infrastructure. Their economies are improving but are still fragile, and the shortage of disposable income affects the production and dissemination of educational materials. School book publishing is impeded by the small size of the national markets, which are further reduced by the presence of minority language groups.

Latvia is beginning to pay attention to ethnic minority education and, above all, the integration of Russian language schools. Lithuania is supporting the decentralization of education. There are some text-book and work book shortages in Estonia, and all countries feel serious shortages of teachers' guides and supplementary materials, including reference books. In all three countries, the annual number of textbook titles published had increased substantially by 1997 over output even two years earlier.

As in other states of the former USSR, the collapse of the old regime in Ukraine, Belarus, the Republic of Moldova and the Russian Federation was followed by the collapse of political, economic and cultural structures, and by disruption of commerce and distribution against a background of hyper inflation.

The large size of *Ukraine* and the division between its Ukrainian and Russian-speaking areas exacerbated the difficulties of transition. The government controls the selection and issue of every textbook but lacks the funds to meet all requirements. Old textbooks need to be replaced and, in general, instructional materials are in serious demand.

Economic reform and privatization in Belarus are proceeding more slowly than in the Russian Federation or the Baltic states. The country is closely tied to the Russian market and heavily dependent on it. The publishing sector remains state-owned. The Ministry of Education has the ultimate control over text-book provision and state-owned publishers retain their monopoly. Russian textbooks from before 1990 are still in use.

In the Republic Moldova national educational standards and curricula are being revised. There is a critical shortage of text-books and teachers' guides, and supplementary materials are non-existent. An experimental textbook rental scheme was severely undermined by the Russian economic crash of August 1998.

In the *Russian Federation*, estimates of the shortage of text-books in primary and secondary schools range from 100 to 300 million books, depending on whether one counts physical numbers of books in the schools or considers quality and appropriateness. History books from the 1980s are still in use and falling apart. In the early 1990s educational funding was devolved to the eighty-nine blasts (provinces) and the Ministry of Education was expected to recommend two or three suitable textbooks for each subject/level.

Competition might have been expected to blossom, but the market remains dominated by the massive state publishing house Prosvescheniye, which benefits from hidden subsidies despite efforts to commercialize it. Another large textbook publishing company is said to have links with the mafia. Despite all obstacles, the quality of books in general is being improved through competition and consumer demand. In 1998 competitions for textbooks were launched and forty new titles approved, with the result that by 1999 the federally approved list had two and often three titles for each subject/level. Teachers' guides and supplementary materials remained in short supply, however.

Textbook shortages in the countries of Albania, Bulgaria and Romania are a direct result of slow political, economic and social reforms. Only recently, with the arrival of democratic governments have changes begun. The governments are committed to privatization, but progress is impeded by low wages, inflation and declining purchasing power.

Financial support for textbooks from international agencies, such as the World Bank and the Soros Foundation, has been decisive during the past several years. Even so, budgets are not always sufficient to meet needs for textbooks and work books, most of which are being replaced by new editions. Supplementary materials are still in scarce supply. Bulgaria has developed new textbooks for most grades and to finance them has begun selling them to families.

In *Romania*, competition in textbooks has been introduced with World Bank funding. In *Albania*, much of the countryside is remote and difficult to reach, and 87 per cent of the schools are in villages. Textbook production and provision is controlled by the Ministry of Education using monopoly state-owned publishing and distribution enterprises. There is a shortage of text-books, and teachers of all grades require guides to the revised curriculum.

Wars have destroyed schools as well as the national economies and infrastructures and have fragmented what was once one national market. In Bosnia and Herzegovina, international funding for education has initially been directed towards repairing damaged schools. The already small book market is divided in three by language and differing publishing policies. As a result production costs are high and print runs low. There is no system at cantonal level for inventory control and distribution of textbooks to schools. Croatia's education system has remained completely centralized and under funded. Curricular reform has been hampered by disputes between Croatians and the Serb minority.

The Former Yugoslav Republic of Macedonia has undertaken educational reform and tested new methods, but lacks finances to support the desired change. Development of new learning materials is impeded by an underdeveloped publishing industry and gradually increasing costs. Moreover, the constitution guarantees the Albanian, Turkish and Serb minorities instruction in their mother tongues at the elementary and secondary levels. Textbooks of equal quality are required in all subjects at the same price in the three minority languages as well as Macedonian. Many print runs are small as a result, but costs are amortized across the four editions to achieve a common sales price. Supplementary materials are basically nonexistent.

In the aftermath of Kosovo, the educational infrastructure of Yugoslavia must be reconstructed. The school systems are strictly controlled by a totalitarian state, using old teaching methods. Textbooks are sold. No curricular reform was in place before the war and there is little evidence that publishing of any kind will receive immediate attention.

Most countries permit choice and competition in the production of educational materials, Belarus and Ukraine being notable exceptions. Ministries of education in all countries decide what textbooks are approved for use in schools. Alternative textbooks may be used without Ministry approval, as in Lithuania, or only with approval of the Ministry, as in Bulgaria. In the Former Yugoslav Republic of Macedonia, the Ministry intends to allow schools, an element of choice in the textbooks they use for most if not all subjects.

In the *Russian Federation*, teachers are free in principle to choose among Ministry-approved and any other published textbooks, but information about what is available is scarce sample copies are hard to come by and teachers continue to rely on the old books and methods with which they are familiar.

In the *Russian Federation*. Hungary and Estonia, textbooks that are not recommended by the Ministry tend to be more expensive for parents to buy. The highly centralized Yugoslav system of education did not allow choice of textbooks before the war with Kosovo. In Albania, there is practically no choice. Privatization in the publishing industry has been initiated in many countries. Most of the former state publishing houses in Estonia are privatized, including the former textbook publishing monopoly Koolibri.

In *Latvia*, privatization is also complete and Zvaigne, the former state textbook monopoly, is having to compete with a small number of private houses. Most of the publishing industry of Romania has been privatized but the textbook market is still dominated by a single state-owned educational publishing house.

The biggest publishing houses in Bosnia and Herzegovina are still state-owned, however. In Macedonia, the state publisher Prosvetno Delo still has the textbook monopoly but discussions concerning its privatization have been completed. In Ukraine; private publishers are beginning to get a share of the educational market but are constrained by high prices for paper and printing because of dependence on Russian suppliers.

The Albanian government has approved the privatization of state enterprises. Systems of textbook distribution differ, but all have problems, pre-eminently delays in payment to publishers. In several countries, state systems have been replaced by the private sector. In Estonia and Poland, publishing companies work with private wholesalers. In Poland, textbooks are chosen by teachers and bought by parents, usually in bookshops.

In *Estonia*, the former state distribution and retail book selling monopoly has been replaced by private wholesalers and booksellers. In Romania, publishers are responsible for distributing the books to the schools and are paid only on delivery. The state distribution organization still exists in Latvia but no longer has a monopoly and many of its bookstores have been privatized or closed.

In *Lithuania*, the state distribution organisation has been privatized but textbook distribution has been taken over by the Ministry of Culture and Education and remains state-controlled. In Belarus and the Russian Federation, textbooks are distributed to schools by governmental firms. In Albania, textbooks are delivered in bulk by the state printing house to local state warehouses in the thirty-seven administrative districts and from there are redistributed by school-appointed representatives, usually teachers. In the Former Yugoslav Republic of Macedonia, the state publisher has recently been supplying textbooks directly to the schools instead of through retail bookshops.

In *Croatia*, distribution channels have been badly neglected and in Ukraine, the distribution system has disintegrated.

Some countries have successfully introduced market rules and free competition in the creation of educational materials (Table 13). Elsewhere, the debate over the state's role is heated. Many governments struggle to balance stretched budgets and a continuing commitment to provide textbooks free of charge. In some countries, parents buy books on a black market simply because the state has failed to deliver what is needed. In Slovenia, parents pay for all books; in Romania and Belarus, educational authorities pay for textbooks and parents pay for supplementary materials that have not been approved by the Ministry of Education.

In *Bulgaria*, the state provides free schoolbooks in the first years of education but parents complain about the high prices of textbooks for subsequent grades. In Albania, pupils pay a nominal charge for the use of schoolbooks, which are returned for reuse. Some countries subsidize textbook prices generally, and most subsidize text-books for handicapped children, minority groups and vocational schools.

8

Indian Scenario

The priorities outlined by the National Policy on Education 1986 have continued through the 1990s. This has been reflected in the higher allocation of resources as well as in terms of clearly defined strategies to achieve the goals of education for all.

In 1990, The World Declaration on Education For All -gave further fillip to the national commitment for reaching basic education for all children. The Jomtien Declaration together with several positive developments within the country brought to the central stage the need for viewing basic education as a fundamental right of every citizen. India is one of the few countries where during the stabilization phase of structural adjustment, expenditure on education has been stepped up.

Achievements during the last fifty years are not insignificant. An estimated 95% of the rural population living in 826,000 habitations have a primary school within 1 km. and about 85% population have an upper primary school within 3 km. More than 150 million children are currently enrolled covering around 90/0 of the children in the age group of 6-14 years. Recent surveys on literacy rates indicate a phenomenal progress in the 90s. Basic education policies and programmes in the recent years have gone beyond the mere emphasis on numbers to focus on quality concerns in basic education, on the education of girls and disadvantaged sections of the society, the need for people's involvement in basic education programmes and decentralisation of educational management.

It is also during this period that World Bank and other international donor agencies began providing additional funds for speeding up the process of universalisation of elementary education. Despite such significant achievements and positive goal orientation in the recent years, it is realised that there are serious problems of gender, regional, sectional and caste disparities in UEE. A significant proportion of students continue to dropout due to socio-economic and cultural factors as also due to lack of adequate infrastructure, shortage of teachers and unsatisfactory quality of education provided. The country still is the home for more than 300 million illiterates.

The challenges have been many. Therefore, the review of progress made in the 90s represent this struggle to resolve some of the basic problems and make concrete progress towards the goal of EFA against all odds.

Though the progress made is not insignificant, the country realises that the challenges ahead at the turn of the century are quite daunting, demanding not only continued commitment but also an enhanced attention and resources to meet the challenges in the coming years.

The government is fully seized of the fact that nothing less than a whole hearted national effort both in the public and private sectors would be necessary if India is to emerge as a fully literate and economically vibrant nation of the 21st century.

The review of progress presented in this section is mainly according to the framework provided by UNESCO in order to generate a common comparative picture of progress made by different countries. The core set of data base used in the review relate to the 18 EFA Indicators identified for this purpose. However, wherever found relevant, quantitative and qualitative information on various other aspects of EFA, which are considered important in the Indian context, have been used to describe the progress made and the challenges ahead.

National Policy on Education-1986 recommended for strengthening ECCE programmes not only as an essential component of human development but also as a support to universalisation of elementary education and a programme of women's development. The programme is expected to provide necessary maturational and experiential readiness to the child for meeting the demands of the primary curriculum. It also indirectly enhances enrolment and retention of girls in primary schools by providing substitute care facility for younger siblings. The national policy envisages ECCE as a holistic input fostering health, psychological and nutritional development of children.

It is an inter sectoral programme which seeks to directly reach out to children from vulnerable and remote areas and give them a head-start by providing an integrated programme of health, nutrition and early childhood education. Its package of services includes supplementary nutrition, immunization, health check-up, referral services, non-formal pre-school education and community participation for children below six years and to pregnant and nursing mothers. The scheme is funded by the central government.

Though ICDS is the major programme catering to the ECCE needs, several other schemes have also been initiated by the central and state governments mainly to supplement the ICDS provisions, in content and coverage. For instance, 'Creches and Day Care Centres Scheme' was started in 1975 to provide day care services for children below five years. It caters mainly to children of casual, migrant, agricultural and construction labourers.

The programme in the scheme is primarily custodial in nature. Similarly, 'Early Childhood Education Scheme' was introduced as a distinct strategy to reduce the drop-out rate and to improve the rate of retention of children in primary schools. Under this scheme, central assistance is given to voluntary organisations for running pre-school education centres. In addition to these schemes that reach out to the rural, urban slums and tribal areas, there are innumerable private, fee charging nursery schools which cater to the needs of the parents living in urban and semi-urban areas. At present, there is no system of licensing or recognition of such institutions.

The spread of ECCE facilities, particularly in terms of ICDS centres, has been phenomenal during the recent years covering all the 5,320 community development blocks in the country. However, the actual out reach and coverage in respect of early childhood education component has been rather poor. This is evident from the fact that the GER of 10.33 in 1990 has improved only to 16.9 in 1997-98. Further, the coverage is very uneven across different part of the country. Bihar and Uttar Pradesh represents a serious situation with less than 10 percent coverage.

Most states in the north-east seem to be doing well in this regard. Proper understanding of the variations in the levels of participation of children in the ECCE facilities will require additional data related to different dimensions of community life and development viz., demographic, social, cultural, political and economic. Apart from the quantitative expansion of facilities, there have also been efforts to create alternative models of ECCE under different EFA programmes. The efforts made in this direction particularly in the states of Assam, Madhya Pradesh, Rajasthan, Andhra Pradesh and Karnataka are worth mentioning. In addition, there have also been attempts to create convergence between the ongoing programmes of ICDS and the early childhood education activities, essentially by expanding the scope of the ICDS programmes.

In spite of all these efforts, the challenge in extending the ECCE facilities to all children is enormous and has to be made an integral part of all EFA projects in the years to come. Another point emphasised in this regard is to strengthen the linkage between early childhood education programmes and primary education programmes. Towards this end, many state governments are establishing pre-primary units attached to primary schools. In fact a massive effort of this kind with corporate funding support is going on in the city of Mumbai. It is recognized that inter-sectoral convergence and co-ordination is crucial for the success of any ECCE/ECE programme and its linkage with primary education. Setting up of state level coordination committees by state governments to prepare state specific plans is being promoted as a viable convergence strategy.

To facilitate this and periodically review the situation, constitution of a National Advisory Group for ECCE is being proposed with representation from different regions and different sectors related to ECE.

Primary School Level

With vast area to be covered and the huge, still burgeoning, population to be reached, it has not been easy to provide access for all children to primary schools. However, considering the difficult socio-economic conditions in which a large number of people particularly in rural areas live, it has been the endeavour of the government to provide primary schooling facilities within easy access of all children. Though this may imply providing smaller schools with relatively less facilities, it is considered that expecting parents to send their children long distance for centralized schooling facilities may prove counterproductive. This is particularly true in case of girls. Keeping this in view, following norms have been drawn in terms of distance and population within which primary schools have to be provided:

- Provision of primary schools in all habitations having a population of 300 persons within a walking distance of 1 km. for children of 6-11 years age group. Further, relaxation has been made in case of difficult/hilly terrain and areas with ethnic minority population.
- Provision of upper primary schools in all habitations having a population of 500 persons within a walking distance of 3 km. for the children of 11-14 years.

For instance, the Education Guarantee Scheme (EGS) initiated by the Madhya Pradesh government has demonstrated how a demand based provision with the community at the centre stage can help in much faster progress. Under the Scheme, any community, which has a group of at least 25 school-going age children, can demand from the government to provide a primary school within their habitation.

As a reciprocal measure, the community has to find a place for conducting the school and also ensure the attendance of the children enrolled in the EGS school, as consistently low attendance would lead to closure of the school. Of the 19289 schools which were started under the EGS upto September 1998, 10325 (54 per cent) were in tribal pockets, which is indicative of the efforts directed to the schooling of children of socially disadvantaged groups.

Similar efforts based on micro-planning and school mapping exercises have been attempted under Lok Jumbish, the EFA project in Rajasthan. Other major projects such as DPEP have also focused on improving the access to primary school facilities in remote and un-served habitations.

Schooling facility at the upper primary stage has also increased over the years. The facilities of upper primary schooling, though widespread are comparatively less accessible, as the norms for establishment specify a radius of 3 km. At this stage, 85 per cent rural population has schooling facilities within a distance of 3 km. In terms of rural habitations the access to upper primary schooling facilities is 76.15 per cent.

The access to these facilities of upper primary schools has improved considerably as 23,000 upper primary schools (Middle Schools) have been established during the period from 1992-93 to 1996-97, indicating an increase of 14.8 percent, raising the per cent of rural population served by upper primary section to 90.95. In fact, a major programme for further improvement of upper primary schooling facility is being worked out within the framework of DPEP. Improvement in the availability of upper primary schools is also indicated by the changing ratio of upper primary schools to lower primary ones. Specifically, in 1957, there was only one upper primary school for every six lower primary schools.

This situation has gradually improved. In 1987, the ratio of lower primary schools to upper primary schools was 4:1 which further improved to 3:1 by 1993. This improvement, indirectly also indicates the considerable increase in the demand for upper primary education and improvement in transition rates from lower primary to upper primary classes.

The goal is to improve the situation further and provide at least one upper primary school to every two lower primary schools.

Increase in Students

The progress made in the provision of schooling facilities during the last few decades has, undoubtedly, been quite impressive. Mere existence of schooling facility does not guarantee the participation of children in schooling. This is clearly brought out by the large variations among the States/ UTs in respect of access to elementary education (primary and upper primary schooling). For instance, the highest percentage of unserved population by a primary school/section within 1 km. distance, is that for Himachal Pradesh, though this is a State with literacy rate much above the national average (57.3 in 1991 and 72 in 1997).

In contrast, in respect of Bihar, the percentage of population unserved by primary school/section is only 4.49 which is quite low comparatively, though Bihar has the lowest literacy rate in the country, via., 35.1 which indirectly indicates that a large section of the population has not been making use of the schooling facility available. What is the progress made in terms of student enrolment and attendance in the present decade? How big is the demand for additional places in the primary schools if all children are to be enrolled in school?

Growth of School System

India embarked on the task of building a mass education system fifty years ago after becoming independent from British colonial rule. Since then the system has grown several folds ill size both in terms of number of schools and the total enrolment of children in primary schools.

Enrolment in primary level of education has increased by about six times between 1951-1997 while the enrolment in upper primary level increased by about eleven times during the same period. The increase in case of girls had been nine times in primary level, and twenty four times in upper primary level.

The primary school system in India has grown in size consistently reaching an enrolment of nearly 150 million. This poses a major challenge not only for efficient management but also for mobilizing resources needed to maintain even a reasonable level of quality. Though the enrolment of girls has grown at a much faster rate than for boys during the last ten years, the difference continues to be very large with only six girls for every eight boys in the school. This calls for urgent action from the planners to devise innovative strategies and bridge the large gender gap.

Though the size of total enrolment in schools is very impressive, the population growth during the last few decades has also been high. Comparison with the total population in the school going age shows that several million children are still outside the fold of primary schooling.

Ratio of Attendance

Official entry age for primary school in India is 6 years and the country is also committed to give free education for all children upto the age of 14 years. How many of the children in this age group of 6-14 years are really in the schools? While it is difficult to give a precise answer to the question several indicators can help assess the situation. The most important indicator pointing to the participation of children in schooling is the enrolment ratio.

Gross enrolment ratios have remained relatively static during the decade. One of the factor is that, children are not enrolled exactly at the official age specified by the state, which also varies from one state to another. While in the states of Kerala and Tamil Nadu, more than 60 per cent children are enrolled in Class I when they are five year old, the level of enrolment is highest at six year in most of the states, and is quite high even for the seven year old category. This could be due to lack of school readiness and the fact that the number of first generation learners is very large in educationally backward States. Further, special enrolment drives carried out to bring even older children into the primary schools have also influenced the age composition of the school going population.

Seventeen States/UTs have a lower NER than the country's average while fifteen states/UTs have a higher NER than the national average. Whatever be the reasons for slow growth and even if computation methods are responsible for certain amount of under-reporting, the enrolment ratios indicate the major challenge that the country faces in bringing all children to school.

Betterment in Situation

Mere provision of access and enrolment of children in the school are not enough for achieving the goal of education for all. These should be coupled with suitable measures to ensure that children stay in the school to complete the full cycle of primary education. Though most states of India have done well in enrolling more and more children in the school, lack of capacity of the schools to retain the children in the school has been a serious problem. Efforts have been made for last several decades to ensure that children do not drop-out from the school after initial enrolment.

Regular information on drop out and retention of children is not collected in all the states. Therefore getting accurate data on the regular participation level of children in the schools and their progress through various classes to completion of the full cycle is not possible to compute as this is also affected by failure rates. This is further complicated, as most of the states follow a principle of automatic promotion in the initial classes of the primary cycle. However, in order to assess the progress made during the last decade, five indicators have been computed, namely, rate of drop-out, rate of repetition, rate of survival from class I through class V, efficiency index in terms of average number of years taken by a learner to complete the initial five year cycle and rate of transition from primary to upper primary stage.

The technique of 'school mapping' is Lok Jumbish's special contribution to the task of mobilizing people for education. This begins with LJ workers (or a local NGO) building a rapport with members of the community who are interested in improving education standards in the village. These members called the prerak dal (inspirational group), are given a short training for the task of mapping, which they undertake along with the LJ workers or the NGO. School mapping refers to the exercise of depicting every household in the village visually on a simple map. Small symbols indicate the schooling status of every household member in the 5-14 age group.

The whole exercise is an occasion for interacting with the community. When the map is ready, it is possible to see which household needs special help, and to discuss the schooling facilities required in the village. The prerak dal and the local community draw up a set of proposals based on the mapping data. The proposals usually relate to two issues: the need for new schools and non-formal centres and the improvement of the existing ones These proposals are sent to a block level committee, which is the sanctioning authority. The school mapping allows the ordinary, even non-literate villager to participate in a field survey and make proposals – a tremendous capacity-building exercise. Prompt follow-up to these proposals further builds up the confidence of the community.

It may be observed that the repetition rate is very small to the tune of only around 5-8 per cent. This is possibly due to the automatic promotion policy followed in most of the states. Low repetition rates may, however, be leading to lack of attention to learner achievement and in turn affecting the learning levels of the children as well as their motivation to attend regularly.

In fact, statewise data computed on this factor show considerable variation among the states in terms of repetition. One can also observe a slight rise in the repetition rate at grade III level as many States conduct external examination from that grade. Some states such as Uttar Pradesh and West Bengal show a very low efficiency level, schools in certain others such as Kerala and Punjab seem to be functioning at higher levels of efficiency.

Uttar Pradesh and West Bengal also show a high drop-out rate of 40.4 and 38.4 percent respectively. Interestingly there is not much difference between the drop-out in terms of 'years input per graduate' for boys and girls in almost all the states.

Exceptions again are Uttar Pradesh and West Bengal which show a fairly large difference between boys and girls. Himachal Pradesh which has recorded a quick progress in recent years show a lower drop-out rate for girls in comparison to boys. This reinforces the well recognized fact that progress in EFA goals demands special focus on girls education.

The more children are staying in the system for longer number of years. But the situation is still far from satisfactory. Following are some issues that need particular attention:

- It is clear that only 7 out of 10 children enrolled in the school stay in the school system. This acquires a serious proportion when this is seen along with the fact that the net enrolment ratio is only 70 percent.
- As in case of enrolment, there are wide disparities among different states in the efficiency with which the school system functions. One can identify certain states, which have remained chronically difficult.
- Again, the situation as it stands now shows that girls are at a disadvantage. However, a positive feature is that the reduction in dropout has been faster in case of girls than for boys in the recent years. This is possibly due to the special attention paid to girls' education in the recent years in general and in all the EFA projects, in particular.

- There is an urgent need to improve the transition rates. This problem gets compounded when viewed in conjunction with problem of unenrolled children and the extent of drop out in the lower primary classes. Here again education of girls needs special attention.

Drop-out Problem

The problem of dropping out of the school without attending the full cycle of primary education has been fully recognized by the planners and several measures have been initiated in this regard. Achievement made in this regard has to be seen against the fact that the drop-out rate was as high as 60 percent in early eighties. Some of the important measures that are being implemented to address this issue have to be noted. Poverty is one of the major reasons for children dropping out of school.

Many of these children are likely to be engaged in productive work and the opportunity cost involved in attending the schools is substantial for the parents. In order to address this issue, all states have been implementing a number of incentive schemes such as free textbooks and uniform, and attendance scholarship for children from socio-economically deprived sections.

Educational development of the children cannot take place without adequate attention to their health and nutritional status. It is in view of this that the government of Tamil Nadu initiated a programme of nutritious meal for all school going age children more than a decade ago. Following the significant impact the scheme made on the participation of children in the school, a national programme of mid-day meal is being implemented by the Government of India in all the states since 1995.

The Programme of Nutritional Support to Primary Education, popularly known as the Mid-day Meal Scheme, was launched in August 1995 on a nationwide basis. The Programme intends to boost universalisation of primary education by increasing enrolment - retention and attendance and to improve the nutritional status of children in primary classes. The Programme covers all the children studying in government, local body and government aided schools. The number of beneficiaries covered is estimated to be more than 97 million studying in about 688,000 primary schools.

Considering that girls continue to remain at a disadvantage, special attention is given to education of girls. Innovative efforts are being made to meet the socio-emotional and educational needs of the girls. It is noted that cultural factors also come in the way of higher participation of girls in schooling. Keeping this in view, state and central governments operate separate girls' schools wherever necessary; special scholarships are provided to girls; in several states, education of girls is free at all levels, including university education. Also, teacher recruitment procedure in almost all the states envisages that at least fifty percent positions are filled by women teachers.

Many children who join schools in rural areas as first generation learners come from poorer socio-economic background. Many among these tend to drop-out unable to adjust to the formal structure of the school functioning. Studies have shown that preschool programmes can create greater readiness among such children and help them adjust to the primary school set up. It is in this context that special measures are being made to promote the expansion of preschool programmes including the ICDS implemented by the government and other programmes for early childhood education in the non-government sector.

Notwithstanding the efforts to reach out and provide schooling facilities for all, children from nomadic groups and special ethnic communities living in remote hilly and forest areas are unable to get primary education.

Even those who get enrolled tend to drop out. In order to meet the educational needs of such children, special residential schools known as ashram schools are established in all such areas. Though the effectiveness of such schools is not found to be uniform, it is proposed to improve their functioning and expand the network to cover more areas. Another problem faced by schools located in small remote habitations is that of teacher reluctance to work in such schools. It was found that due to irregularity of teaching in such schools many children tended to drop out. To meet the requirement of such schools a novel experiment called Shiksha Kami Project has been tried out in Rajasthan.

With the success experienced during the initial years the project has expanded to cover a large number of habitations in the state. Since the problem is not unique to Rajasthan, several other states are beginning to adopt this model on a fairly large scale.

To overcome the problem of teacher absenteeism, the concept of 'barefoot teachers' was introduced by the Shiksha Karmi Project (SKP) which is being implemented in Rajasthan since 1987 with financial assistance from Swedish International Development Cooperation Agency. The idea was to substitute the absentee primary school teacher by a 'local educational worker'. The project aims at universalisation and qualitative improvement of primary education in remote and socio economically backward villages in Rajasthan, with primary attention being given to girls. The project works on the following assumptions:

- that a 'barefoot teacher' belonging to a local community can work effectively to reach every child in the locality;
- that if a person is willing to work as a social worker, the lack of formal training requirement can be made up by intensive in- service education and training; and
- that education must have community support and local ownership in order to meet the needs of the deprived sections of the rural areas.

Major factors include a curriculum, which is not relevant to the life of the children and an uninteresting teaching-learning process, which gives undue emphasis to rote learning and memorization of facts. In order to overcome this problem, improvement in teaching learning material and pedagogic practices have received very high priority in DPEP as well as all other ongoing EFA projects.

Goal of EFA is to bring all children into the fold of primary education. In 1997, 35.06 million children of age group 6-11 years were out of school. This number would, as per estimates, swell to 39.25 million. Therefore net additional enrolment of this order will be required in order to achieve the goal of EFA. The data clearly shows how varied the requirement is among different states. One can also observe that the bulk of the children to be enrolled are in a few educationally backward states.

Of the additional net enrolment of 39.25 million, a large portion consisting of 30.45 million children are estimated to be in eight States, viz., Andhra Pradesh, Bihar, Gujarat, Maharashtra, Madhya Pradesh, Orissa, Uttar Pradesh and West Bengal. The net additional enrolment required in these eight States is 77.58 percent of the total net additional enrolment estimated. Even among these eight states five states, namely, Andhra Pradesh, Bihar, Maharashtra, Uttar Pradesh and West Bengal account for 67.86 per cent of the total net additional enrolment required.

Improvement in Quality

Redefinition of universalisation of elementary education in the National Policy on Education – 1986 as consisting not only of enrolment and attendance but also of learner achievement brought focus on quality of primary education in a significant manner. The emphasis laid on achievement indicators by the Jomtien Declaration gave further impetus to this and brought quality concerns and improvement in learner achievement to the centre stage of policy making and planning for basic education in the country.

Quality improvement is a complex question, unlike improvement in infrastructure, appointment of teachers or even of equipping schools with better academic facilities. It is not that there were no quality improvement measures in primary education in the past. However, learning from the past efforts, it is realised that there is no single factor solution for the problem.

With this in view, the government has pursued a five-fold strategy following the recommendations of the NPE consisting of

(a) Improvement in provision of infrastructure and human resources for primary education;

(b) Provision of improved curriculum and teaching-learning material;

(c) Improving the quality of teaching-learning process through the introduction of child-centred pedagogy;

(d) Attention to teacher capacity building; and

(e) Increased focus on specification and measurement of learner achievement levels.

Quality improvement in education cannot be carried out on a turn-key basis in a pre-specified time-frame. Persisting with efforts to move ahead on all fronts mentioned in the strategy above is seen as the most important factor.

Keeping this in view a number of programmes and schemes have been initiated by the central as well as state governments. Also, quality improvement component has been given high priority in all the EFA projects such as DPEP and Lok Jumbish.

Human Resources Development

In the traditional framework for providing classrooms and teachers, number of students has been the main determining factor. Under this framework, small schools located in remote areas and invariably serving marginalised groups suffer from serious inadequacies.

Breaking away from this framework, following the recommendations of the NPE, a national programme called 'Operation Blackboard' was launched around 1990 to equip every school with certain basic infrastructure and human resources. As a part of this programme, every school was to have a minimum of two teachers and two classrooms and certain other basic teaching-learning and other school equipment.

Government of India has spent on an average about Rs. 400 million per year during the last ten years on this Scheme. More than

182,000 classrooms have been built and 149,000 additional teachers appointed. Besides, 42,000 posts of teachers have been sanctioned to add a third teacher to primary schools with more than 100 enrolment. A standard set of school equipment has also been supplied to all primary schools. An important dimension of this whole exercise is the element of community involvement. In most cases, under DPEP as well as Lok Jumbish, emphasis is laid on the role played by community members through village education committees or special school building construction committees. For instance, more than 5000 new school buildings are to be constructed in the seven DPEP states.

With the expansion of educational facilities, the number of teachers has also increased over the years. The policy of the Government is to provide 2 teachers to every Primary School initially and ultimately the endeavour is to provide one teacher for every class or section in Primary Schools. In the Upper Primary Schools the teachers are provided on the basis of subject teaching and teaching workload.

Curriculum Renewal

Curriculum prescription and textbook preparation for schools is essentially a subject handled by state governments within a national curricular framework prepared by the NCERT. The state level authorities decide on the specific curricular inputs and teaching-learning material to be followed in all the state supported schools. The last ten years have witnessed a variety of activities in the area of curriculum and teaching-learning material preparation in all the states.

The purpose of the exercise has been mainly to make the material more relevant, interesting and child friendly. The specification of Minimum Levels of Learning in early 90's at the national level also prompted the states to take up the task of curriculum and textbook revision. A series of activities in all the states with EFA projects as well as others were set in motion. The exercise has been guided by the following principles:

- Facilitate a two-way interaction between teacher and child to promote learning
- Promote self and peer group learning
- Be child-centered and activity based
- Be bias-free in terms of gender, ethnic, social and cultural considerations
- Be attractive and interesting to children
- Be related to children's context of learning and living
- Avoid information over-burden.

Three factors have characterised the process of material development. First, a participatory approach has been the high point of textbook development processes involving teachers, field personnel and experts from SCERTs. Secondly, people involved in textbook development have been periodically exposed to 'good practices' of other states and also NGOs. For instance, an attempt was made in Madhya Pradesh to conceive and produce jointly by the SCERT and Ekalavya, which has been well recognized for its long experience in producing innovative teaching-learning material. Thirdly, in most states, field trialling of textbooks and other material have been undertaken to identify gaps that could be corrected before large-scale introduction took place.

Process of Teaching and Learning

In the final analysis, quality of education depends on the nature of teaching- learning process. In fact, studies have also brought out that non-attendance of children in schooling and subsequent dropping out from school for many of them is determined by the nature of the teaching-learning process. It is in this context that a number of activities to improve the quality of classroom interaction and making it child centered and joyful have been initiated during the last several years.

The main thrust in the area of action is to help teachers make the classroom processes more contextualised to the local conditions characterizing the school and the community. It is recognized that many schools have to continue working under minimal infrastructure and without adequate learner support material.

In spite of additional teachers being appointed in many project schools, majority of the schools in the country – around 80 to 85 percent, adopt multi-grade teaching. This perhaps, is inevitable with more schools in smaller habitations being opened. Adapting to such conditions and making the teaching learning process still effective is a big challenge faced by a primary school teacher. This has been the main focus of all the EFA initiatives in the country.

A major project initiative called "Shikshak Samakhya" (Teacher Empowerment) was initiated in early 1990s in Madhya Pradesh with UNICEF support, which emphasized teacher creativity and autonomy for classroom organization and teaching with a view to making learning a joyful experience for the children. The experiment has influenced the pedagogic renewal process in many other states, viz., Ananddayi Shikshan in Maharashtra and Guru Mitra Yojana in Rajasthan. Similarly, following the model evolved by the Rishi Valley Education Trust in Andhra Pradesh, a small effort for resetting the teaching learning process in a block in Mysore district.

After extensive trialling and adaptation to local conditions, the DPEP in Karnataka is attempting to extend the initiative to other districts in the state. In fact, this process of effective dissemination of experiences from across state boundaries and their meaningful adaptation in larger areas is an important feature of the efforts for pedagogic renewal process under the EFA projects of 1990s.

Teachers have to be equipped to deal with multi-grade teaching, as even in the foreseeable future the multi-grade situation will continue to be the norm rather than the exception. Training programmes to deal with multi-grade situations have hitherto concentrated on how the teacher should divide her time among children of different grades, without sufficient thought being given to how optimum use can be made of the time available to the child for learning activities. This is not the real spirit of multi-grade teaching, which brings children of different grades and abilities together in one class room. The HD Kote project reflects what is possible in a multi-grade situation.

The project which drew inspiration from the experiment conducted by the Rishi Valley Education Trust, Madanapalli, Andhra Pradesh has been in operation with UNICEF support since 1995 in 270 schools of HD Kote block in Mysore district. Two major strategies developed are:

- improved classroom interaction through a graded curriculum which sets learning tasks along a continuum, replacing textbooks with activity based material to make learning individualized, child centred and interactive and bridging attainment gaps so that all children achieve predetermined levels of learning.
- improved teacher commitment and involvement through development of all teaching and learning material through teacher participation, enhancing the creativity and competence of teachers by giving them a say in material production and development of monitoring and evaluation tools to ensure accountability. The major strengths of the programme are:
- There is a sense of ownership of the programme by teachers as they have been participants at all stages.
- All actors, especially inspectors, AEOs and BEOs understand and identify with the methodology.
- Cluster resource persons are very carefully selected and provided constant support and guidance.
- The methodology is based on sound principles of learning and is appropriate to multi-grade situations.

The programme has resulted in significant improvements in enrolment, increase in retention rates and appreciable increases in learning achievement. The experiment is being upscaled to cover six additional blocks of Mysore district with DPEP assistance in 1998.

Capability of Teachers

Whenever questions of quality are raised, all fingers invariably point towards the teachers, their capacity and motivation. While this is natural, what kind of academic support do primary school teachers get on a continuous basis? Placed as they are working in difficult circumstances it is perhaps impractical to expect high levels of performance from all the teachers without external support and monitoring. It is with this in view, the National Policy on Education recommended decentralizing the technical and academic support mechanism by establishing a District Institute of Education and Training (DIET) in each district exclusively to cater to the development needs of elementary education of the particular district. The country has moved ahead considerably in this process of decentralization of academic support to teachers.

Before 1987, the main source for academic support and training for teachers in the elementary schools was the State Council of Educational Research and Training in each state. This was proving to be woefully inadequate to meet the capacity building needs in most of the states. The establishment of a DIET in each district following the NPE-1986 was therefore a major step in taking the support system nearer to the field.

During the last 10 years more than 400 such district level institutions have been established. This process of decentralization has been further extended under the externally aided EFA projects through the establishment of Block Resource Centres (BRCS) and Cluster Resource Centres (CRCs). The main function of these sub-district level institutions is capacity building among teachers. Recent reviews of DPEP report the creation of 414 BRCS and 5224 CRCs across different states of the country.

Another important feature of the in service teacher training programmes in the recent years has been the partnership between government bodies and NGOs with field experience in teacher training. For instance, Lok Jumbish has been working very closely with Sandhan, Allaripu and Digantar and several other NGOs in their programmes for teacher capacity building as well as for training of other field level personnel working for quality improvement in school functioning. The Rajiv Gandhi Shiksha Mission which implements DPEP in Madhya Pradesh has been taking the help of Ekalavya. Attempts are being made in other states also to work in collaboration with NGOs for teacher training and other related activities.

It is realised that even with the establishment of an extensive institutional network, continuous upgradation of knowledge and skills cannot be done effectively in view of the perpetually expanding system of schools and teachers. With this in view, a major move has been made in the 1990s to use modern technology and distance education mechanisms to reach out to the school teachers on a continuous basis. Two programmes in this regard need to be mentioned. One is the expanding programme of reaching out to teachers and teacher educators through satellite based tele conferencing network.

The second is the fairly large sized Distance Education Project within the framework of the DPEP. Both the programmes are operated in a collaborative fashion involving various organizations such as IGNOU, NCERT, SAC and several other national and state level organizations. In fact, one can see that distance education is gradually emerging as an effective means of providing academic and technical support to school teachers on a continuous basis.

The 1990s have also witnessed a high level of importance and attention given to assessment of learner achievement. The first prompting for this came from the special emphasis given to learner achievement in the NPE. However the main thrust for activity in this regard came from the specification of Minimum Levels of Learning at the national level through an expert body set up by the Government of India. Following this, most of the state governments with the help of NCERT and SCERTs not only revised their curriculum and textbooks but also initiated programme for measuring learner achievement on a regular basis. The Government of India supported 16 large scale projects to study and streamline this process and work out the processes needed for achieving of competencies by all children.

The National Policy of Education, 1986, brought to the forefront the need for focusing not only on quantitative aspects but also on quality in terms of achievement levels.

Towards this end, a committee constituted by the Ministry of Human Resource Development specified the basic competencies to be achieved by all children at the primary stage in the form of Minimum levels of Learning (MLLs) in selected subjects such as Language, Mathematics and Environmental Studies across the country. Currently, 12 states are implementing the programme through the institutional mechanism of around 200 DIETS and the programme is being up-scaled. Under this scheme, financial assistance is being provided to the state governments for a wide range of activities such as preparation of competency based textbooks, training of teachers, preparation of teaching learning materials, orientation of education personnel and conducting benchmark surveys. The programme aims to lay down learning outcomes expected from basic education at a realistic, relevant and functional level, prescribes the adoption of measures that would ensure that all children who complete a stage of schooling achieve these outcomes.

The endeavour is to monitor learning achievement, to direct greater resources where levels of learning are lower, and to consciously accelerate the pace of development in the needy areas, thereby reducing disparities, equalising standards and determining inputs for quality improvement and enhanced efficiency of the system. A second set of efforts in this direction emerged with the launching of EFA projects which carried out baseline studies to assess the achievement of learners in various classes of the primary school. Some of the projects have even set targets for raising the learner achievement levels in a phased manner. For instance, DPEP has set the target of raising achievement levels by 25% during the project period.

Towards monitoring the programmes to raise the achievement levels, periodic surveys have been carried out both in DPEP and Lok Jumbish. Have these efforts help increase the levels of learner achievement? It is difficult to respond categorically to this. First of all, there is no all India survey done to determine the current levels of achievement. Further, since the programme content as well as context of schooling is quite different in each state, it will be difficult to generalize on the progress made in this regard. Finally, though the initial results show positive change in the learning levels of children different project schools, both under Lok Jumbish and DPEP, one cannot expect any dramatic upswing in the learner performance in the short term.

Performance of learners does not depend only on inputs provided in the school. They are also influenced by many other socio-economic contextual factors, which do not fall within the purview of education development projects. Also, it may be counter-productive to anchor all quality improvement efforts only to improvement in performance of learners in achievement tests in selected subject areas. They have to be coupled with focus on learner growth and development in other areas which are not necessarily performance based and measurable.

9

Official Policies

The broad objective of education is to create a sizeable population of such educated men and women who could understand the world well enough and are able to bring about a change leading to adequate health and education services, a better environment, and elimination of ignorance and deprivation-limitations- which continue to strangulate the developing societies. The Policy, therefore, adhering to the principles of equity, quality and efficiency place added emphasis on the education of the people, who are under privileged and live in misery.

They will not only be required to achieve skills in reading, writing and arithmetic, but also would be enabled to understand the factors which have historically contributed to their unsavoury place in society. Consequently, basic education for all shall be pursued not merely as a sectoral target, but as an integral part of human development plan. The ultimate aim is to eliminate disparity.

Considering the low literacy rates and low participation at the primary level, the sub-sectors retain a high place on the priority list of educational development. The dilemma is essentially due to limitations of finance; the costs involved are almost prohibitive. Yet, the policy places equal emphasis on universal primary education and adult education. However, it proposes to attract private finance by shifting most of the adult education programmes to non-governmental organizations to be supported through 'incentive' grants.

Only a limited progress has been made in reducing rural urban educational disparities. If anything, the disparities have accentuated in terms of access to quality institutions. The policy proposes a strategy to remove the inequalities by providing more schools in rural areas.

Women education continues to be a difficult area to tackle. Social, cultural and economic factors have put off the women participation rates. For improvement of female education, innovative approaches, both in the formal and non formal sectors, are clearly warranted. The Policy, recognizing the difficulties attendant upon this vital issue, proposes to make a shift in the hitherto used approaches in the education of females both in the formal and non-formal sectors.

Accordingly, increased access of females to general and vocational education through a wider spread of educational facilities, use of a mix of non-formal and distance education modes based on new education technology, expansion of the non-governmental sector through financial incentives, and motivation campaigns through print and broadcast media, among others, are the measures which will form the basis of new Policy parameters.

The curriculum plays a pivotal role in the process of education. The development of curriculum is a dynamic process which assumes its best shape if it is leavened with professional inputs both in content and design. The knowledge explosion demands an equally rapid turnover of curricula and textbooks. The policy considers the curriculum as a central covenant of educational development, and calls for sweeping reforms such as:

(a) starting a new cycle of curriculum development at all levels of education by professionals who are trained in the science of curriculum development;

(b) bringing about cognitive compatibility between one level of curriculum and the next;

(c) eliminating unnecessary overcrowding of subjects in curricula, and

(d) allowing the production of textbooks in the private sector with the possibility of different books to be prescribed by different institutions.

In order to stand up to the future challenges, fulfil the needs and demands of the country and also to honour international commitment in EFA, Education Policy 1992 was revised in the form of National Education Policy (1998-2010). Similarly, Social Action Programme Phase-I was replaced by Social Action Programme Phase-II and 8th Five Year Plan by 9th Plan. In addition to that Pakistan 2010 programme also focuses on basic education for all.

Policy for Future Education

Based upon these policy prospects and framework the following guiding principles for future policy in EFA particularly basic education have been evolved:

- Forging a link between basic education and development strategies;
- Improvement and enhancement of the relevance of training programmes for teachers;
- Modernization of Planning and Management;
- Shifting the focus of the Curricula from disciplines to basic Learning Needs;
- Building new alliances for basic education and increasing the roles of the traditionally less involved actors in basic education;

- Strengthening the participatory dimension in the provision of basic education;
- Diversification of the financial resource base of basic education;
- Introduction of the pre-school programmes as part of the efforts to improve the achievement of pupils at the primary school level;
- Implementation of special programmes aimed at the indigenous sectors in the rural areas;
- Modernization of the concepts and programmes of literacy which are to be anchored on integrated literacy education;
- Maximization of the roles of the family, schools, community, non-governmental organizations and the media in the provision of basic education;

According higher priority in the provision of basic education to the out-of-school children, illiterate adults, those who have relapsed into illiteracy; females, rural population, inhabitants of settlements, tribesmen, nomads special children;

Programme for Social Action

In both its first and second phase the SAP education sector programme has placed greatest emphasis on improving the quantity and quality of primary schooling. In particular its objective was to rapidly increase the proportion of children attending primary school, and also make efforts to improve the quality of education. In particular, children of poor households, girls and rural areas were identified as requiring special attention under the programme.

The strategy involves a range of measures designed to:
- improve the efficiency;
- increase access to schools; and
- improve the quality of schooling;

Against the expectation of increased political commitment to the provision of public education services, these objectives were transformed into three areas of focus for education sector programmes in the different provinces and regions of the country. These include:

- improving the implementation of education sector programmes,
- improving planning, and
- improving the level of effort required to implement the programme.

National Education Policy (1998-2010)

The current primary education policy has been based on agreed themes and strategies of Social Action Programme (SAPP-II) such as improving the quality, expanding access for out of school children, especially disadvantaged groups, improving management and supervisory services, capacity building, institutional development and financial sustainability.

Salient characteristics of the current education policy in primary education include:

Aims and Objectives

(i) Enactment for compulsory primary education.

(ii) 90% enrolment at primary level by the year 2002-3 and 105 percent by 2010.

(iii) Retention/completion of primary education cycle upto 90 percent students (both boys and girls) by the year 2010.

Achievement of minimum level of learning by 90 percent primary class students by the year 2010.

Quality of elementary education shall be improved.

Access to elementary education shall be increased through effective and optimum utilization of existing facilities and services as well as provision of new facilities and services.

Character-building oriented towards humanism, tolerance, and moral-building-up on Islamic lines at elementary level shall be assigned top priority.

Teachers' competence shall be improved and the relevance of training programmes for teachers shall be ensured.

Katchi class at primary level shall be introduced as a part of the effort to improve the achievement of pupils. The role of the family, school, community, non-governmental organizations and the media in the provision of elementary education shall be maximized. Disparities and imbalances of all types shall be eliminated so as to promote equity.

High priority shall be accorded to the provision of elementary education to the out-of-school children.

Financial resource base of elementary education shall be diversified.

Non-formal system shall be adopted as complementary to formal system.

A monitoring system shall be developed to obtain timely and reliable information on enrolment, retention, completion and achievement. In addition, qualitative monitoring of achievement shall be introduced.

Management and supervision shall be improved through greater decentalization and accountability.

Strategy for Implementation

Policy goals and objectives shall be achieved through the following programmes and strategies:

Revise regulations and create stronger and more transparent personnel management mechanisms to promote merit-based hiring. Assign teachers to schools on the basis of empirical need and reduce transfer rate by recruiting local teachers for local schools.

Revise, strengthen and enforce attendance and leave regulations and strict action to check teachers' absenteeism.

Revamp in-service training for existing teachers, and over a period of five years all primary school teachers shall be provided with in-service training opportunities, and then institutionalize in-service on a 3 years cycle. Raise the entry qualification for Primary Teacher Certificate from Secondary School Certificate to Higher Secondary School Certificate gradually.

Reform pre-service teacher training, and include the revision of the curricula, revamping textbooks, and instructional materials in the training programmes.

Institute a clear career structure for teachers at the primary and middle levels that includes promotion possibilities, revise and enforce the standards of professional behaviour.

Ensure a better distribution and optimum utilization of teachers.

Institutionalize the incentives and accountability system for teachers to improve their performance.

Relaxation of qualification where no female teacher is available.

Relaxation of age limit for females to facilitate entry into the profession.

Substantial increase in the non-salary recurrent expenditures on texts, basic school supplies, and learning materials; and improving procurement and distribution mechanisms.

Ensure an adequate supply of basic textbooks and learning materials' availability at the start of the school year, and free of charge for the poor children.

Develop a new and more logical, demanding, and challenging curricula taking into account the provincial differences; involve the stakeholders in the process which should precede updating of text books and revamping of teacher training.

The span of Primary education including katchi class shall be six years duration. Construction of new schools and classrooms where objective demographic criteria indicate their urgent need.

Area/District based targets and Programmes shall be developed for the promotion of elementary education and literacy which may be supervised by District Education Authority.

An incentive tied approach may be adopted for the communities, villages and areas proportionate to their degree of accomplishment and success in elementary education.

Enactment and enforcement of free and compulsory Primary Education Act, in a phased manner.

Building work shall be given priority to the existing school: (a) build rooms for shelter less schools; (b) replace dilapidated schools; (c) add new classrooms in overcrowded schools; (d) repair inadequate schools; and (e) construct facilities (water supply, boundary walls, toilets of suitable design).

Complete major repairs wherever it is needed, in cooperation with Village Education Committees.

Deploy larger number of Learning Coordinators and Supervisory Staffs, retrain the existing staff, and certify that the graduates meet the minimum standards.

Train DEOs, ADEOs and LCs in management and VEC organization so as to improve the quality of administration of teaching in the schools.

Bring about a coherent system of elementary education (Grades 1-8) by putting together government primary and middle schools.

Decentralize selection management functions in elementary education towards the district, the school, through the community, while helping communities and local bodies organize their efforts more effectively. Work on National assessment capacity by laying down a set of procedures to monitor the aggregate performance at grade four level;

Revise Monitoring the evaluation systems that will enable provincial officials to assess school-level performance and study the associated reasons for their success and failure.

School-level assessment capacity for teachers to measure accurately the student learning.

Reform the current examination system administered at the end of elementary school.

Literacy : Provisions

The policy of democratization of education, through the expansion of elementary education both through formal and non-formal methods, and expanded programmes of adult education, literacy and functional literacy programmes, as a basic requirement for economic development, modernization of social structure and for providing equality of opportunity for all citizens.

Pakistan's international commitment to double the rate of Literacy by the year 2000 could not be possible because of non-achievement of Universal Primary Education (UPE). This will be achieved by complementing the formal primary school system by a strong Non-Formal Basic Education initiative.

A massive Non-Formal Basic Education Programme, on a war footing, will be launched to provide access economically and expeditiously to all the (5-9 years old) children that are at present out-of-school. The 10-14 year old adolescents and youth who have missed primary education will be given a second chance through a crash condensed course to enable them to complete primary education cycle in 2-3 years time.

The Asian Development Bank sponsored pilot project for 15-25 year old rural women on successful completion will be replicated nationwide. Attainment of literacy, social and occupational skill training programmes will equip the beneficiaries with appropriate income generating skills to ensure socio-economic development of Pakistan.

Educated unemployed adults will also be able to benefit from these skill training programmes.

Additional strategies, such as the tested Quranic Literacy Programme and other methods in collaboration with the other sectors, will be used to achieve universal literacy. A Literacy Fund is planned to be created give a boost to the literacy drive.

10

Book Industry

Every country has a publishers' association, most of them founded since 1989. Those in Estonia and Latvia have been particularly active.

In many countries, the printing industry lacks modern equipment that can provide short print runs economically. With the exception of the Russian Federation most countries need to import paper. Printing prices in the Republic of Moldova, which had been a major printing centre in the Soviet Union, are low in comparison with those in neighbouring countries and there is substantial demand for its services from Romania. Bulgaria and the Russian Federation. Many countries must find financing for short-run textbooks to meet minority needs. There is an urgent need for training in writing, publishing and distribution of textbooks, and for training of teachers in their use.

The Open Society Institute and the local Soros Foundations for Open Society have been running numerous regional and general programmes addressing educational reforms, textbook publication and translation of materials. The British Know How Fund has also organized training workshops in Albania and Romania. In the early 1990s the Soros Foundation supported some 400 writing projects in the Russian Federation, most of them supplementary materials that have found their way to the country's more progressive schools.

The World Bank is supporting the publication and distribution of selected primary and secondary school core textbooks in Bosnia and Herzegovina. In Romania, it supported an education reform project that introduced new textbooks and competition. It is negotiating with Albania an education reform loan that would include competitive textbooks. It has also provided support for textbooks in the Russian Federation, the Former Yugoslav Republic of Macedonia, and the Republic of Moldova. A Bank project in the Russian Federation involved direct loans to oblasts to provide working capital for publishers to produce federally approved textbooks, but it faltered, just as agreement was to be signed, after the ruble was devalued in August 1998. Strategies for developing, publishing and distributing text-books and other learning materials must be devised to meet local conditions and needs. They should be based on what is appropriate and practical locally, not on an imported model. None the less, some thirty lessons may be drawn from the achievements and the failures of the decade since Jomtien.

Depending on the quality of their binding and paper, if they are well used and well cared for they may last three years, or even five. Where, children carry them home each day over hilly paths, in seasons of heavy rain, to homes without shelves, they may not last that long. In northwestern Pakistan, the simple saddle-stitched textbooks are not expected to last longer than one year and those for the early grades, whose owners have not yet been trained in book care, often must be replaced part-way through the year.

Textbooks must also survive domestic hazard. Younger siblings are always a threat and an extremely unlucky student may find his illiterate father has torn a page from a textbook to roll his tobacco in or his mother has taken a page for wrapping the sugar she is selling. In time, moreover, and regardless of their physical condition, textbooks grow obsolete as the curriculum changes and so must be replaced. As a result, textbooks have never fit comfortably into the large-scale projects and procurement procedures of the World Bank and other funding agencies' institutions that were designed initially to help fund long-lasting capital projects such as dams, bridges and roads.

Open competitive bidding that is based principally on cost can be used in procuring the paper and printing for textbooks, but fails when it is applied to textbooks that are individually unique and cannot truly be compared as simple commodities. While the World Bank has never stipulated that it looks for the cheapest price, procurement has been affected by a shortage of qualified staff and a less than perfect implementation of general guidelines for procurement, including a trial set of guidelines for procurement of textbooks issued in 1994.

In countries where state institutions wrote, produced and distributed a single textbook for each subject/level, the systems generally have been found to be inefficient and ineffective. Sida found that in the programmes it supported, by and large government publishing has not functioned well. State-aided companies are frequently hampered by inefficient bureaucracy, unawareness of real costs, or lack of motivation on the part of the staff. Other observers have noted that hidden subsidies masked true costs. Civil servants often well versed in educational theory but unskilled in printing and publishing techniques made decisions that might be pedagogically appropriate but unnecessarily costly. Books were produced in uneconomical page sizes and in wasteful designs.

Distribution systems failed because of inadequate funding for transportation from regional warehouses to the schools. Everywhere, books were frequently late in reaching the schools, if they arrived at all; too often they remained in regional and district storerooms, ill protected from water, mould, insects and vermin.

Textbook provision suffered from the common maladies of a civil service. Functions were sometimes scattered among different departments or units, with little co-ordination. Personnel were poorly motivated to meet schedules or save money. Staff development and promotion followed civil service procedures, often oblivious to publishing professionalism: staff were transferred to publishing units on the basis of seniority or availability rather than knowledge or merit. Rules and procedures for procurement were cumbersome. Funding was principally by an annual legislative grant, making forward planning difficult if not impossible. The contents of textbooks often reflected the values and policies of the government that controlled the purse strings and appointments.

Private Level

Shareholders are more likely to be concerned about achieving economies and making use of professional skills than civil servants who have no personal stake in textbook provision beyond their own survival in office. Of course there are many civil servants who are just as dedicated and professional as any private-sector manager, but even they are likely to be overcome by the inertia of large bureaucracies and the indifference or unwillingness of their superiors to make changes. Publishing, in contrast to bureaucracy, benefits from a personal style that marries innovation and professionalism. It is also unusually complex in the number of 'product lines' each book constituting a separate product that must be managed simultaneously in development or revision, production, and distribution.

Because the private sector sells textbooks, either to the government or on the open market, it has funds to reinvest in the next year's sales and a powerful motivation the need for financial turnover to make that reinvestment. Books that are available this year, therefore, are likely to be available next year if the sales potential this year is realized. The difference between public and private sector publishing was illustrated dramatically in French-speaking sub-Saharan Africa, where several countries agreed on common syllabuses in mathematics and, with help from French aid organizations, co-operatively developed textbooks for common use. Two approaches to publication were followed. In the primary-level series, the intergovernmental co-ordinating committee that developed the books acted as publisher and retained the copyright. It offered film for plate making to countries that signed an exclusive five year agreement with it.

The countries then had to secure their over funding, by grants or loans, and arrange production of the books. The series was adopted by only three countries. In Benin, the government took three years to find funding. The state printer was given the contract for books at the first two levels but could not fulfil it for technical reasons and subcontracted it to a foreign printer at a high cost. Benin subsequently chose books for the next two levels from a French publisher. In Mali, the contracted printer delivered the books a year late. Because the financing did not cover distribution, only part of the stock was supplied to schools, mainly in the capital and its neighbourhood. The Democratic Republic of the Congo also needed three years to find funding, then chose a European printer and faced similar problems in delivery and distribution.

None of the three countries had funds to reprint books in following years. In contrast, the committee that developed the secondary-level textbooks assigned the copyright to a single publisher, the Hachette subsidiary EDICEF. The secondary series was adopted in twelve countries and sold in the open market, helped by a French subsidy to lower the sale price. About 1.5 million copies were bought, either in bookshops or within the framework of a bid, at the equivalent of US$5 per copy, about half the price of a comparable Ghanaian book, also the recipient of development aid. The books continue to be available throughout the countries because they are in the copyright of a publisher with an interest in their commercial longevity.

The foundation for a sustainable publishing industry that can meet continuing local needs while reflecting local conditions and experiences. The importance of school books extends far beyond the classroom. A large and relatively stable continuing demand for them, year after year, can provide the financial underpinning for a more general publishing industry. With the capital generated from educational books, publishers can engage in works of fiction and poetry, and in works of nonfiction books that examine the country's history, society, economy, ecology, and culture that will help to develop a sense of national identity and self-awareness.

Most important in this context, they can develop books in all these genres written specially for children and young adults, and sell them in the marketplace to a book-hungry population. In short, publishers who have financial resources from school books can provide the books that will maintain literacy once schooling ends.

Textbooks are particularly important to publishing in countries that do not have a well-developed reading culture. In industrialized countries, textbooks and learning materials represent between 25 and 50 per cent of all publishing income. In developing countries where textbooks are sold, they can represent up to 95 per cent of the local publishing market. In sub-Saharan Africa overall, they account for 75 per cent of publishing revenue.

When the state dominates the provision of learning materials, the general publishing industry languishes. This was clear in many countries of Africa and Asia, where the imposition of a state monopoly devastated publishing. As one publisher explained it, 'a book industry without access to the textbook market is a dying industry, because the textbook market is the side of the bread that is buttered for the publisher and bookseller.'

A public monopoly may appear attractive because it cuts out the retailer and concentrates production, leading to apparently lower costs for the consumer, whether that is the government or the family. The true cost to the country is great, however, commercial publishing lacks a financial base on which to build. Bookshops do not develop because they have no books to sell. The quality of textbooks deteriorates from lack of competition.

Book industries stagnate or die. 'It is not surprising,' Brickhill and Priestley observed, 'that book development... is weakest where monopolies are strongest.' In contrast, when textbook provision is opened to commercial competition, even partially, industries grow.

Children's book production, for example, increased notably in Kenya, Nigeria and Uganda during the 1990s, in number of titles and in copies per title printed. The ownership local or foreign of commercial publishing houses that produce textbooks is not an issue so long as their publishing activity is truly locally based and locally oriented. Locally produced books are likely to be cheaper than imported books from Europe or North America, and far more likely to be appropriate in content, illustration and emphasis.

In contrast, the foreign imported children's books the most common form of children's literature in the bookshops of many African countries have been described by Chinua Achebe as 'poisons wrapped in between beautiful covers'.

The president of the United Republic of Tanzania has said that it is 'incumbent upon African publishers to protect African value systems and ways of life'.

Official Policies

Government policies for book provision are often impeded by other government policies and practices. Not infrequently the policies of other departments impede the policies of educational authorities.

Most notable are high tariffs imposed by the Ministry of Trade or Finance on imported paper, other raw materials, printing equipment and replacement parts. Such tariffs are particularly onerous in countries that have acceded to the Florence Agreement on the free movement of books and charge no duty on imported finished books but levy high tariffs on the materials for publishing books at home.

Tariffs may be used to shield inefficient domestic paper mills as well as to raise revenue. An ADEA/APNET study on the intra-African trade in books has illustrated the contradictions in taxation and legislative practices that can work against the development of the book chain in countries committed to Education for All. High interest rates set by the central bank also inhibit book development by commercial publishers, who may be further penalized by government subsidies to parastatal publishing and printing houses with whom they and their printers compete.

The Ministry of Culture or Education may require textbooks to be produced in two, three or even eleven local languages, a policy that is pedagogically sound but adds greatly to the investment involved in book development. The absence of intellectual property legislation, or governmental indifference to its infringements, encourage piracy of books and fragment markets that may already be marginal.

When there is no co-ordination among ministries in policy or regulation, the cost of providing school books generally rises. In times of fiscal austerity, that usually means that fewer books will be produced or bought, and the textbook pupil ratio grows unacceptably high.

Production of Books

Books cannot be considered independently but only as part of a process involving many players and policy issues. A school book is part of a continuum that begins with the students needs, as defined by a curriculum institute, and ends with the student's use, inside or outside the classroom. In between there are many stages: curriculum development and authorization, identification and commissioning of authors, drafting and revising of a manuscript, preparation of illustrations, evaluation by the publisher in field tests, evaluation by the Ministry of Education, possible revision and further evaluation leading to authorization for use of the book in schools, production (typesetting, printing and binding) and, finally, shipping to a government warehouse and from there to individual schools or, alternatively, shipping to wholesale and retail outlets that will sell the book to families. This is not an exhaustive list of processes or players.

The World Bank or another funder may be involved, with its own procedures and guidelines which may be different from the government's development agencies and civil society organizations may supply paper or expertise. Teachers will need training in the use of a new text-book and teachers' guides must be prepared following all the same steps simultaneously for them. Any weak links in this book chain will, as we have seen, affect the availability of books in the classroom.

The policy issues that must be examined have been set in detail by several authors. They include:

- selection of subjects requiring textbooks (core subjects or all subjects);
- use of national and local languages in instruction and text books; timing of reforms and revisions;
- rewards for authors;
- target textbook pupil ratios (if books are provided by the state);
- technical specifications for paper, printing and binding;
- procedures for evaluation and authorization of textbook by the Ministry of Education that are and are seen to be objective, thorough, comprehensive, fair, timely concerned with social content and in the public interest;
- affordable and sustainable financing;
- open competitive bidding for printing and/or publishing;
- practical and economical distribution;
- professional development for publishing personnel and educators;
- identification and provision of supplementary reading and other learning materials, including their development, publication, distribution and financing;
- support for public and school libraries, and the training of teacher librarians; and
- positive industrial policies affecting publishing.

Failures in planning and co-ordination will affect the provision of textbooks and learning materials adversely. External support will be meaningful only if it is rooted in detailed strategic plans, rather than based simply on general policy statements.

Large-scale loans in the past have unquestionably reduced the pupil-to-textbook ratio in many countries from extreme scarcity to a more effective level. But book provision, as Bgoya has pointed out, is not the same as book development. Textbooks have too often been viewed as commodities to be delivered in the short run to meet immediate needs. As a World Bank team leader once remarked with passion: 'All care about is getting books into the children's hands!' If the government receiving a loan for textbook provision is still unable to fund its needs when those books must be replaced, a second loan must be negotiated.

The World Bank acknowledged, in its draft policy released in 1998, that 'many book provision efforts over the last 25 years, some with Bank support, may have achieved their immediate objectives but have been unable to maintain the service over the longer term to sustain the educational impact that textbooks help to achieve'. This has also been true of loans by the Asian Development Bank. Newton has pointed out that is not only funders that have been responsible for short-term solutions. Ministers of Education have generally been avid for the votes that come with the promise of free books in the coming year. An insistence on international competitive bidding for all contracts above a certain threshold, while understandable from the viewpoint of the funders, has exacerbated the effects of short-term provision by channelling most of the loans for text-books out of the recipient country. Reports to APNET indicate that in book procurement programmes supported by World Bank lending, the ratio of books from local publishers to those from foreign-based publishers is 1 to 50.

A book purchase made on the basis of a one-off cost import is not a good bargain when we consider: the opportunity cost of jobs lost to the economy, since the book was not produced locally; the cost of discouraged innovative trading, which would have resulted from higher turnover and increased profitability; the cost of capacity not built; and the cost of lost spill over benefits, which in turn would have invigorated the textbook industry. As a result, these books are not cheap.

Very few governments fully understand the critical role indigenous publishers can play in national culture and, more specifically, in textbook provision, nor have they paid serious attention to the conditions that would encourage an indigenous publishing industry. Publishers have a responsibility to raise awareness of these issues if they want change. An experienced textbook publisher, now a consultant, recommended to the Canadian International Development Agency that any project related to educational books be preceded by an in-depth analysis of the book sector; be designed to cover a minimum of ten, and preferably fifteen, years; be co-ordinated with other agencies; view textbook provision within an overall framework of developing local capacities in publishing, production and distribution; give priority to financial sustainability and substantial private sector involvement; and use experts in curriculum development, publishing, production and distribution in the project's planning, implementation, monitoring and evaluation.

Foundation's principles for support of the book sector show the same holistic approach: using the commercial potential of a book wherever possible to keep subsidies to a minimum and to provide an incentive for efficiency; leaving as much initiative as possible to the publishers; avoiding monopolies; and making support part of an educational process that aims at reducing dependence on external help through carefully focused training and business planning. These are desiderata that any funding agency should consider.

States in Picture

The state has the initiative and ultimate responsibility for the timely and adequate provision of textbooks in any publicly funded education system. It decides what textbooks will be used, how they will be published and how they will be paid for. These responsibilities remain even when some functions are performed by the private sector. The International

Commission on Education for the Twenty-first Century defined the state's role as follows:

> Education is a collective asset that cannot be left only to market forces. Thus, whatever the organization or degree of centralization or diversification of a system, the state must assume certain responsibilities to its citizens, . . .
>
> That role . . . must not, however, be exercised as a strict monopoly. It is more a matter of channelling energies, promoting initiatives and providing the conditions in which new synergies can emerge. It is also a matter of insisting on equity and quality in education . . . . more specifically, the state should play a re-distributive role, to the benefit of minorities and the underprivileged especially. Guaranteed educational quality moreover implies the establishment of general standards and various monitoring devices.

Ingemar Gustafsson, then head of Sida's education division, defined a further public responsibility, to ensure that text-books reflect the culture of the student-users' own country. This in turn requires each country to have some control over and capacity to produce its own school books.

At a minimum, the state must be expected to prepare clear and detailed curriculum guidelines; make them available for the development of textbooks; establish an objective process of evaluation and authorization of textbooks; decide the channels to be used in funding and distributing textbooks to the schools; set minimum physical standards of production; perform the same functions with respect to other learning materials, including teachers' guides and supplementary reading; train teachers in the use and care of textbooks and learning materials; and protect intellectual property rights through appropriate legislation.

The state may also be expected to support libraries and promote literacy through community-based campaigns. Beyond this, the state may play a role in any of the permutations outlined by Searle and described in the preceding pages. Experience suggests that no option is perfect and that what is best for one country may be unsuitable for another.

Financing and Distribution

Too often, inexperienced managers and editors ignore ways to save money in textbook printing that are standard practice among trained professionals. The size of a book's page can have surprising implications for its cost, especially when paper represents a high proportion of total production expenditures.

The most economicai page size is determined by the size of the sheet of paper used in printing, which in turn is related to the size of the printing press being used. Any mismatch between press and sheet, or between sheet size and page size, results in waste. Production costs can also be reduced by restricting the number and size of illustrations, the use of colours other than black, and the total number of pages. More generally, governments can reduce costs to state and families by limiting the number and size of textbooks required.

Public and Private Sector Together

Privatization has been successful in providing a long-term supply of textbooks. Where the government opted for a system of purchase by families at both primary and secondary levels and concentrated production in a very few hands. In 1991 the country's two textbook publishers, le Centre edition et distribution africain (CEDA) and les Nouvelles editions ivoiriennes (NEI), both parastatal partnerships between the government and French publishers, were technically bankrupt following an economic crisis and social disorder. In order to obtain new capital they were transformed into private companies.

In both, the government retained 20 per cent of the shares and further shares were set aside for individual Ivorians to ensure majority local control. The balance of NEI shares was held by three French companies and the balance of CEDA shares by one French and one Canadian company. The new companies were granted exclusive rights, shared equally between them, to publish primary school textbooks, teachers' guides and work books, all written in the Ministry of Education. The two companies are also active at the secondary level, where the state issues a list of approved textbooks.

The state regulates the retail prices of textbooks and in the first two years of the agreement negotiated substantial decreases; prices were frozen even after the devaluation of the CFA franc increased the cost of imported materials substantially. The price of textbooks to disadvantaged areas is subsidized. Through its share holding and regulation, including quality control, the state acts as 'school protector' while remaining committed to economic liberalism. The results of the Ivorian policy are substantial. Textbook prices are said to be the lowest in all French-speaking Africa, except where prices are artificially lowered by external subsidies.

The two national publishers sell more than 4 million primary school books each year for a school population of about 1.5 million students, and there is an additional market in second hand books. It is estimated that 75 to 95 per cent of students, depending on their level and where they live, own French and mathematics textbooks, although fewer own books in other disciplines. The system has encouraged the development of the only major printing industry in French- speaking sub-Saharan Africa and of a distribution network of wholesalers, bookstores and other sales outlets. The companies have returned profits. The World Bank is supporting free distribution of the textbooks in 116 marginalized zones.

The Ivorian policy is based on a single textbook for each subject/level. The quality of a textbook determines how well the needs of the users are met and a good quality textbook in a single-textbook system is probably better than several competing textbooks of poor quality. Many educators and publishers argue, however, that a multi-textbook system is preferable because competition encourages publishers to innovate and improve their textbooks and teachers' guides.

Gaston de Bedout, a Colombian commercial publisher, presents another reason for moving away from a single compulsory textbook in each subject, whether published by the government or bought by the government from a friendly publisher. In the final analysis, 'education through a texto unico will result in a mass of people desolately uniform, indoctrinated by the official history, philosophy, science, grammar, chemistry, biology, and even the official calligraphy.

Personnel must be trained in manuscript development, editing, design, illustration, field testing, production control, marketing, warehousing and distribution. Authors must be identified and they too must be trained to meet the special demands of writing textbooks and teachers' guides. Training tended during the 1990s to focus on the more obvious needs of writing, editing, design and illustration. Less attention was paid to preparing publishers for the underpinning skills of operational and financial management, marketing, and evaluation' an imbalance that is gradually being redressed.

Typically, a textbook takes three years from inception to the classroom roughly, one year or more to commission authors and for them to write a first-draft; one year for field testing, revision and evaluation by the Ministry of Education for authorization; one year to produce final books and, especially where distribution is difficult, get them to the schools. The process can be accelerated, but only if the commercial sector is sufficiently established to meet the challenge.

It can be impeded by difficulties in securing capital or credit and, too often during liberalization, by bureaucratic foot dragging. Uganda's experience illustrates the time an industry takes to develop. Up to 1993, the National Curriculum Development Centre had a monopoly on textbook production and the few books it produced were assigned to two transnational publishers.

Other textbooks bought under a World Bank project were all imported. In 1993 the centre's monopoly was removed and selection was devolved to the schools, choosing from a centrally approved list. By the end of the decade, ten publishers were sharing the market.

A result of a general government policy of economic liberalization, lobbying by a newly formed book publishers' association and pressure from the principal funder of a primary-level textbook provision scheme, the United States Agency for International Aid (USAID).

About US$20 million was spent under the project between 1993 and 1997 and publishers responded with vigour. Sales representatives combed the countryside, visiting schools and addressing teachers' meetings no easy job in a country with more than 8,000 government-aided primary schools, many of them in remote areas with poor roads.

Local publishers built sales and skills. Some mutually beneficial joint ventures developed with foreign partners. The quality of textbooks improved. Publishers from abroad set up offices employing local people. Bookshops expanded from five in Kampala in 1990 to twenty-five and others upcountry publishers met teachers directly to offer guidance in the use of their books.

The Ugandan book chain is developing, but its local base even after more than half a decade of such activity is still narrow. The number of local publishers is small, and the sales of textbooks have not yet been matched in other kinds of books. More than 90 per cent of the primary-level textbooks are still published by British-based trans nationals who have local partners that are basically only marketing agents. Most of the printing is done abroad, because local printers lack the capacity and' in a chicken-and-egg situation' cannot afford to build capacity without the lucrative textbook jobs. The government still procures textbooks centrally, consolidating orders from the various schools, and delivers them to the schools free of charge. As a result, bookstores reap no benefits, nor does the infrastructure for general publishing.

Local publishers find it difficult to obtain credit because banks are reluctant to lend money to businesses with only one customer, even if it is a government ministry. After six years of rapid development, the book sector is still heavily dependent on external inputs. Without any attempt at cost recovery, the provision of primary-level textbooks remains dependent on external funding.

The Ugandan experience is not atypical. Publishing is not an industry that can be jump-started. Capital is a particularly high barrier to local publishing development and there have been several suggestions that governments guarantee loans to publishers, as in the Dag Hammarskjold scheme, or extend cheap credit to publishers as many do to farmers for the purchase of seeds and machinery, or obtain concessional credit for publishers through the World Bank and regional development banks. Government-guaranteed loans have proved their value in the development of the Canadian publishing industry for more than twenty years.

Zimbabwe, which has a long history of liberalization in textbooks, passed an 'import substitution' regulation in 1983 which stipulated that any textbook required in a quantity of more than 1,000 copies must be locally published. In effect, foreign publishers who wanted to tap the Zimbabwean market had to license their books to a local publisher; as a result, import expenditures were reduced and the local industry was given a powerful boost.

Mozambique, recognizing that textbook shortages were too severe to be met by local development, adopted a similar policy in 1998, under which it may authorize licensing, adaptation and co-editions of books published elsewhere, but no more than 2,000 copies of any foreign book may be imported. To meet greater demand, books must arrive under the imprint of a Mozambican publisher and/or only with special permission from the Ministry of Education. Ghana encourages joint ventures between local and foreign publishers but insists that Ghanaian authors and illustrators comprise 70 per cent of any writing team and that Ghanaian printers do 60 per cent of the printing. Still, without competition at the international level, quality can suffer. A self-sustaining but complacent local industry may fossilize, as happened in Algeria.

A transition from state monopoly to private competitive provision of textbooks cannot occur without a welcoming political climate and a clear, well-designed and open policy preferably one that has been developed in consultation with the book industry. A favourable environment for commercial publishing requires decentralization of funds (or at least purchasing authority) to enable schools to select the textbooks and other resources they want to use and buy; capacity-building of new publishers to increase choice of textbooks and competition in quality and price; an objective and open system for approving textbooks for purchase; training in assessment, selection and purchasing of textbooks for school administrators and teachers; adequate information systems for procurement of textbooks; and effective commercial distribution systems.

The same authors argue that a multi-textbook system can be completely successful only if book purchasing is done at the lowest level and if all the books that are approved have an equal opportunity to be purchased.

When one publisher dominates the market, the second condition cannot be met. This has happened when the state continues to produce textbooks through a commercialized parastatal that may enjoy special benefits, such as subsidies or access to subsidized government printing, in competition with small private publishers who have difficulty in obtaining credit and raw materials. This situation has occurred in many countries of Eastern and Central Europe and in some countries of Africa.

Even when the state withdraws from publishing, the field will not necessarily be level. If local commercial publishers are unprepared to deliver textbooks in sufficient quantity and quality, transnational publishers will be quick to fill demand, as in Uganda.

Countries that use a metropolitan language for instruction are especially open to transnational domination. 'Ultimately, it will be simply a matter of who is able to develop, publish, and place the manuscripts on the market more quickly'.

Publishing in Collaboration

For nascent publishing industries, the fastest route to sustainability may be through co-operation. It may be through adaptation of a textbook produced in a neighbouring country, such as the science series developed on a Kenyan model that gave Fountain Publishers of Uganda rapid access to a newly liberalized market. Or it may be a joint venture between a local publishing house and a well-established house in an industrialized country, involving the transfer of know-how as well as capital, as happened in Jamaica, Mali, Cameroon and Namibia.

An impressive example of co-operation between local and non-local companies is the partnership of Heinemann Educational Publishers of the United Kingdom and New Namibia Books. When it began in 1990, the local partner consisted only of its owner, who had recently returned from England with no resources.

By 1997, the collaboration had produced two core textbook courses, in primary and junior secondary school science, for a country that had been almost totally dependent on South African imports. New Namibia Books had eight qualified employees and an extensive list of other books that it had developed with profits from textbooks.

Intergovernmental co-operation is also possible. In examples described above, several countries of French-speaking sub-Saharan Africa established common curricula and developed common textbooks in order to achieve economies of scale. The potential of intergovernmental co-operation was also recognized by a group of

English-speaking and Portuguese speaking policy and decision-makers, educational planners, curriculum developers and textbook development managers from ten African countries at a seminar in 1991.

They suggested co-operation was particularly appropriate for countries and island communities whose populations were too small to make the local production of school books, economical or sustainable.

Sub-regional clusters of such countries could form common examination councils and develop standardized curricula, opening possibilities for regional negotiations with publishers for bulk supply and bulk prices. Regional adoptions to achieve economies of scale in procurement were subsequently recommended for the countries of the Organization of Eastern Caribbean States. Few programmes along these lines have been implemented, however. A common textbook implies a common language of instruction, normally a metropolitan language as in the francophone example, in contrast to a trend towards use of local languages. Brunswic and Hajjar have observed, moreover, that in their experience co-operation is more difficult to develop between governmental institutions than between commercial publishers.

In principle, co-operation between publishers in neighbouring countries should be practicable. Curricula differ across borders, but in many instances are similar enough for transactional companies to adapt the textbook used in one country for adoption in another. Local publishers should be able to do the same. Co-operative ventures are impeded, however, by lack of information, poor communications, ineffective marketing, national bias, customs and tariff barriers, foreign exchange restrictions and cumbersome bureaucracies.

In higher-level subjects such as science and mathematics, imported books will probably continue to play an important role. In primary-level subjects, especially those without a major socio-cultural component, co-publication and adaptations should be expected to increase. Within Africa, the value of trade in books of all kinds between countries doubled between 1992 and 1996, and the Zimbabwe International Book Fair annually reports increasing international business. At this year's fair, just over one-third of exhibitors and visitors responding to a questionnaire said they had come to negotiate, confirm or revisit co-publishing agreements.

Until then, Jordanian statistics had been gathered centrally on an outdated mainframe computer, in flat files not easily amenable to statistical applications, in a form principally dictated by the Educational Statistics Yearbook. The Ministry of Education and twenty-three regional directorates collected their own information and held it in their own locations, usually in manual records. To complicate matters further, the identification number of each school changed every year.

The system could report gross enrolment and student flow rates, but the aggregated data could not be disaggregated for analysis or for comparison, for example, between districts or schools or between schools and an absolute standard. For the new system, personal computers were bought, relational database programmes installed, staff trained at the central and regional levels, and EMIS operations gradually transferred to the regional offices. At the end of five years, data entry time had been reduced from about six months to two weeks and the accuracy of data was substantially improved.

The Jordanian experience demonstrates that, with proper initial technical assistance and guidance, and even modest means, a developing country can improve its educational information-gathering dramatically.

Innovation in curricula is necessary to introduce new learning and new methodology. But abrupt or frequent changes can throw the textbook provision system into disarray and discourage publishers from investing in textbook development. The provincial textbook boards in Pakistan, for example, used to complain about the almost annual small revisions that issued from the federal curriculum developers in Islamabad, forcing minor but expensive changes in the textbooks published provincially. In the Philippines, a Secretary of Education decided to reinstate science as a subject in the first two primary grades just two years after his predecessor had removed it from the curriculum; science was therefore officially on the curriculum, but there were no textbooks to teach it and relatively few teachers trained to teach it without such help.

Commercial textbook publishers in particular seek stability in curricula. In order to keep the price of textbooks as low as possible, they are anxious to amortize the substantial costs of development (writing, editing, design, illustration, typesetting, and field testing) over three to five years of sales. If the curriculum changes significantly during that period, they cannot recoup their investment. If they have printed books in anticipation of sales under the old curriculum, they will have a warehouse full of unsaleable books. For these reasons, when the Philippines moved from state to commercial production of textbooks in 1995, the publishers requested and were granted a guarantee that no substantial changes would be made in the curriculum for five years.

The impact of abrupt change on commercial publishing may be seen in South Africa, where the government of Nelson Mandela made two major changes in educational structure and policy. The first was to unite the fragmented apartheid system of eighteen education departments into one national department that sets policy and nine provincial departments that are responsible for operations.

The second was to promulgate a new curriculum that is outcomes-based, a radical shift from the authoritarian system that existed under apartheid. The new curriculum was to be introduced at the rate of two grades per year. The schedule was stretched out subsequently, but publishers initially set out to develop, write, design and produce textbooks for Grades I and 7 in just 18 months and to do so in most, if not all, of the eleven official languages. That they achieved as much as they did was remarkable, although most were forced to cut back to three to five languages besides English and Africans.

When the date for implementation in Grade 7 was deferred, publishers were faced with development costs but no sales. There were problems with the selection and authorization of textbooks, in part because of inadequate training of evaluators and in part because of bureaucratic rigidity, and decisions were inconsistent between and within provinces.

Books were often delivered after the beginning of the school year. Budgets for buying books were far less than expected. The government had promised a free and equal education for all children up to Grade 9, with a book on every child's desk; in fact, however, the money for textbook acquisition dropped more than 80 per cent between 1996 and 1998 as the bulk of the educational budget was consumed by increased teachers' salaries, and a promised increase in 1999 fell far below what was required.

The consequences to what had been a well-established and confident publishing industry have been devastating. Companies faced with high overhead costs for the development of new textbooks and severely reduced markets have started retrenching. An estimated 44 per cent of the educational publishing industry has been lost in the last eighteen months a demonstration of the fragility of an industry that depends upon a single customer.

State purchase of textbooks for free distribution through the schools is desirable to ensure equity in education, but few of the countries surveyed have been able to meet a target textbook: pupil ratio of l:l or 1:2 throughout their jurisdiction or to sustain that level even with external assistance. To maintain free distribution, the state must commit funds annually to production or purchase, distribution, warehousing and supervision.

Few have been willing to do so in the requisite amounts and budgetary shortfalls usually affect the districts already most disadvantaged. Both Jamaica and Mexico did achieve the target during the early 1990s, but at the cost of inferior books in Jamaica and ballooning cumulative expenditures in Mexico. Furthermore, free distribution discourages private booksellers who are the key to continuing literacy and engenders a belief that books should never be paid for. Even politicians begin to consider books free commodities.

Unless a state has the both the tax base and the political will to allocate sufficient amounts of public money for the provision of learning materials, it will continue to be dependent on external support or have to attempt some form of cost recovery. Both may be necessary.

The state can relieve itself of all or part of the financial burden of textbook provision by expecting families to pay for the text-books their children use, just as they may be expected to pay for uniforms or work books. This approach penalizes the disadvantaged. Poor families may not be able to afford to buy textbooks and families living in remote areas may have no access to them for lack of retail outlets stocking them.

Families may have to choose which children to educate, usually at the expense of girls. They may also discriminate between subjects, buying textbooks only in those subjects that seem most likely to lead directly to future employment. This system does encourage private bookselling and instils the book buying habit. Governments can subsidize the cost of production to reduce the cost to families, as happened in Cote d'Ivoire after the radical devaluation of the CFA franc.

Book rental schemes, in which books owned by the state or school are lent to students for the school year on payment of a fee, reduce the cost to families because the cost of the books can be amortized over three or more years. It is possible, moreover, to allocate funds to the schools so they can buy textbooks and learning materials through local booksellers, thus supporting the retail part of the book chain. The system is a compromise between state purchase and family purchase with benefits of both, but requires durable books, safe storage between school years and educational staff trained to handle money, manage stock and supervise loans.

It works only if the fees go into a revolving fund, the fund is used only to replace worn-out or obsolete materials, the books last as long as expected, teachers and children are trained in book care and repair, few copies are lost or stolen, book prices and enrolments do not rise abruptly, revisions to the curriculum are not too frequent and families can pay the rental fee. The system is usually cost-effective, given that the cost of a book that will last for three to five years is probably no more than 50 per cent greater than the cost of the same book produced with poorer paper and binding that will last only one year.

However, book rental was found to be a less than perfect solution in a study of representative primary-level public schools, urban and rural, in Guinea. Only 32 per cent of the books available in the schools were actually rented to pupils. Most of the pupils came from poor families, or families that were illiterate in French.

The parents already had to spend money for exercise books, pencils and other school expenses, all at the beginning of the school year. Some parents were reluctant to spend a substantial amount of money for books that might be lost or damaged by their children.

Problems have also arisen with late payment of fees and accountability in financial management, as reported, inter alia, in a forthcoming ADEA publication, Financing Textbooks and Training Materials in Africa. One consultant with considerable international experience suggests that revolving funds work best in small discrete communities where the disbursement and accounting pathways are relatively short, as at the school or local level or in small island nation. Once again, the government can reduce the cost to families, this time by annual grants to the revolving fund.

Many projects in support of textbook provision have subsidized the supplier usually the government in ways that have either reinforced a state monopoly or distorted the market. Subsidies for production, whether in cash or in materials such as paper, tend to mask the real costs of production. Unless special care is taken, they result in prices that cannot be maintained if external assistance ends. They can help to solve short-term problems if applied with care, but may have no positive long-term results. In general, subsidies should be applied only to the one-time costs that are incurred before printing begins.

Subsidization of state monopolies has usually in the past reinforced the monopoly without building sustainability. Subsidization of individual (possibly state-owned or parastatal) publishers in a competitive market has given the recipients a competitive advantage and discouraged the entry of other publishers.

Subsidizing the supplier may, moreover, prove ineffective if the subsidy is inadequate. Read reports that in one country where books were sold, supply-side subsidies succeeded in reducing the cost of the textbooks by half, but sales did not increase; the books had simply been made cheaper for the elite who could afford them already.

Increasingly, funders are turning to demand-side subsidies as a more effective way to assist in the provision of textbooks. The subsidization becomes more effective the further down the education ladder it reaches. Direct subsidies to parents or pupils help to keep the cost to them of textbooks low and open opportunities for competition among publishers without creating market distortions. If it is impractical to provide subsidise to families, the money may be given to individual schools; and if that is impossible, selection can be placed in the hands of the schools even if the responsibility for finances and procurement is at a higher level.

Under a scheme supported by the International Development Association, for example, stipends are paid to young women in Bangladesh who are preparing for the secondary school certificate. Education among women in Bangladesh is among the lowest in the world and access to the examination had been restricted to those who could afford examination fees, stationery and private tutoring. The stipend includes a book allowance and also covers tuition, school fees, uniforms, shoes, umbrellas, transportation and other costs.

Stipends are paid twice a year into bank accounts in the names of the students, who thus also learn to manage money. Parents must agree that their daughters will attend school for at least 75 per cent of the school year, a condition that recognizes that about 90 per cent of rural girls work as household helpers. The students must obtain at least second-class marks and remain unmarried until they earn the secondary school certificate. A similar scheme is under way in Guatemala.

Alternatively, supply-side subsidies are being targeted directly to disadvantaged populations. The development of local-language textbooks for minority groups in China and Mexico was mentioned in Part III. In both the Philippines and Bangladesh, ADB is funding textbook provision only in the poorest provinces, leaving it to the national government to fund free provision elsewhere in the country. Namibia introduced a policy of positive discrimination in 1998 under which it provides textbooks, posters, maps, wall charts and encyclopedias to disadvantaged schools.

Advances have been made in respect to gender equity and sensitivity to minority groups, but much remains to be done. Some ministries of education have established social content guidelines for the authors, publishers and evaluators of textbooks. Even when efforts are made, however, stereotypes slip past.

In Zambia, textbook writers included many examples of role reversal and balance, and female assertiveness. But in one book a man and a woman are still seen introducing themselves by saying 'I am a man' and 'I am a woman', the man with his hands hanging freely at the side, the woman with hands cupped in a posture of general deference.

The provision of textbooks in local languages is a matter of pedagogical as well as social concern, for programmes that teach people in their own language have been proved to be more effective in both Latin America and Africa than those using the language of a former colonial power. Where local languages are extensively used, as Hausa is in Nigeria, the economics of local language publication are manageable. For small language groups, the problems are more formidable because the print runs are so much smaller.

There may be additional difficulties in securing type faces for special scripts, or in agreement on orthography, or in finding writers and editors with the requisite knowledge of subject and language. There is, however, considerable scope for South-South co-operation, building on experience in the Pacific and elsewhere, and in the late 1990s there has been renewed interest in Africa in publishing in cross-border languages.

Training of Teachers

In the concern over the inadequate provision of textbooks and learning materials, too little attention has been paid to the use of those materials and the continuing training of teachers in their use. Generally, pre-service training should be reinforced by in-service training through various channels and by school inspectors. Some countries have tried to establish resource centres to help teachers improve the learning environment in their classrooms; others have established teacher clusters to provide peer support and in-service training. Not all such initiatives have been maintained, however. When teachers fail to use books well, they deprive themselves and their pupils of a fundamental tool for promoting reading.

In particular, pre-service training in many countries fails to give due emphasis to the preparation and use of teaching and learning aids. This failure may result from lack of hours in the programme, or the inadequacy of teacher trainers in this area, or both. Creative teachers, properly trained and motivated, can overcome a lack of professionally produced materials by making their own teaching and learning aids, often with the help of the pupils or even community members. Parents do not have to be literate to participate, as long as the meaningfulness of the work is clearly explained.

Nevertheless, few teachers in the eight countries in the UNESCO/Danida case-study survey made any effort to make teaching and learning aids, even though they seemed aware of their importance. Jamaica was the only country in which a majority of teachers made their own aids and involved children in the activity.

Locally made aids are most likely to be appropriate for the needs and experience of the children concerned. Their value does not, however, remove government's responsibility for providing both educational materials of good quality and in service training in the preparation and use of teaching and learning aids. Training programmes in future must also prepare teachers to use many forms of educational technology and techniques, both traditional and non-traditional, including electronic media, music, dance, drama, folk theatre, newspapers and games.

Teachers will also have to become increasingly aware of intellectual property rights, in particular with respect to material found on the Internet. In Africa, Asia, Latin America, and Central and Eastern Europe, teachers have proved reluctant to use new textbooks, especially those embodying new methods. Those accustomed to a jingle 'official' textbook tend to stick with it even when other books are approved and available. Human nature is essentially conservative, but is more so than normally when people are under qualified and insecure.

Where competition among textbook publishers is active and the publishers experienced, the publishers undertake the training of teachers in the use of the materials they have for sale. That is part of their marketing. Where the state is the provider and in-service training is inadequate (as it frequently is), this important stage in the introduction of new materials is too often ignored, as is constructive supervision of teachers by principals and school inspectors.

In the Republic of Korea, reluctance to use new textbooks surfaced when a new curriculum in the national language was introduced that changed the emphasis in teaching from repetition and detailed reading of set passages to speaking, listening, and writing. The single textbook in Korean that had been used at each level was replaced by a set of three and the number of pages doubled. The change was made after wide consultation, research and pilot testing, but the teachers resisted it, complaining that they now had more content to cover without an increase in the time available. Over several years, they gradually changed their opinion and recognized the value of the new books.

That change coincided with a change in teaching methods towards individualized instruction. The experience demonstrated that it is easier to change textbooks than teachers' preferences and habit. In contrast, teachers in Kazakhstan were given intensive training in the methods incorporated in a new generation of textbooks and are reported to have welcomed the new materials with enthusiasm (UNESCO/Danida case-studies: Kazakhstan).

The parallel trends towards multiple choice in textbooks and decentralization place parallel responsibilities on the state. The first is to ensure that all the books bought with public money, or recommended by the schools for purchase by families, meet minimum standards. There must be a process of evaluation and authorization that is not only objective and thorough, but can be demonstrated to have these qualities. This in turn requires a governing board with some members from outside the Ministry of Education, a set of uniform standards, a corps of trained evaluators including teachers from different parts of the country, open invitations to submit manuscripts, procedures that guarantee anonymity in submissions and confidentiality for the names and reports of the evaluators, and full and rapid reporting to publishers.

The South African criteria for selection have been described by one publisher as often seeming arbitrary and sometimes bizarre. In the Philippines, publishers complained that approvals were not only inconsistent but that evaluators tended to reject textbooks that exceeded the minimum learning competencies.

The director of the government body that supervises evaluation admitted that evaluators were sometimes appointed through friendship rather than merit and that there had not been enough time to train them.

The second responsibility of the state is to ensure that teachers and principals who have been empowered to select books can make well-informed choices. At a minimum, each school must have a full list of the textbooks and other learning materials that have been authorized for use. If possible, the list should be annotated as a guide to teachers, especially those in remote areas that may receive few visits from publishers' representatives. The notes might point, for example, to textbooks specially designed for rural schools or for the needs of minority groups. Teachers and principals (who may have the final say in any selection) must be provided with suggested criteria for choosing among textbooks and the skills of selection should become a regular part of in-service training and the training of new teachers.

Experience suggests that this is the point at which devolution of selection breaks down, especially when the transition from monopoly to choice is abrupt. Teachers who are accustomed to a single textbook throughout their career, and who may be poorly qualified in many of the subjects they teach, are ill prepared for this new responsibility. Where educational structures have traditionally been hierarchical, teachers and principals tend to be influenced in their selection by their superiors. There is no evidence that any country undergoing liberalization has adequately met the challenge.

Process of Decentralization

Under state provision, the preparation and publishing of textbooks cannot be abruptly devolved from the central administration to regional or provincial offices without taking into account local capacities. In Ethiopia, under a new policy of decentralization, regional educational bureau were given the mandate for developing new primary-level textbooks. Few regions had the trained staff to produce camera-ready copy or the printing capacity to produce the books. As a result, all regions except the national capital returned the production of English-language textbooks to the Institute of Curriculum Development and Research, which in turn had a British adviser do most of the writing. In other subjects, in general, one textbook was written centrally and translated into the ten other languages of instruction. This in effect neutralized the expected benefits of local preparation and production. The books were all printed in Addis Ababa.

Distribution Hassles

The physical difficulties of distribution of textbooks to the schools will not disappear. It will always be arduous and expensive to reach remote areas. In urban areas where access is easy and the market is large and concentrated, distribution is estimated to account for 25 to 30 per cent of the cost of a textbook; in remote areas, distribution may cost twice as much as the textbook itself.

In many countries where the state is responsible for distribution, public funds have proved inadequate to the task. The last part of the journey, from district or regional warehouses, has usually been left to the initiative of individuals' inspectors, principals, teachers and parents using whatever means of transportation are available.

The Discrepancies in the Textbook : Pupil ratio between urban and rural schools throughout much of the world testify to the failures of the system. Occasionally, the army has carried books to remote areas by helicopter. Distribution by the state has been hampered as well by human failings that should be amenable to improvement. Books have been damaged because they were inadequately wrapped or stored in insecure locations. Systems for estimating needs, accounting for inventory and recording shipments have been poorly designed or maintained.

Consolidation of orders for economy has resulted in delays when one title of several was late in delivery. Books have been slipped from central warehouses months after the school year began because there was not enough staff or money to do better. Large-scale textbook projects have not always allowed adequately for the recurrent costs of distribution. Some of these problems can be reduced by decentralizing book procurement.

Distribution through the private sector faces many of these hurdles and is further hindered by the lack of retail outlets in rural areas. Supplementary materials will be stocked only selectively, because few shop owners have the capital to hold large inventories of slow-selling goods. If there is sufficient profit to be made, however, retail outlets will spread not necessarily bookshops, more likely shops that sell stationery and other dry goods that would, for a few months of the year, stock text-books promising a rapid turnover and relatively stable market. The ubiquity of certain soft drinks proves that profitable goods will find even the most remote markets.

Social Factors

The editors of a recent World Bank publication on curbing corruption observe that 'corruption is a pervasive phenomenon that can be found in countries of widely varying ideology economic conditions and social development.' They continue: Although some societies may be more vulnerable than others and may suffer more devastating effects, no country in the world today is immune from corruption's corrosive influence. Yet for all its seeming prevalence, there is no clear evidence that corruption has become more widespread today. It has been around, in one form or another, from the earliest days of social organization. What has changed is that information about corrupt practices has become more available as governments have been increasingly unable to conceal evidence of wrongdoing; the level of public tolerance for corruption has declined; and the spread of democracy seems to afford less fertile ground in which corruption can flourish.

They go on to say that malfeasance, in general, is most likely to occur where the public and private sectors meet, as they do in public procurement, contracting and licensing activities that relate directly to textbooks and other materials used in government-supported schools. Those who award contracts or procure goods may demand bribes, kickbacks, percentages or other 'gifts' from those seeking government business and sales. At a more petty level, underpaid and greedy civil servants demand their own bribes and in turn must often pay their superiors for the privilege of holding public office.

This should come as no surprise, but the potential for corruption in providing learning materials may astonish even a nation accustomed to abuses of power. After the private sector took over the provision of learning materials to the public schools of the Philippines in 1998, the newspapers carried sensational stories of bribery and misuse of funds, involving all levels of government from minor clerks to congressmen and, in one instance, the office of the president. Increased funding for learning materials has simply increased the amount of bribery, according to the reports.

Funds were diverted from textbooks to supplementary materials that carry a higher mark-up and a higher rate of bribery, despite declining text-book: pupil ratios. A new undersecretary of education has instituted various internal controls and stringent bidding procedures that he predicts will double the number of books for the country's public schools, but he admits that no system is entirely foolproof and some abuses will occur.

Abuse of another kind occurs when a cartel of suppliers forces the government to negotiate with it for want of any other source of goods. This happened in Bangladesh, where the textbooks for government schools were produced by more than 400 small printers. The government adopted an open bidding procedure to meet funder's requirements, but ultimately acceded to the cartel because no single member of it could produce all the country's needs alone. Printers who have large and largely under-used web presses do not bid for textbooks for fear of industrial action by the small printers that would close them down.

The president of Transparency International suggests four types of strategy to reduce corruption. The first is to work within the underlying structure of government programmes and focus on improving government integrity, enforcing the existing law, designing effective penalties for bribers and bribe-takers, and developing international support mechanisms. The second is to reform the procedural basis of government to increase transparency and discourage corruption.

The third is to address government programmes that may give rise to corruption because they are poorly designed or unnecessary for example, by standardizing specifications, limiting discretion of civil servants and establishing new public-interest criteria for bidding. The fourth is to encourage self-regulation within the private sector and changes in public attitudes concerning accountability and transparency.

The International Commission on Education for the Twenty-first Century argued that one of the main aims of educational reform should be to involve stakeholders in decision-making. Decentralization, it said, would encourage innovation and participation by all. It would also allow further consideration to be given to the cultural and linguistic aspirations of minority groups and it could enhance the relevance of education through carefully worked out appropriate programs.

It has been suggested that funds generally are used more efficiently the closer decision-making is to the actual user of the material. O'Connor argues that corruption is inevitable when there is only one customer for textbooks, as in centralized procurement by the state: 'The most effective influence on the purchase decision of a sole customer is not quality of product or value for money but the size of a more or less overt 'commission' to persons of influence . . . All textbooks publishers, both indigenous and international, in countries where centralized textbook approval and purchasing systems operate are compelled to adopt these practices . . . they cannot do otherwise; it is a matter of marketplace survival, not business ethics.'

She agrees that the most positive effects of donor provided textbooks seem to occur when the process of selection is at the lowest possible rung of the education system. Parents' associations can act as watchdogs to ensure that money allocated to schools is spent appropriately and in response to the community's needs.

In Bolivia, for example, community participation and decentralization are considered essential parts of the national educational reform, not only to encourage respect for cultural diversity and multilingual education, but also to help curb corruptions by providing a channel for social censure. The school community has been involved in demand-side financing of textbook provision in Armenia and Guinea, helping to decide which families or students are neediest and should receive financial assistance. A similar strategy has been proposed in Cambodia.

Decentralization is far from a perfect answer, of course. Brick-hill and Priestley recognize that, especially in rural areas, books and reading are not part of the social and cultural life, which may limit the effectiveness of local surveillance of book acquisitions. Pope warns that efforts to reduce corruption by decentralizing can backfire badly unless a strong and honest team is appointed to oversee and audit public procurement. Even the strongest advocates of stakeholder participation acknowledge that civil society is a player in corruption, although it is also the major victim.

But Kisubi, a former senior adviser to the Ministry of Public Works in Uganda, argues that where genuine anti corruption attempts have failed, one ingredient has invariably been missing, and that is the involvement of civil society. Any attempt to develop an anti-corruption strategy that neglects fully to involve civil society, he says, is neglecting one of the most potentially useful tools available.

Teaching Aids

Everything that has been learned from experience with textbooks applies also to the other kinds of learning materials. Indeed, even more vigilance may be necessary because of the wide range of supplementary materials and the much more limited resources available to buy them.

The benefits of careful planning in the purchase of books for school libraries has been demonstrated in Bolivia. The country has 32 languages, of which 3 are major. In 1995, it began building classroom and school libraries for 11,000 urban and rural schools and for 1,800 resource centres where teachers could be trained and exchange information. Each classroom library under the scheme contains 45 titles, one-third of them produced locally. Each school library contains 10 reference books and each resource centre, 150 titles. In all, nearly 6.5 million books were acquired through competitive bidding. Procurement followed several stages. A year before bidding was announced, the Ministry of Education made contact with more than 100 publishing houses in the Spanish-speaking world. In response to the call for bids, 120 publishing houses from 16 countries submitted proposals. About 5,000 sample books were received and reviewed by 50 readers, all classroom teachers. After six months, 798 books were selected for further review, this time by schoolchildren, parents and teachers at book fairs in three regions.

The number of selected titles was winnowed to 730, at which point their 51 publishers were asked to submit prices. Ultimately, 370 titles from 48 publishers were bought in quantities of 1,800 to 22,000 copies. About one-tenth of the titles were translations from Spanish into one of the main indigenous languages. To ensure that a reasonable number of Bolivian authors would be included, the Ministry organized a national literary contest, paid for first-time rights to the 123 winning manuscripts and edited them for publication.

The value of Bolivia's multi-stage strategy can be seen by comparing its results to similar projects in Chile, where only 16 publishers participated, and in Peru, where 24 did. School libraries are expensive to build and maintain. They require basic storage facilities, pre-service and in-service training of teacher-librarians, and efficient systems of distribution, management, inspection and supervision. Book box libraries have proved more cost-effective in some projects.

National agencies have been started in some countries to direct and assist the development of school libraries by providing training, books and advice. These school library services began in Africa with independence but, despite initial enthusiasm for the concept, they have failed to maintain their early promise.

The activities of those that were established in Ghana, the United Republic of Tanzania, and Nigeria declined; in some other countries, a service was planned but never came into being. Finances have been blamed for the failure, but indifference was also a factor.

In oil-rich Nigeria of the 1980s, for example, money went to tertiary-level libraries but not to school libraries. School library services that were located in the National Library rather than the Ministry of Education proved less effective because they did not have the strong support of educational administrators. Others failed because they did not gain the support of teachers, who did not recognize the value of libraries and who were focused on formal instruction based on the textbook.

Computers and other instruments that are common in the industrialized countries are beyond the budgets and the infrastructure of much of the world. The use of new educational technologies normally depends on reliable, high quality telecommunications connections, which are seldom found in developing countries. Even where they are available, the countries may lack the necessary pedagogical and technical support to implement programmes successfully. Many respondents to the AREA/ UNESCO survey dismissed non print media as irrelevant while textbooks and other basic learning materials remain scarce.

The lessons taught in school will dissipate if there nothing to support them outside the classroom. Continuing literacy requires a literate community, which in turn will enable people to continue learning. The availability of books and other printed material leads to social and political awareness and to continuous self-learning in practical matters such as health, nutrition, agricultural practices and small business operations. In countries in which the book trade has been destroyed by war or economic collapse, in many countries of Africa, and in remote regions everywhere, the need is great.

Henry Chakava, a distinguished Kenyan publisher, has said that 'There is talk in the North about a 'bookless' society, meaning a post-book society, while for us in Africa 'bookless' societies are indeed 'pre-book societies.' It is difficult with donor funding to increase access to written materials in everyday life, but funding agencies and civil society organizations are making the effort.

The Swedish International Development Co-operation Authority (Silo) has had a broad programme for support of a literate environment, ranging from the supply of Braille presses to workshops for writers of literacy materials and the development and production of supplementary readers, science kits and radio programmes. It has supported the various links in the book chain, from the collection and publication of oral literature, through writing and publishing, to promotional events such as book weeks and book fairs.

It has helped to fund libraries and reading rooms in Botswana, Ethiopia, Mozambique, Nicaragua and the United Republic of Tanzania, language projects in Sierra Leone, Zimbabwe, the Lao People's Democratic Republic and Panama, and authors and authors' organizations such as PEN International. It has bought and distributed children's books, and has supported libraries, reading campaigns and the training of librarians and teachers in Gaza and the West Bank. It has also supported adult literacy and post-literacy classes, often with accompanying assistance to village reading rooms, rural newspapers, and other materials for new-literates.

The Children's Book Project in the United Republic of Tanzania directly addressed the absence of books for children in a country where even textbooks in rural schools were scarce.

To encourage the development of local writing and publishing, in 1991 it launched the buy-back scheme mentioned in Part III, guaranteeing to purchase 3,000 copies of selected new children's titles if the publisher would put at east another, 2,000 copies on the open market. The 3,000 copies were distributed to rural libraries and primary schools, and their purchase was just enough to ensure the publisher a return on the initial investment; the additional copies sold would be profitable.

The project was conceived by CODE and supported by Sida, Danida, the Netherlands Embassy. The British Council, the Canada Fund and the Aga Khan Foundation. The project included training courses for writers, publishers, editors and illustrators. Ninety titles were produced by twenty-seven publishers and several were reprinted. The infusion of 270,000 books into rural areas created a demand for more. There were problems m the implementation, but a review team in 1995 recommended further support and the participating donors considered it one of the most successful publishing initiatives in Africa.

In India the Rajiv Gandhi Foundation is building networks of village libraries and stocking them with books and newspapers in the local language. The libraries are run by village committees that are responsible for providing suitable premises fox the library, identifying a librarian, and general financial management. They are expected to become financially self-sustaining through low membership fees municipal grants, and donations.

The foundation supplies initial financing, furniture, training for the librarian and a collection of about 400 books, chosen with community assistance. Efforts are made to integrate the collection with other local rural development projects, Books are lent among libraries to obtain diversity at minimum cost.

The libraries are intended to lend books for reading at home. There is not enough accommodation in most villages for reading rooms and there is concern that women might hesitate to use a reading room that becomes a place where men congregate. In Egypt, Mme Suzan Mubarak, the wife of the president, initiated a national project called 'Reading for All' in 1990, to encourage reading among schoolchildren during their summer vacation. Children win awards for reading in various subjects, competitions are held among schools, simplified low cost books are published in a 'Family Library' and mobile libraries provide access to book in remote villages.

Additional Reading

Bhaskara Rao, Digumarti (1994). *Scientific Aptitude,* New Delhi: Ashish Publishing House. ISBN 81-7024-658-X.

Bhaskara Rao, Digumarti (1995). *Animal Kingdom.* New Delhi: Discovery Publishing House. ISBN 81-7141-274-2.

Bhaskara Rao, Digumarti (1995). *Batracology.* New Delhi: Discovery Publishing House. ISBN 81-7141-279-3.

Bhaskara Rao, Digumarti (1997), *Scientific Attitude.* New Delhi: Discovery Publishing House. ISBN 81-7141-308-0.

Bhaskara Rao, Digumarti (1996). *Scientific Attitude vis-à-vis Scientific Aptitude.* New Delhi: Discovery Publishing House. ISBN 81-7141-308-0.

Bhaskara Rao, Digumarti, Editor (1996). *Encyclopaedia of Education for All,* 5 Volumes. New Delhi: APH Publishing Corporation. ISBN 81-7024-759-4 (set).

- Vol. I *Education for All: The World Conference.* ISBN 81-7024-760-8.
- Vol. II *Education for All: The EPA-9 Summit.* ISBN 81-7024-761-6.
- Vol. III *Education for All: Quality Education for All.* ISBN 81-7024-762-6.
- Vol. IV *Education for All: Planning and Monitoring.* ISBN 81-7024-763-4.
- Vol. V *Education for All: The Indian Scenario.* ISBN 81-7024-764-0.

Bhaskara Rao, Digumarti, Editor (1996). *Global Perceptions on Peace Education,* 3 Volumes. New Delhi: Discovery Publishing House. ISBN 81-7141-319-6.

Bhaskara Rao, Digumarti, Editor (1996). *National Policy on Education*. 2 Volumes. New Delhi: Anmol Publications Pvt. Ltd. ISBN 81-7488-323-1.

Bhaskara Rao, Digumarti, Editor (1997). *Care the Child*, 2 Volumes. New Delhi: Discovery Publishing House. ISBN 81-7141-394-3.

Bhaskara Rao, Digumarti, Editor (1997). *Education for the 21st Century*. New Delhi: Discovery Publishing House. ISBN 81-7141-389-7.

Bhaskara Rao, Digumarti, Editor (1997). *Reflections on Scientific Attitude*. New Delhi: Discovery Publishing House, ISBN 81-7141-319-6.

Bhaskara Rao, Digumarti, Editor (1997). *Success Story of a Primary Education Project*. New Delhi: APH Publishing Corporation. ISBN 81-7024-850-7.

Bhaskara Rao, Digumarti, Editor (1997). *World Food Summit*. New Delhi: Discovery Publishing House. ISBN 81-7141-386-2.

Bhaskara Rao, Digumarti, Editor (1998). *Adolescence Education*. New Delhi: Discovery Publishing House. ISBN 81-7141-432-X.

Bhaskara Rao, Digumarti, Editor (1998). *Community and School Nutrition Education*. New Delhi: Discovery Publishing House. ISBN 81-7141-435-4.

Bhaskara Rao, Digumarti, Editor (1998). *District Primary Education Programme*. New Delhi: Discovery Publishing House. ISBN 81-7141-396-X.

Bhaskara Rao, Digumarti, Editor (1998). *Earth Summit*, 2 Volumes. New Delhi: Discovery Publishing House. ISBN 81-7141-435-4.

Bhaskara Rao, Digumarti, Editor (1998). *National Policy on Education: Towards an Enlightened and Humane Society*, New Delhi: Discovery Publishing House. ISBN 81-7141-426-5.

Bhaskara Rao, Digumarti, Editor (1998). *Reforming School Education*. New Delhi: Discovery Publishing House. ISBN 81-7141-403-6.

Bhaskara Rao, Digumarti, Editor (1998). *Teacher Education in India*. New Delhi: Discovery Publishing House. ISBN 81-7141-406-0.

Bhaskara Rao, Digumarti, Editor (1998). *World Summit for Social Development*. New Delhi: Discovery Publishing House. ISBN 81-7141-420-6.

Bhaskara Rao, Digumarti, Editor (2000). *Education for All: Achieving the Goal*, 3 Volumes, New Delhi: APH Publishing Corporation. ISBN 81-7648-152-1.

Vol. I *The Global Consensus*. ISBN 81-7648-155-6.

Vol. II *Mid-Decade Review Reports of Regional Seminars*. ISBN 81-7648-154-8.

Vol. III *Issues and Trends*. ISBN 81-7648-155-6.

Bhaskara Rao, Digumarti, Editor (2000), *International Encyclopaedia of AIDS*, 11 Volumes in 13 Parts. New Delhi: Discovery Publishing House. ISBN 81-7141-6 (Set).

Vol. 1 *Introduction to HIV/AIDS*. ISBN 81-7141-523-7.

Vol. 2 *HIV/AIDS—Issues and Challenges*, 2 Parts. ISBN 81-7141-524-5.

Vol. 3 *HIV/AIDS—Socio Economic Realities*. ISBN 81-7141-524-3.

Vol. 4 *HIV/AIDS—Law Ethics and Human Rights*, 2 Parts. ISBN 81-7141-526-1.

Vol. 5 *AIDS and NGOs*. ISBN 81-7141-527-X.

Vol. 6 *AIDS and Home Care*. ISBN 81-7141-528-8.

Vol. 7 *STD Case Management*. ISBN 81-7141-529-6.

Vol. 8 *HIV/AIDS Prevention and Care—Teaching Modules for Nurses and Midwives*. ISBN 81-7141-530-X.

Vol. 9 *HIV Prevention Education for Education for Educational Institutions*. ISBN 81-7141-531-8.

Vol. 10 *Instructional Modules for AIDS Education*. ISBN 81-7141-532-6.

Vol. 11 *School Health Education to Prevent AIDS and STD—A Package for Curriculum Planners*. ISBN 81-7141-5338-4.

Bhaskara Rao, Digumarti, Editor (2000). *International Encyclopaedia of Science and Technology Education*, 11 Volumes. New Delhi: Discovery Publishing House. ISBN 81-7141-548-2 (Set).

Vol. 1 *Science and Technology Education*. ISBN 81-7141-568-7.

Vol. 2 *Science Education in Developing Countries*. ISBN 81-7141-570-9.

Vol. 3 *Organisational Structure of Science*. ISBN 81-7141-570-9.

Vol. 4 *Science Education in Asia and the Pacific*. ISBN 81-7141-571-7.

Vol. 5 *Science and Technology Education for All*. ISBN 81-7141-572-5.

Vol. 6 *Values, Ethics, Talent and Girls in Science and Technology Education*. ISBN 81-7141-573-3.

Vol. 7 *Popularization of Science and Technology Education*. ISBN 81-7141-574-1.

Vol. 8 *Science, Power and Society*. ISBN 81-7141-575-X.

Vol. 9 *Information Technology*. ISBN 81-7141-576-8.

Vol. 10 *Teacher Training in Science and Technology Education*. ISBN 81-7141-577-6.

Vol. 11 *Teacher Training in Science and Technology: A Curriculum Framework*. ISBN 81-7141-578-4.

Bhaskara Rao, Digumarti, Editor (2001). *Distance Education in Different Countries*. New Delhi: APH Publishing Corporation. ISBN 81-7648-229-3.

Bhaskara Rao, Digumarti, Editor (2001). *Decentralised Management of Education (Management of Education in Panchayati Raj and Municipal Bodies)*. New Delhi: Discovery Publishing House. ISBN 81-7141-617-9.

Bhaskara Rao, Digumarti, Editor (2001). *Electrochemistry for Environmental Protection*. New Delhi: Discovery Publishing House. ISBN 81-7141-619-5.

Bhaskara Rao, Digumarti, Editor (2001). *Global Educational Studies*. New Delhi: Discovery Publishing House. ISBN 81-7141-616-0.

Bhaskara Rao, Digumarti, Editor (2001). *Global Synthesis of Educational Assessment*. New Delhi: Discovery Publishing House. ISBN 81-7141-613-6.

Bhaskara Rao, Digumarti, Editor (2000). *International Encyclopaedia of Human Rights*. 7 Volumes in 13 Parts. New Delhi: Discovery Publishing House. (Royal Size). ISBN 81-7141-567-9 (Set).

Vol. 1 *International Instruments of Human Rights*, 2 Parts. ISBN 81-7141-595-4.

Vol. 2 *Regional Instruments of Human Rights*. ISBN 81-7141-604-7.

Vol. 3 *Human Rights and the United Nations*, 2 Parts. ISBN 81-7141-605-5.

Vol. 4 *Fact Files of Human Rights*, 3 Parts. ISBN 81-7141-605-3.

Vol. 5 *Study Stories of Human Rights*, 3 Parts. ISBN 81-7141-607-3.

Vol. 6 *International Meetings on Human Rights*, 2 Parts. ISBN 81-7141-608-X.

Vol. 7 *Professional Training in Human Rights*. ISBN 81-7141-609-8.

Bhaskara Rao, Digumarti, Editor (2001). *Jomtein Decade of Education*. New Delhi: Discovery Publishing House. ISBN 81-7141-618-7.

Bhaskara Rao, Digumarti, Editor (2001). *Nuclear Materials: Issues and Concerns*, 2 Volumes. New Delhi: Discovery Publishing House. ISBN 81-7141-611-X.

Bhaskara Rao, Digumarti, Editor (2001). *World Conference on Education for All*. New Delhi: APH Publishing Corporation. ISBN 81-7141-274-9.

Bhaskara Rao, Digumarti, Editor (2001). *World Conference on Higher Education*, New Delhi: Discovery Publishing House. ISBN 81-7141-610-1.

Bhaskara Rao, Digumarti, Editor (2001). *World Conference on Science*. New Delhi: Discovery Publishing House. ISBN 81-7141-612-8.

Bhaskara Rao, Digumarti, Editor (2003). *Inspiring Experience in Teacher Education*. New Delhi: Discovery Publishing House. ISBN 81-7141-656-X.

Bhaskara Rao, Digumarti, Editor (2003). *International Studies in Education*, 3 Volumes, New Delhi: Discovery Publishing House. ISBN 81-7141-647-0.

Bhaskara Rao, Digumarti, Editor (2003). *Military Conversion: Impact on Science and Technology*, New Delhi: Discovery Publishing House. ISBN 81-7141-578-4.

Bhaskara Rao, Digumarti, Editor (2003). *United Nations Millennium Summit*. New Delhi: Discovery Publishing House. ISBN 81-7141-632-2.

Bhaskara Rao, Digumarti, Editor (2003). *World Assembly on Aging*. New Delhi: Discovery Publishing House. ISBN 81-7141-637-3.

Bhaskara Rao, Digumarti, Editor (2004). *World Conference on Human Rights*. New Delhi: Discovery Publishing House. ISBN 81-7141-661-6.

Bhaskara Rao, Digumarti, Editor (2003). *World Education Forum*. New Delhi: Discovery Publishing House. ISBN 81-7141-639-X.

Bhaskara Rao, Digumarti, Editor (2004). *Education Employment and Human Resource Development*. New Delhi: Discovery Publishing House. ISBN 81-7141-681-0.

Bhaskara Rao, Digumarti, Editor (2004). *Successfully Schooling*. New Delhi: Discovery Publishing House. ISBN 81-7141-677-2.

Bhaskara Rao, Digumarti, Editor (2004). *European Education and Teachers*. New Delhi: Discovery Publishing House. ISBN 81-7141-702-7.

Bhaskara Rao, Digumarti, Editor (2004). *Teachers in a Changing World*. New Delhi: Discovery Publishing House. ISBN 81-7141-694-2.

Bhaskara Rao, Digumarti, Editor (2004). *Learning to Live Together*, 4 Volumes. New Delhi: Discovery Publishing House.

Vol. 1 *International Conference on Learning to Live Together.*

Vol. 2 *Globalisation and Living Together.*

Vol. 3 *Curriculum for Learning to Live Together.*

Vol. 4 *Science Education for the Contemporary Society.*

Bhaskara Rao, Digumarti (2004). *International Guidelines on Open and Distance Education*, New Delhi: Discovery Publishing House.

Bhaskara Rao, Digumarti, Editor (2004). *Adult Learning in the 21st Century*. New Delhi: Discovery Publishing House.

Bhaskara Rao, Digumarti, Editor (2004). *Educational Practices: Research and Recommendations*. New Delhi: Discovery Publishing House.

Bhaskara Rao, Digumarti, Editor (2004). *Chernobyl: Never Again*. New Delhi: APH Publishing Corporation.

Bhaskara Rao, Digumarti, Editor (2004). *Virology and Immunology*. New Delhi: APH Publishing Corporation.

Bhaskara Rao, Digumarti, C.A.P. Swami and B.S.V. Dutt (1997). *Self-Evaluation in Student Teaching*. New Delhi: Discovery Publishing House. ISBN 81-7141-374-9.

Bhaskara Rao, Digumarti and B.S.V. Dutt, Editors (2003). *Education: Programmes and Policies*. New Delhi: APH Publishing Corporation. ISBN 81-7648-470-9.

Bhaskara Rao, Digumarti and D. Naresh Kumar (2004). *School Teacher Effectiveness*. New Delhi: Discovery Publishing House.

Bhaskara Rao, Digumarti and D. Sridhar (2002). *Job Satisfaction of School Teachers*. New Delhi: Discovery Publishing House. ISBN 81-7141-652-7.

Bhaskara Rao, Digumarti and Digumarti Pushpa Latha (1994). *Achievement in Biology*. New Delhi: Discovery Publishing House. ISBN 81-7141-264-5.

Bhaskara Rao, Digumarti, C. Sridevi and K. Vijaya (1995). *Achievement in Social Studies*. New Delhi: Discovery Publishing House. ISBN 81-7141-281-5.

Bhaskara Rao, Digumarti and Digumarti Pushpa Latha (1995). *Achievement in English*. New Delhi: Discovery Publishing House. ISBN 81-7141-283-1.

Bhaskara Rao, Digumarti and Digumarti Pushpa Latha (1994). *Achievement in Science*. New Delhi: Discovery Publishing House. ISBN 81-7141-280-70.

Bhaskara Rao, Digumarti and Digumarti Pushpa Latha (1995). *Achievement in Mathematics*. New Delhi: Discovery Publishing House. ISBN 81-7141-278-5.

Bhaskara Rao, Digumarti and Digumarti Pushpa Latha, Editors (1998). *International Encyclopaedia of Women*. 5 Volumes. New Delhi: Discovery Publishing House. ISBN 81-7141-410-9.

Vol. 1 *Status of World's Women*. ISBN 81-7141-494-X.

Vol. 2 *Women, Education and Empowerment*. ISBN 81-7141-498-1.

Vol. 3 *Women Challenges and Advancement*. ISBN 81-7141-497-4.

Vol. 4 *Women and Family Health*. ISBN 81-7141-497-4.

Vol. 5 *Women and International Action*. ISBN 81-7141-498-2.

Bhaskara Rao, Digumarti, Digumarti Pushpa Latha and Digumarti Harshitha, Editors (2001). *Biological Warfare*. New Delhi: Discovery Publishing House. ISBN 81-7141-597-0.

Bhaskara Rao, Digumarti, Digumarti Pushpa Latha and Digumarti Harshitha, Editors (2001). *Women as Educators*. New Delhi: Discovery Publishing House. ISBN 81-7141-602-0.

Bhaskara Rao, Digumarti and Digumarti Harshitha, Editors (2001). *Education in India*. New Delhi: APH Publishing Corporation. ISBN 81-7141-207-2.

Bhaskara Rao, Digumarti, Digumarti Pushpa Latha and Digumarti Harshitha, Editors (2001). *Assessing Learning Achievement*. New Delhi: Discovery Publishing House. ISBN 81-7141-601-2.

Bhaskara Rao, Digumarti, Digumarti Pushpa Latha and Digumarti Harshitha, Editors (2001). *Energy Security*. New Delhi: Discovery Publishing House. ISBN 81-7141-598-9.

Bhaskara Rao, Digumarti, Digumarti Harshitha and K.R.S.S. Rao, Editors (1999). *Advanced Biotechnology*. New Delhi: Discovery Publishing House. ISBN 81-7141-516-4.

Bhaskara Rao, Digumarti and K.R.S. Sambhasiva Rao, Editors (1996). *Current Trends in Indian Education*. New Delhi: Discovery Publishing House. ISBN 81-7141-311-0.

Bhaskara Rao, Digumarti and K. Vijaya (1995). *A Text Book of Evaluation*. Ambala Cantt: The Associated Publishers.

Bhaskara Rao, Digumarti and N.V.M. Mohana Rao (2002). *Problems of Mentally Handicapped Children*. New Delhi: Discovery Publishing House. ISBN 81-7141-645-4.

Bhaskara Rao, Digumarti and S. Chandra Mohan (2002). *Sports Management*. New Delhi: APH Publishing Corporation. ISBN 81-7648-467-9.

Bhaskara Rao, Digumarti and Sk. Johni Basha (2004). *Teachers' Population Education Awareness*. New Delhi: APH Publishing Corporation.

Bhaskara Rao, Digumarti, V.V. Rao, V.V. Lakshmi and V.V. Krishna, Editors (1999). *Status and Advancement of Women*. New Delhi: APH Publishing Corporation. ISBN 81-7648-169-6.

..bu, P.C., Author and Digumarti Bhaskara Rao, Editor (2004). *Flowers of Wisdom*. New Delhi: Discovery Publishing House. ISBN 81-7141-695-0.

Bhagya Lakshmi, Lingineni, Author and Digumarti Bhaskara Rao, Editor (2000). *Reading and Comprehension*. New Delhi: Discovery Publishing House. ISBN 81-7141-543-1.

Bhuvaneswara Lakshmi, Gadde, Author and Digumarti Bhaskara Rao, Editor (2000). *Attitude Towards Science*. New Delhi: Discovery Publishing House. ISBN 81-7141-541-6.

..raj, T.A.S., Author and Digumarti Bhaskara Rao, Editor (1997). *Trace Analysis of Uranium and Thorium*. New Delhi: Discovery Publishing House. ISBN 81-7141-375-7.

Durga Rani, K., Author and Digumarti Bhaskara Rao, Editor (2000). *Educational Aspirations and Scientific Attitudes*. New Delhi: Discovery Publishing House. ISBN 81-7141-555-55.

Dutt, B.S.V. and Digumarti Bhaskara Rao (2001). *Empowering Primary Teachers*. New Delhi: Discovery Publishing House. ISBN 81-7141-615.2.

Ediger, Marlow and Digumarti Bhaskara Rao (1996). *Science Curriculum*. New Delhi: Discovery Publishing House. ISBN 81-7141-321-8.

Ediger, Marlow and Digumarti Bhaskara Rao (2000). *Teaching Mathematics Successfully*. New Delhi: Discovery Publishing House. ISBN 81-7141-552-0.

Ediger, Marlow and Digumarti Bhaskara Rao (2001). *Teaching Science Successfully*. New Delhi: Discovery Publishing House. ISBN 81-7141-600-4.

Ediger, Marlow and Digumarti Bhaskara Rao (2001). *Teaching Social Studies Successfully*. New Delhi: Discovery Publishing House. ISBN 81-7141-596-2.

Ediger, Marlow and Digumarti Bhaskara Rao (2002). *Philosophy and Curriculum*. New Delhi: Discovery Publishing House. ISBN 81-7141-631-4.

Ediger, Marlow and Digumarti Bhaskara Rao (2002). *Improving School Administration*. New Delhi: Discovery Publishing House. ISBN 81-7141-633-0.

Ediger, Marlow and Digumarti Bhaskara Rao (2002). *Elementary Curriculum*. New Delhi: Discovery Publishing House. ISBN 81-7141-658-6.

Ediger, Marlow and Digumarti Bhaskara Rao (2003). *Language Arts Curriculum*. New Delhi: Discovery Publishing House. ISBN 81-7141-657-8.

Ediger, Marlow and Digumarti Bhaskara Rao (2004). *Teaching Language Arts Successfully*. New Delhi: Discovery Publishing House. ISBN 81-7141-678-0.

Ediger, Marlow and Digumarti Bhaskara Rao (2004). *Teaching Mathematics in Elementary Schools*. New Delhi: Discovery Publishing House. ISBN 81-7141-687-X.

Ediger, Marlow and Digumarti Bhaskara Rao (2004). *Teaching Science in Elementary Schools*. New Delhi: Discovery Publishing House. ISBN 81-7141-709-4.

Ediger, Marlow and Digumarti Bhaskara Rao (2004). *School Curriculum and Administration*. New Delhi: Discovery Publishing House. ISBN 81-7141-709-4.

Ediger, Marlow and Digumarti Bhaskara Rao (2004). *Modern Elementary School*. New Delhi: Discovery Publishing House.

Ediger, Marlow and Digumarti Bhaskara Rao (2004): *Relevancy in Elementary Curriculum*. New Delhi: Discovery Publishing House. ISBN 81-7141-751-5.

Ediger, Marlow and Digumarti Bhaskara Rao, (2004). *Teaching Social Studies in Elementary Schools*. New Delhi: Discovery Publishing House.

Ediger Marlow, B.S.V. Dutt and Digumarti Bhaskara Rao (2004). *Teaching English Successfully*. New Delhi: Discovery Publishing House. ISBN 81-7141-707-8.

Harshitha, Digumarti and Digumarti Bhaskara Rao, Editors (2004). *Educational Innovations*. New Delhi: Discovery Publishing House.

Indira Devi, Author and J. Prasanth Kumar and Digumarti Bhaskara Rao, Editors (2004). *Values in Language Text Books*. New Delhi: Discovery Publishing House.

Jayasree, Kandi, Author and Digumarti Bhaskara Rao, Editor (1999). *Correlates of Socialisation*. New Delhi: Discovery Publishing House. ISBN 81-7141-517-2.

John Babu, Chikati, Author and T.J.R. Prasad, G.M. Madhukar and Digumarti Bhaskara Rao, Editors (1996). *Problem Solving in Mathematics*. New Delhi: APH Publishing Corporation. ISBN 81-7648-273-0.

Lalitha, T., Author and K.S. Prabhakaram, D.S.N. Sastry and Digumarti Bhaskara Rao, Editors (2004). *Educational Philosophic Beliefs*. New Delhi: Discovery Publishing House. ISBN 81-7141-765-5.

Madhu Bala, Jampala, Author and Digumarti Bhaskara Rao, Editor (2004). *Adjustment Problems of Hearing Impaired*. New Delhi: Discovery Publishing House.

Marja, Talvi and Digumarti Bhaskara Rao, Editors (1996). *Educational Leadership and Social Changes*. New Delhi: Discovery Publishing House. ISBN 81-7141-320-X.

Nirmala Jyothi, M., Author and Digumarti Bhaskara Rao, Editor (2003). *Non-detention Systems in School Education*. New Delhi: Discovery Publishing House. ISBN 81-7141-654-3.

Prabhakaram, K.S., Author and Digumarti Bhaskara Rao, Editor (1998). *Concept Attainment Model in Mathematics Teaching*. New Delhi: Discovery Publishing House. ISBN 81-7141-424-9.

Prasanth Kumar, J., Author and Digumarti Bhaskara Rao, Editor (1998). *Effectiveness of Distance Education System*. New Delhi: Discovery Publishing House. ISBN 81-7141-437-0.

Prasanth Kumar, J., Author and G. Sundara Rao and Digumarti Bhaskara Rao, Editors (2000). *Open University Student Support Services*. New Delhi: Discovery Publishing House. ISBN 81-7141-550-4.

Ramatulasamma, K., Author and Digumarti Bhaskara Rao, Editor (2002). *Job Satisfaction of Teacher Educators*, New Delhi: Discovery Publishing House. ISBN 81-7141-655-1.

Rama Krishnaiah, D., Author and Digumarti Bhaskara Rao, Editor (1998). *Job Satisfaction of College Teachers*, New Delhi: Discovery Publishing House. ISBN 81-7141-438-9.

Rama Kumar Ratnam, M., Author and Digumarti Bhaskara Rao, Editor (1998). *Dukka: Suffering in Early Buddhism*. New Delhi: Discovery Publishing House. ISBN 81-7141-653-5.

Rathaiah, Lavu and Digumarti Bhaskara Rao, Editors (1996). *International Innovations in Education*. New Delhi: Discovery Publishing House. ISBN 81-7141-359-5.

Ramesh, Ganta and Digumarti Bhaskara Rao, Editors (1998). *Environmental Education: Problems and Prospects*. New Delhi: Discovery Publishing House. ISBN 81-7141-423-0.

Rathaiah, Lavu and Digumarti Bhaskara Rao (1997). *Achievement Correlates*. New Delhi: Discovery Publishing House. ISBN 81-7141-385-4.

Reddy, Sudhakar Y., Author, and Digumarti Bhaskara Rao, Editor (2003). *Creativity in Adolescents*. New Delhi: Discovery Publishing House. ISBN 81-7141-659-4.

Reddy, M.S., Author and Digumarti Bhaskara Rao, Editor (2004). *Creativity in College Students*. New Delhi: Discovery Publishing House. ISBN 81-7141-697-7.

Radramamba, B., Author and Digumarti Bhaskara Rao, Editor (2003). *Problems of Teaching*. New Delhi: APH Publishing Corporation. ISBN 81-7648-462-8.

Sanjeeva Rao, P.C., Author and Digumarti Bhaskara Rao, Editor (1996). *A Text Book of Geology*. New Delhi: Discovery Publishing House. ISBN 81-7141-313-7.

Satya Narayana V., Author and Digumarti Bhaskara Rao, Editor (2001). *Physical Education, Social Attitudes and Leadership Qualities*. New Delhi: Discovery Publishing House. ISBN 81-7141-593-8.

Srinivasulu Reddy, M., and K.R.S. Sambasiva Rao, Authors and Digumarti Bhaskara Rao, Editor (1999). *A Text Book of Aquaculture*. New Delhi: Discovery Publishing House. ISBN 81-7141-482-6.

Srinivasa Rao, Mandalapu, Author and Digumarti Bhaskara Rao, Editor (2004). *Achievement Motivation and Achievement in Mathematics*. New Delhi: Discovery Publishing House. ISBN 81-7141-674-8.

Vanaja, M. Author and Digumarti Bhaskara Rao, Editor (1999). *Inquiry Training Model*. New Delhi: Discovery Publishing House. ISBN 81-7141-515-6.

Vanaja. M. and N. Sneha Latha, Authors and Digumarti Bhaskara Rao, Editor (2004). *Student Shyness*. New Delhi: APH Publishing Corporation.

Valeri V. Koustiouk, Author and Digumarti Bhaskara Rao, Editor (2002). *A Text Book of Cryogenics*. New Delhi: Discovery Publishing House. ISBN 81-7141-642-X.

Valeri V. Koustiouk, Author and Digumarti Bhaskara Rao, Editor (2004). *Refrigeration and Environment*. New Delhi: APH Publishing Corporation.

Veena Kumari, Balusu and Digumarti Bhaskara Rao (1996). *Operation Black Board*. New Delhi: Ashish Publishing Corporation. ISBN 81-7024-711-X.

Veena Kumari, Balusu, Author and Digumarti Bhaskara Rao, Editor (2000). *Psycho-Social Correlates of Achievement*, New Delhi: Discovery Publishing House. ISBN 81-7141-547-4.

Vanaja, M., Author and Digumarti Bhaskara Rao, Editor (1999). *Inquiry Training Model*. New Delhi: Discovery Publishing House. ISBN 81-7141-515-6.

Venkata Rao, P. and Digumarti Bhaskara Rao (1989). *A Text Book of Zoology—Junior Intermediate.* Guntur: Vignan Publishers.

Venkata Rao, P. and Digumarti Bhaskara Rao (1989). *A Text Book of Zoology—Senior Intermediate.* Guntur: Vignan Publishers.

Venugopala Rao, K., Author and Digumarti Bhaskara Rao, Editor (2000). *Teacher Morale in Secondary Schools.* New Delhi: Discovery Publishing House. ISBN 81-7141-551-2.

Vidya, C., Author and Digumarti Bhaskara Rao. Editor (1996). *A Text Book of Nutrition.* New Delhi: Discovery Publishing House. ISBN 81-7141-309-9.

Vidya Bharathi, D., Author and Digumarti Bhaskara Rao, Editor (2000). *Educational Philosophies of Swami Vivekananda and John Dewey.* New Delhi: APH Publishing Corporation. ISBN 81-7648-309-9.

Books in Telugu Language

Bhaskara Rao, Digumarti (1986). *Dhrushya Sravana Bodhanapakaranalu* (Audio Visual Teaching Aids). Guntur: Nagarjuna Publishers.

Bhaskara Rao, Digumarti (1993). *Jeevasashtra Bodhana* (Teaching of Biology). Guntur: Nagarjuna Publishers.

Bhaskara Rao, Digumarti (1995). *Vignanasasthra Bodhana* (Teaching of Science) Guntur: Nagarjuna Publishers.

Bhaskara Rao, Digumarti (1997). *Vidya Manovignana Seshtram* (Educational Psychology). Guntur: Creative Press.

Bhaskara Rao, Digumarti (1998). *DSC Study Material.* Guntur: Nagarjuna Publishers.

Bhaskara Rao, Digumarti (1998). *Upadhyayudu Vidya.* (Teacher and Education). Guntur: Nagarjuna Publishers.

Bhaskara Rao, Digumarti (1998). *Vidya Drukpadalu* (Prespectives of Education). Guntur: Nagarjuna Publishers.

Bhaskara Rao, Digumarti (1999). *EdCET Teaching Aptitude.* Guntur: Nagarjuna Publishers.

Bhaskara Rao, Digumarti (2001). *Bharata Samajamulo Upadyayudu Vidya* (Teacher and Education in Emerging Indian Society). Guntur: Nagarjuna Publishers.

Bhaskara Rao, Digumarti (2001). *Bhoutika Sastra Bodhana Paddathulu* (Methods of Teaching Physical Science). Guntur: Nagarjuna Publishers.

Bhaskara Rao, Digumarti (2001). *Jeeva Sastra Bodhana Padhathulu* (Methods of Teaching Biology). Guntur: Nagarjuna Publishers.

Bhaskara Rao, Digumarti (2001). *Vidya Manovignana Sastram* (Educational Psychology). Guntur: Nagarjuna Publishers.

Bhaskara Rao, Digumarti (2003). *Patsala Yajamanyam/Paripalana* (School Management and Administration). Guntur: Nagarjuna Publishers.

Bhaskara Rao, Digumarti (2004). *Vidya Sanketika Sastram mariyu Computer Vidya* (Educational Technology and Computer Education). Guntur: Nagarjuna Publishers.